3.25

TWAYNE'S WORLD AUTHORS SERIES

A Survey of the World's Literature

Sylvia E. Bowman, Indiana University

GENERAL EDITOR

ITALY

Carlo Golino, University of California, Riverside

EDITOR

Petrarch

TWAS 81

TWAYNE'S WORLD AUTHORS SERIES (TWAS)

The purpose of TWAS is to survey the major writers —novelists, dramatists, historians, poets, philosophers, and critics—of the nations of the world. Among the national literatures covered are those of Australia, Canada, China, Eastern Europe, France, Germany, Greece, India, Italy, Japan, Latin America, New Zealand, Poland, Russia, Scandinavia, Spain, and the African nations, as well as Hebrew, Yiddish, and Latin Classical literatures. This survey is complemented by Twayne's United States Authors Series and English Authors Series.

The intent of each volume in these series is to present a critical-analytical study of the works of the writer; to include biographical and historical material that may be necessary for understanding, appreciation, and critical appraisal of the writer; and to present all material in clear, concise English—but not to vitiate the scholarly content of the work by doing so.

Petrarch

By THOMAS G. BERGIN

Timothy Dwight College
Yale University

TWAYNE PUBLISHERS
A DIVISION OF G. K. HALL & CO., BOSTON

To Leone and Mirillo Cattani

Italy in Petrarch's Time

Contents

About the Author

Thomas Goddard Bergin, Sterling Professor of Romance Languages, Yale University, has taught at Western Reserve, State Teachers College at Albany, New York, Cornell, where he was for eight years Curator of the Willard Fiske Dante and Petrarch Collections, and Yale where he was for nine years Chairman of the Department of Spanish and Italian and for fifteen years Master of Timothy Dwight College. Among his publications are three books on Dante, translations of the *Divine Comedy*, Machiavelli's *Prince* and various contemporary Italian poets. He has edited a selection of Petrarch's *Sonnets, Odes and Letters* and the complete sonnets of Petrarch, translated by various hands, including twenty-eight versions of his own.

Foreword

THE purpose of this book is to offer to the general reader a concise survey of Petrarch, the man and the artist. I have attempted to set forth the background of his times and the events of his life as briefly as possible, bearing in mind, however, that his peregrinations and vicissitudes are not unrelated to the inner crises that are at the source of his works; conversely too, one could well argue that, to a greater degree than many writers, Petrarch shaped his own life, made of it, one might say, one of his works—and not the least significant of them. I have also attempted an assessment of each item in the Petrarch canon so far as this isolation is possible. For this section in particular I have had in mind the service that this book may hope to offer simply as a work of reference. Finally I have attempted a synthesis, dealing with the impact of the poet humanist on his own and succeeding times.

The facts of his life are readily available in his own letters; as for the critical opinions herein expressed they represent my own conclusions. But this is not to say that I am not very grateful to scholars and historians who have gone before me; without their lighting of my way I should frequently have stumbled on the road; indeed I suspect I should not have undertaken the journey. I have acknowledged their assistance at various places in the text and the bibliography will indicate others to whom my indebtedness while difficult to particularize is nonetheless great. Above all, I am most grateful for the information and illumination contained in the numerous volumes of Ernest Hatch Wilkins, the insights offered by Morris Bishop, and the over-all guidance I found in Umberto Bosco's compact monograph.

I wish to thank the Rockefeller Foundation for the hospitality of the Villa Serbelloni, generously offered me for the final weeks of the preparation of this book.

THOMAS GODDARD BERGIN

Bellagio
February 1969

Acknowledgments

I wish to thank the following publishers for kind permission to reproduce the items indicated:

Chicago University Press: for the lines quoted from E. H. Wilkins' *Petrarch at Vaucluse* (1958) and *Life of Petrarch* (1961); University of Illinois Press: for the quotations from Jacob Zeitlin's *The Life of Solitude by Francis Petrarch* (1924); The University of Indiana Press: for the quotations from Morris Bishop's *Letters from Petrarch* (1966); The Mediaeval Academy of America: for several quotations from E. H. Wilkins' *Petrarch's Eight Years at Milan* (1958). I am grateful to the Yale University Press for permission to reprint the translations of sonnets xxxv and clxxvi, first published in *Lyric Poetry of the Italian Renaissance*, edited by L. R. Lind, New Haven, 1954; to Appleton-Century-Crofts for permission to reprint "To Italy," first published in *Petrarch: Selected Sonnets, Odes and Letters*, edited by Thomas G. Bergin, New York, 1966; and to the *Cesare Barbieri Courier* for permission to reprint the versions of *Carmen bucolicum* iii and viii and *Ep. Met.* I, 14, originally published in vol. IX, no. 2 of that magazine, Hartford, 1969; and to the Society for Promoting Christian Knowledge: for the letters quoted from *Francesco Petrarca, The First Modern Man of Letters, His Life and Correspondence*, London, The Sheldon Press, 1925–26.

*   *   *   *

I am grateful to Prof. Charles Garside, Jr., for reading Chapter 1 and to Dr. Carlo Golino for encouraging supervision during the preparation of this book. I should like also to express my special thanks to Mr. Roger C. Haile of Bronxville, N.Y., who prepared the map for this book.

Chronology

1304   Born at Arezzo July 20.
1309   Clement V moves papal seat to Avignon. Robert "the Wise" becomes King of Naples.
1311   With family at Pisa; meets Dante.
1312   Family settles in Carpentras after journey through Genoa, Marseilles, Avignon. Begins study of *trivium*.
1313   Death of Henry VII of Luxembourg. Birth of Boccaccio.
1314   Death of Philip IV of France. Battle of Bannockburn.
1316   Begins study of law at Montpellier. John XXII made Pope.
1320   Continues legal studies at Bologna.
1321   Death of Dante.
1324   The *Defensor Pacis* of Marsilius of Padua.
1326   Settles in Avignon following his father's death. Begins ecclesiastical career (he never went beyond the minor orders).
1327   April 6, Holy Week, sees Laura in Church of Santa Chiara in Avignon.
1328   Lewis IV crowned Emperor in Rome; creates Nicholas IV anti-Pope.
1330   In Gascony with Bishop Giacomo Colonna; later returns to Avignon under protection of Cardinal Giovanni Colonna. (Earliest *Rhymes* are of this period.)
1333   Travels in France, Germany, Flanders.
1334   Benedict IV becomes Pope.
1336   Climbs Mont Ventoux. Travels in Italy (first visit to Rome January, 1337).
1337   Retires to Vaucluse. Birth of his son Giovanni (mother unknown). Boccaccio writes the *Filostrato*. Beginning of the Hundred Years' War. Birth of Froissart. Death of Giotto.
1338   Begins *Africa, De viris illustribus,* perhaps *Triumphs*.
1340   Birth of Chaucer.

1341 Crowned Poet Laureate on the Capitoline in Rome.

1342 Takes up Greek. Begins the *Secretum.* Boccaccio writes the *Fiammetta.* Clement VI becomes Pope.

1343 On embassy for Pope at the court of Naples. His illegitimate daughter Francesca born. Death of Robert of Naples, succeeded by Joan I.

1344 Begins *Liber rerum memorandarum* at Parma.

1345 Escapes from Parma; attacked by bandits at Reggio. Puts son to school in Verona. Discovers Cicero's letters *Ad Atticum.* Returns to Vaucluse.

1346 Begins *De vita solitaria* and *Bucolicum carmen.*

1347 Visits his brother in the Charterhouse of Montrieux. Starts for Rome to salute Cola di Rienzi, who has made himself master of the city but stops at Genoa on learning of Cola's reverses.

1348 Year of the plague. Death of Laura. Boccaccio begins the *Decameron.* (Petrarch in Parma and Verona).

1349 Prepares first "edition" of *Rime,* starts to collect his letters.

1350 In Verona, Mantua, Rome, Arezzo, Florence. Charles IV imprisons Cola di Rienzo in Prague.

1351 In Padua, where Boccaccio delivers invitation to lecture in Florence. Refuses; returns to Vaucluse. War between Florence and Milan.

1352 Works on the *Triumphs.* Innocent VI becomes Pope.

1353 Moves to Milan where he remains eight years, guest of the Visconti. War between Genoa and Venice.

1354 Begins *De remediis.* Final fall of Cola di Rienzo.

1355 Finishes *Contra medicum quendam.* Charles IV crowned Emperor at Rome.

1356 Ambassador to imperial court at Prague. Created Count Palatine. Releases *De vita solitaria* and *De otio religioso.* Battle of Poitiers.

1357 Releases *Bucolicum carmen.*

1358 *Itinerarium syriacum.* Chigi edition of *Rime.*

1361 In Paris on political mission. Returns to Milan, then moves to Padua; thence to Venice, where he is given a palace by the Senate.

1362 Urban VI made Pope. Langland's *Piers Plowman* (first version).

1364–5 Arranges his letters.

Chronology

CHAPTER 1

A World Confused

"O miseris perplexum ambagibus orbem!"

THE fourteenth century in which Petrarch lived and wrote is a kind of halfway house. If all centuries are in some ways transitional, we may say, borrowing the phrase from Orwell, that some centuries are more transitional than others. And to the fourteenth more than any other, the term may be accurately applied. We can see this best perhaps by looking a little before and a little after. In the Middle Ages mankind, or at least the articulate part of it, lived with its eyes raised to the world of eternity, and heaven was not only its destination but its pattern. Theology and metaphysics absorbed the philosophers, who were indeed exclusively men of the church. The scheme of earthly things (insofar as they were worthy of consideration), it was assumed, should follow the plan of the divine. As there was a hierarchy in heaven so there should be one here below, and the feudal concept responded to this need. The Emperor regarded himself as the supreme prince on earth, and lesser kings did not quarrel with the theory however much they may have opposed it in practice. For authority and leadership men looked above. Classes were rigidly fixed; duties, obligations, and even habits of dress were carefully prescribed. The goal of mankind was a disciplined unity disposed in an almost military order for the achievement of salvation in the world to come. The arts reflected this objective. As the great cathedrals bore witness to the aspirational in human effort, so, broadly speaking, the great works or art and philosophy were dedicated to synthesizing—one need but refer to the works of Thomas Aquinas and Dante for examples—even as in the political sphere the Crusades themselves, however imperfectly, exemplified the zeal for a united Christendom in the service of God. Flawed as it was at the top by the ambiguous relationship of Pope and Emperor, shaken by recurrent heresies and chronic dynastic rivalries, the ethos of the Middle Ages remained serene, constant, and firm, consistently faithful to its mission, which was to unify and coordinate the struggling humanity of this earth and so to prepare it for its true destiny above. "Christians are right and pagans are wrong," *The Song of Roland* proclaimed with a kind of embattled serenity, and Dante in Purgatory hears the same message, essentially, from the lips of his master: "Be ye content, oh human race, with the *quia* . . ." [1] The Middle Ages preserved, too, a sense of the continuity of human endeavor. Through the apostolic succession the Pope could and did believe himself a direct inheritor of the authority of Peter. The emperors likewise traced their claim back to Augustus. In Dante's mythology indeed, these great directors of human affairs go back respectively to David and Aeneas, contemporaries, Dante believed, and both having a similar sanction from providence. If we look now to the Renaissance, which for our purposes we may define as the second half of the fifteenth century and most of the sixteenth, the differences are immediately visible. The secular authority of the emperors has been replaced by nationalism, and the Reformation is in process of fragmenting the spiritual unity of Christendom. Where men once looked above for guidelines with which to shape human institutions, by force if necessary, we find that philosophers and artists are now vigorously and enthusiastically studying the world about them, finding beauty in the transitory world of nature and putting the delights of liberty above the security of order. However fruitful the work of William of Occam (to give one example) may have been in other respects, it certainly had the effect of corroding the rational foundation which Thomas had so magnificently used to support the true faith. One may see something of the same destructive effect in the work of Marsilius of Padua (even in the fourteenth century), while giving it all due credit for its vitalizing influence on the political theory of the future. Like Dante, Marsilius argued against the Pope's political and temporal supremacy, but Dante had sought his sanctions from above while Marsilius discovered the source of political authority lay in the people: a fatal thrust at the whole hierarchical structure. In the arts too the change is no less revolutionary and no less readily apparent to the naked eye. A medieval cathedral, even a relatively small one, suggests by its design and its profile a reaching beyond the earthly. If, however, we look at St. Peter's, the monument of the Renaissance papacy, we shall see that in spite of its enormous size it is so scaled and planned as to make it human and approachable. But in truth, the concern of the Renaissance is no longer primarily with cathedrals. The great works of this period are in the plastic and pictorial arts, and although the subjects are still more often than not biblical or hagiographical, the treatment is realistic and natural. In terms of Italian literature, where the *Divine Comedy* is written with an ethical purpose and portrays a divinely ordered universe and man's mission within it, the *Orlando Furioso* is a lighthearted social commentary whose principal and perhaps only purpose is to divert. Its tone is skeptical, and its moral may be said to be "What fools these mortals be." By Ariosto's time the feudal hierarchy has been broken up, and the middle class of bankers and merchants for which the scheme of the Middle Ages held no place is in the ascendant. As for continuity and tradition, the Renaissance seems to prefer novelty to both. It is the age of exploration and scientific investigation. We may note another contrast, particularly striking in the arts and having special relevance to Petrarch's case. In the Middle Ages the sense of community was stronger than the desire for self-expression, or at least self-identification. The great cathedrals are largely the work of unknown craftsmen; no one knows who wrote *The Nibelungenlied* or *The Cid* or even *Aucassin and Nicolette*. The beautiful miniatures in the old manuscripts are unsigned. It is notable that even Dante, coming at the end of the Middle Ages, mentions his name but once in his great poem—and then apologetically.[2] But in the Renaissance all is changed: we know the poets and the painters and the architects; indeed we begin to have autobiographies and personal commentaries of all kinds until we get to such monuments of egocentricity as Benvenuto Cellini, a personality that would have been suffocated in the Middle Ages. We may remark here that in this cult of the personal the example of Petrarch counted for much.

All generalizations are, of course, of necessity imperfect. One can find adumbrations of what we call the Renaissance spirit in the *Divine Comedy* and even in the *Roman de la Rose*. The Middle Ages was not in practice as monolithic as it was in concept, nor will any one year serve to mark the ushering in of the new spirit. Ecclesiastical authority, confident in its right and duty to safeguard the faith of mankind, burned Giordano Bruno in Rome in 1600 with the same assurance it had shown in dealing with the Albigensians four hundred years earlier. Whitfield well makes the

point that the teaching of St. Thomas Aquinas, commonly associated with the medieval spirit, had to wait until the Council of
Trent for certification.[3] But with all due allowances for counter-
currents, adumbrations on the one hand and reactions on the
other, the fifteenth and sixteenth centuries breathe a different air,
aim at different goals, and have a different style from those that
characterized the twelfth and thirteenth.

But what of the interval between? In the fourteenth century the
death of Henry VII had put an end to the last serious effort of the
Empire to administer its "garden," as Dante called it. "The Emperors of the fourteenth century were," says Denys Hay, "even when
they could claim descent from an Emperor, elected kings whose
resources were not of those of an empire but of their own German
principality . . . the Emperor was interested in Italy for only
two reasons: to blackmail popes into crowning him; and to extract
as much cash as possible from Italy in return for creating titles.
His descents on Italy were now futile not to say cynical." [4] In
effect he had become just another foreign prince using, and sometimes being used by, the ever varying combinations of the Italian
states to checkmate either the Pope or a rival combination. The
Pope himself had fallen into the hands of the rising house of
France, and for all Petrarch's lifetime was essentially a prisoner of
that monarchy until the attrition of the Hundred Years' War had
sapped its strength. That duel itself is a dramatic illustration of
the displacement in values which was taking place, for it is significant that the great war of the fourteenth century was fought not
on a matter of principle between Pope and Emperor or even between Christian and pagan but was occasioned by territorial and
dynastic rivalry of two secular states.

Philosophy too is in transition. We have alluded to the work of
Occam which was accomplished in our century, though its full
effects were felt later. When Petrarch turned on what he called
"Averrhoism," which was really Thomism, he did not invoke the
name of Occam but rather shifted the argument, extolling the
merits of letters and poetry as against the vanities of philosophers.
There is, in effect, no dominant philosophical current in the century—least of all in Italy. Petrarch's emancipation from philosophical concerns is an evidence of this. Something of the same lack of
distinction is visible in the arts. The great cathedral-building centuries are behind us, even though those of Prague and Milan are

fourteenth-century works and at Florence the Duomo was furthered by Giotto; and the pictorial and plastic arts had not yet
come to flower. With all due respect to the work of the Pisani,
Simon Martini, and Orcagna, the great art of the Renaissance is
still to be born. We cannot say that a century is impoverished in
writers when it produced such great names as Petrarch himself,
his compatriot Boccaccio, Chaucer and Langland in England,
Froissart in France, and the Archpriest of Hita in Spain. Letters
indeed flourished. But here again there is a significant difference.
Where the great work of the Middle Ages had been harmonious,
well organized, and often grandiose in construction, much of the
production of the fourteenth century is fragmentary. The *Decameron* is a collection of stories, not one unified work of art, and the
same is true of the *Canterbury Tales*. Froissart's history is also in
substance an anthology of anecdotes, and one could cite further
examples. It has been remarked that many of the works of this
century are, in complete opposition to the ethical and affirmative
masterpieces of the Middle Ages, generally speaking, works of satire. Again, this is true of Boccaccio and in the broadest sense of
the work also of Chaucer. Petrarch's letters, while not satirical, are
somewhat in the same field, for they are commentaries on contingent affairs and observations, sometimes rather sharply pointed,
on the behavior of his contemporaries. Perhaps it may be said of
all of these works that, while more pointedly realistic and less formalized than the works of the Middle Ages, they tend to lack their
philosophical core and, on the esthetic side, their artistic seriousness and discipline.

It is hardly surprising that historians tend to give tentative and
vague designations to their studies of this period. Titles such as
The Waning of the Middle Ages,[5] *Europe in Transition*,[6] and
even, more graphically, "The Breakdown" [7] have been applied to
Petrarch's century. Perhaps it is not surprising either that "the lack
of guidance available to those who are interested in the history of
late medieval Europe is notorious," as a recent historian has written;[8] as compared to the great number of works which study the
Middle Ages and the even more imposing libraries dedicated to
the High Renaissance, the shelf reserved for this transitional period is somewhat lean, if we except specific studies having to do
with certain literary figures or special items such as the plague or
the Hundred Years' War.

Petrarch has plenty to say about his century; the recurrent motif
in his writings is the expression of distaste and even disgust for the
times in which he is compelled to live. Looking back, he was fascinated by the grandeur of Rome and by what seemed to him the
high level of cultural and social achievements of the classical
world which he saw as a kind of lost paradise. If he turned his
eyes forward, he occasionally allowed himself the hope that some
day a better world would be born; his *Letter to Posterity* is evidence of this hope, which indeed he voiced elsewhere, although
one may look in vain among his works for a statement of any
rational foundation for it. But for his own days he has nothing but
aversion and a contempt so deep at times that it seems to verge on
despair. It is easy to look at his attitude as a mere literary pose or
as an expression of that temperamental petulance from which our
author was not exempt. One's first reaction to Petrarch's irritation
is to wonder whether indeed the fourteenth century in the texture
of its daily life was any worse than those that had gone before.
Dirt, disease, plague, crime, and endemic warfare—these were of
course characteristics of the day-to-day life in the Middle Ages—
and even the educated classes were flawed by ignorance, prejudice, and callousness. Yet one is tempted to think that life in Petrarch's day may have been a little better and certainly no worse
than it was in the time of his grandfathers: we have evidence of
more paved streets, better houses, and perhaps a slightly higher
standard of living. Second thoughts may cause us to reverse our
opinion and to concur with Petrarch, for the fourteenth century
had some very special miseries of its own. It is a century of famine
—not only the so-called great famine of 1315 to 1317, which has
left its name to history—but others coming later in the century
and, no doubt, preparing the way in part for the plague. It was a
century of very bad weather, especially of bitterly cold winters;
Petrarch himself records some of these in his letters. If it is true
that there had always been war, yet the Hundred Years' War with
its consequent ravaging of France and spawning of mercenaries
who devastated France and terrified Italy may claim to have a
kind of primacy among them all. The Black Death alone would
suffice to give the century a gruesome distinction in the annals of
misery. It struck first and hardest in the year 1348 and returned at
almost regular ten-year intervals throughout the century. Europe

had seen nothing like it since the eighth century and has, happily, suffered no such similar scourge since. Although the fourteenth century was not so obsessed with statistics as we are today and all estimates are subject to skepticism, the plague of 1348 seems, on the word of a recent historian,[9] to have carried away about one-third of the total population of Europe, particularly among city dwellers. The population of Florence, for example, was halved; that of England as a whole dropped from 3,700,000 to 2,200,000. Historians are still trying to measure the impact of the plague on economic and social areas. To the contemporaries, the effect on manners and morals was clear and alarming. We may quote profitably here from the account of a singularly gifted eyewitness.

In his introduction to the *Decameron*, Boccaccio describes the impact of the plague in all its horror and then proceeds to speak of the reaction of the citizens; some, he says, believed it was wise to "live temperately" and, shutting themselves away from their fellow citizens, they lived decently enough in their villas.

Others, holding to the contrary opinion, affirmed that the most effective remedy against such an ill was to drink and be merry and to go about singing and roistering, satisfying their appetites as well as they could in every way and laughing and making sport of what was happening. And they put their prescription into effect to the best of their ability, making the rounds of the taverns day and night, drinking without manner or measure, and carrying on in this way more often than not in other peoples' houses, if they heard of anything in them to their taste. And this they could do easily enough, for all men, as if not expecting to live, had given up all care for their goods as indeed for themselves, and most houses had become common property open to all: a stranger could make use of them as easily as the owner if he chanced to come upon them. And following their bestial way of life they continued to keep as far away as possible from the sick. In this great misery and affliction of our city the revered authority of the laws, divine and human alike, decayed and withered, for their ministers and executors, even as befell other men, were all either dead or sick or left without assistants and could not perform their functions, so that every man was free to behave as he chose to.

And because the sick were deserted by neighbors, relatives and friends, and because of the lack of servants, an almost unheard-of usage grew up: no woman, however charming, beautiful or well-born she might be, would think anything of having a man in her service, young, old

or of any kind or condition, or of exposing to him, without shame, any
part of her body, just as she would have to a woman if the needs of her
illness required it. This was perhaps in subsequent times the cause of
less modesty in such women as recovered.[10]

The immediate economic effect of the plague was to put the
working class, artisans or peasants, in a position of advantage, but
the reaction was not long in coming, for if labor was in short supply, so were consumers and they were destined to be so for many
years to come. "The economic and social gulf between masters
and workers widened as economic conditions deteriorated. Europe as a whole was confronted with a problem of overproduc-
tion." [11] And in a feudal society it was bound to be the propertied
classes who would apply the legislative measures necessary to cut
the costs of production. Hence, for the rest of the century workers
and peasants were worse off than before, and their misery and
frustration are the moving forces behind such events as the peasants' revolt in England (1381), the rising of the Jacquerie in
France, and the agitation of the Ciompi in Florence (1378). Such
movements were directed against the aristocracy and the church,
wealthy in its own right and of necessity the most vigorous champion of the existing order. Gradually some kind of equilibrium
was restored—but hardly an easy one. And the collapse of moral
values to which Boccaccio refers has its counterpart too in the
breaking of the old faith between master and man, whether man
meant peasant or artisan, that had characterized the High Middle
Ages. Clearly, too, the plague had its part in the phenomenon of
lawlessness and brigandage of which Petrarch has so much to say
in his letters and of which indeed he had firsthand knowledge. In
sum, the Four Horsemen had their way with continental Europe,
and we must concur with the poet's melancholy assessment of his
age.

Yet however pessimistic his view of the world he lived in and
however hard and frequently he tried to cut himself off from it by
seeking refuge in Vaucluse and burying himself in his own concerns, Petrarch did not abandon it. In fact, he followed public
affairs with the dedication of an impassioned commentator; he
was, furthermore, affected personally both as a man and as an
artist by the events of his time. Some knowledge of fourteenth-
century political history is necessary for a full understanding of his

attitudes and achievements even though we may argue that his greatest work, the *Rhymes,* transcends the era.

To Christendom in general and to Italians in particular the most unusual and disturbing event in the century was the removal of the papacy to Avignon. This dislocation, originally effected by Philip IV of France, was in fact the outward and visible sign of his triumph over the secular pretensions of the Roman Church. At the king's bidding Clement V removed to the Provençal city; once there, even though French power gradually declined, four successive popes after Clement continued to remain in exile. It is hard to measure the effect of this dislocation nowadays; in the fourteenth century it was the source of a profound disturbance in men's minds; one may say, in a sense it was the first deep fissure in the monolithic Christendom of the High Middle Ages and in fact the removal, leading as it did to the Great Schism, contributed to the uneasiness which was at least in part the source of increasing radical heretical movements, and eventually the Reformation. Even as Dante before him Petrarch fulminated against the abandonment of Rome. The Avignon popes themselves were not collectively contemptible either as pontiffs or as men. Clement V (1305–14) was a partisan to be sure, but he was a vigorous pope and was sincerely concerned with the unity of Europe. John XXII (1316–34) reaffirmed the sovereignty of the papacy and triumphed over Ludwig of Bavaria. Benedict XII (1334–42) distinguished himself for his charitable works and his efforts to mediate a peace between France and England. Clement VI was an intelligent patron of the arts (1342–52) and embellished the papal palace at Avignon; Innocent VI was an able administrator (1352–62); Urban V (1362–70), later beatified, was also a patron of letters, and he made an effort to restore the papacy to Rome but found the anarchy of the city intolerable; his successor, Gregory XI (1370–78), also a man of good will, was more successful, possibly because he died only one year after his solemn entrance into the Eternal City. All of these popes were able and one may say even well intentioned, though inevitably their political activities made them on occasion suspect to those who did not share their views. But it must be admitted that it is during the exile that the Church became increasingly venal. "Judicious observers were brought to despair," says Olschki, "by the scandalous financial policy of the pontiffs in Avignon and of their representatives and agents in Italy," describing the brisk and growing trade in indulgences as "the commercialization of Purgatory." [12] The Bull of John XXII (1323) anathematizing any who held that Christ and the Apostles could not have owned property, dramatized the new attitude of the papacy.

Further, since the Avignon popes were all French, all (save for the last) maintained the church in exile, and they were bound to be harshly judged by Italians. Though Petrarch has a kind word to say of some of them, his famous sonnet sequence against the "Spring of all Woe" does not draw any distinctions. The residence of the popes at Avignon is constant and continuous evidence of the times being out of joint.

A hundred years earlier the absence of a pope from Rome would have been an invitation to the Emperor; one can well imagine how eagerly Frederick the Second would have seized the opportunity. But the day of emperors had passed, too. In the Italy of our poet's day there was no central authority and the history of the country, like so many of the literary monuments we have mentioned, is fragmented and without direction. Some detailed consideration of the fragments will be useful here.

In that tormented and recalcitrant peninsula there was one power that was dynastic rather than communal, feudal rather than bourgeois. This was the Kingdom of Naples, in its organization almost anachronistic. During Petrarch's lifetime the realm was governed by Robert (ruled 1309–43) and his granddaughter Joan I, who was suspected of complicity in the murder of her first husband, Andrew of Hungary, and became successively wife to Louis of Taranto, James of Mallorca, and Otto of Brunswick. Petrarch thought highly of Robert, more highly than did Dante, who thought him more fit for the church than for kingship, or for that matter history itself (though it is Villani who calls him "wise").[13] Petrarch was proud of his "friendship" with the King and considered him the only person alive fitted to give him an examination preliminary to his coronation with the laurel. The realm achieved a certain prestige under Robert, in spite of his ill-judged obsession with the reconquest of Sicily, lost to the house of Anjou on the famous occasion of the Sicilian Vespers (1282). His efforts to that purpose were unsuccessful and costly; he did have a brief moment of triumph in the victorious attack on Genoa (1323), but it was ephemeral. And while the King sought glory and political emi-

nence, economic conditions in the Kingdom worsened. Perhaps
there was little hope for it anyway; it was a land lacking in resources, with no industry of its own, with a population made up of
an impoverished aristocracy and an oppressed peasantry, with no
leavening of a progressive bourgeoisie, and with pretensions, in-
herited from the great Charles of Anjou, far beyond its capacities.
Joan's accession was tragic for the Kingdom. The violent death of
her first husband (1345) led to wars with the Kingdom of Hungary and civil war in the realm. Joan indeed was driven to seek
the Pope's protection, for which part of the price was the cession
of Avignon itself to the papacy (1348). But this did not solve
Joan's problems: she was forever at the mercy of subversive and
sometimes bloodthirsty dissension among her own kin and courtiers, the politics of the popes, and the general incompetence of her
administrators. Niccolò Acciaiuolo, the friend of Petrarch, is an
exception: after the restoration of Joan and her second husband to
Naples (whence her Hungarian brother-in-law had expelled her)
Acciaiuoli, the Grand Seneschal of the realm, managed to give
the country a few years of decent administration and almost re-
conquered Sicily for the Crown (and would have done so indeed
save for the intervention of the Emperor and the jealousy of the
Neapolitan courtiers themselves). But he died in 1368 and things
soon fell apart. Strangled by her successor in the gaunt castle of
Muro in Lucania, the unhappy queen left behind her "a nobility
in tumult, a people in incredible misery, and an organization of
the state, set up by Charles I and fortified by Charles II and Robert, no longer in a condition to function." [14] The realm ceased to
have any importance in the politics of the peninsula. The action
was in the north.

Historians concerned with tracing major threads and detectable
trends are not infrequently baffled by the endemic confusion of
northern Italian political events in the thirteenth and fourteenth
centuries. One of them comments: "Boundaries changed continually, weaker units were absorbed by stronger, only to regain
their independence with the fortune of war or the division of a
despot's power between several sons. From year to year the map
resembled not so much a patchwork as some animated biological
diagram, depicting shells in a feverish alternation of union and
fission." [15] It is a deplorable truth that only the foreign domination
that ensued on the French and Spanish invasions in the early six-

teenth century would put an end to this unhappy state of things, although some kind of balance of power was secured briefly in the middle years of the *quattrocento*. For our purposes here, however, a year-to-year account would be as purposeless as it would be confusing; happily the main directions of power thrusts, subject to the vicissitudes alluded to above, are tolerably visible during the period we are considering.

The states on the march in the fourteenth century were Milan and Venice; it was precisely with these powerful governments that Petrarch was largely concerned; since he spent a longer period of his life in Milan than anywhere else, we may well begin with that exuberant region. In Petrarch's time the state was administered by the Visconti, the ablest and most aggressive rulers of Italy. They had at the base of their power the city of Milan, the most populous and the richest city of Europe in the Middle Ages, save only Byzantium. The old Commune which had so vigorously led the Lombard League against the Swabian emperors had in effect ceased to exist in the latter part of the thirteenth century when the della Torre had made themselves tyrants; the designation of Azzo Visconti as "*dominus generalis*" in 1330 merely gave legal ratification to a long existent political fact. The Visconti came to power in the person of the Archbishop Otto; his nephew, given the title of Imperial Vicar (1294), followed the fortunes of the Guelph and Ghibelline struggles, centering around the descent of Henry VII; his son Galeazzo also had a stormy career, being at one time ousted from his domains and imprisoned by Ludwig of Bavaria. Yet the family hold remained unbroken. Azzo, son of Galeazzo, maintained himself for ten years, and on his death administration passed to the very capable hands of his uncles Luchino and Giovanni, the Archbishop of Milan. Giovanni welcomed Petrarch to the city; after his death in 1354 the poet lived on no less comfortably under the regime of the archbishop's nephews, Galeazzo II and Bernabo. Galeazzo II (died 1378) had reached such a peak of prestige that he was able to marry his son Gian Galeazzo to Isabelle, daughter of John II of France and his daughter to Lionel, Duke of Clarence, son of Edward III. For the latter occasion, J. A. Symonds quotes the chronicler Giovio: "Such was the profusion of the banquet that the remnants taken from the table were enough and to spare for 10,000 men"; he adds his own tangential but illuminating comment: "It must have been a strange experience for the brother of the Black Prince, leaving London, where the streets were still unpaved, the houses thatched, the beds laid on straw and where wine was sold as medicine, to pass into the luxurious palaces of Lombardy, walled with marble and raised high above smooth streets of stone." [16] But the Visconti knew how to put their money to other uses too, and by the end of the century Gian Galeazzo had been granted the title of Duke; had he not died before his time (1402) he would in all probability have become king of a realm embracing most of northern Italy.

The territorial expansion of the Visconti domain, if it did not quite keep pace with their lofty ascent on the social ladder, was substantial. In the early years of the century it included all the important cities in Lombardy and by the end of Petrarch's life ran from Verona to Montferrat; indeed for a time (during Petrarch's residence) the Visconti held Genoa and Bologna; if they were dislodged from both, yet such conquests were an indication of the vitality of the little state and a foreshadowing of the dominant role it was to play in fifteenth-century Italy. Both Verona and Padua fell to Gian Galeazzo before the end of the century, though later (1404) they were to be annexed by Venice.

As Milan and the Visconti waxed, the state of Verona and the della Scala waned. The exploits of Dante's patron Can Grande were heroic, and for a time the family defended itself—indeed it maintained its independence during Petrarch's lifetime and at its apogee under Mastino moved to the border of Tuscany. But gradually as the Visconti pressed from the west and the Venetians eroded the eastern shore of the peninsula, the Veronese saw themselves squeezed out; the city had never had the wealth of Milan, and on its other flank could never match the Venetian military genius, itself a reflection of an amazingly well-organized and efficient government.

For Venice was in truth in the *trecento* something of an anomaly. It had never gone through the conventional development of the Italian city-state from feudal fief to commune to despotism. It had never, therefore, been obliged to undergo the anti-feudal bourgeois thrusts that elsewhere were the basis of the communes; in 1310 it had fixed once and for all the status of its citizens before the law with the famous *libro d'oro,* and as a result of an uprising against such definitive regimentation it had established the Council of Ten, all-powerful, secret, and dedicated. It was in effect a totalitarian state and as it had strangled the beginnings of the commune, so in 1355 with equal severity it frustrated the attempt of the Doge Marin Faliero to make himself a despot. ("I had known him for a long time," Petrarch writes, "but I was wrong about him; he had more courage than prudence.") [17] The power was in the hands of an oligarchy, to be sure, but individuals within the oligarchy were subject, like any other citizen, to the law of the state. Even the representative of the church in Venice had to be of Venetian blood. Nor had the Republic ever been interested in the Guelph and Ghibelline conflict, which carried the corollary that it was also exempt from the family blood feuds that characterized the rest of the peninsula. In spite of the sharp distinction between the elite and the disenfranchised the *Serenissima* was a united state, one not without a kind of pragmatic communism: among other things that belonged to the state were the very ships which were the source of its wealth; merchants could sail and trade, but they were leased the ships, which were the property of the Republic. It is in the fourteenth century that the Venetians begin to establish their bridgeheads on the Continent; like those of every other state in that seesaw century their fortunes varied, but in the long run they were there to stay; their conquests on the mainland were, for one thing, content with the clean and efficient administration that Venice gave them. The *trecento* is also the time of the heroic struggle with Genoa: an interminable war fought for the most part at sea and in the overseas concessions and possessions of these great empires. It would go on all century long, but Venice would emerge victorious. (We may in our brief survey here omit Genoa which, even in its moments of triumph, had little effect on the political developments of the mainland.) As we shall see, Petrarch had his voice in the Venetian-Genoese rivalry too.

The only one of the major states in the fourteenth century that might be considered a democracy was Florence, although the electorate was rather restricted. Like Venice, Florence had never had a *Signore* and so was spared the family feuds that were the ruin of Genoa, for example. Unlike Venice, however, Florence had been deeply involved by the very nature of its geographical position in the Guelph and Ghibelline struggle, which in the thirteenth century had led to repeated civil wars within the walls. By the early fourteenth century the city had purged itself of Ghibellines and also of dissident "Whites" and had so been able to present a united front and a strong defense against the Emperor Henry VII. Under the protection of King Robert of Naples the same anti-imperial policy continued, and the city successfully defended itself against the Emperor Louis IV and his vicar, Castruccio Castracane. Broadly speaking, for the rest of the century the Florentine policy vis-à-vis the other Italian states was defensive rather than aggressive, with the exception, of course, of the small neighboring towns of Tuscany, which were in the natural sphere of the great city on the Arno. Here the policy was in part successful. Although some conquests of the Republic were lost under the brief and catastrophic tyranny of the Duke of Athens (1343), yet "by a little past the middle of the century Colle di Val d'Elsa, San Gimignano, Prato, and Pistoia . . . submitted to Florentine control." [18] Late in the century (1384), Arezzo was sold to the Florentines by Louis of Anjou. But both Pisa and Lucca eluded them; the former fell to the Visconti (1399) as did Siena (1387); Lucca, though at various moments conquered, sold, and even pawned, somehow preserved its autonomy through the century and indeed for many years after. When necessary the city would turn to protectors from the outside, as in the case of Robert and, at the end of the century, the English mercenary, Hawkwood; it would form alliances with other states to block the aggressive southern thrust of the Visconti when they pressed on Bologna (1351). It would, when the occasion demanded, laying aside its Guelphism, even be the spearhead of a grand alliance against the aggressive and resurgent papacy in the War of the Eight Saints (1375). The foreign policy of the city may be described in terms familiar to us today as one of successful containment of potentially dangerous aggressors. But Florence could not always contain the restless, unruly temper of her own citizens. Repeated efforts were made during the century on the part of the lower bourgeoisie to have some representation in the government of the city. There were on occasion scenes of violence and bloodshed; and class warfare, sometimes open but always latent, took the place of the dynastic and quasi-ideological troubles that disturbed the peace of other cities on the peninsula. Affairs reached such a point in 1343 that the Florentines called in the aforementioned Walter of Brienne, the so-called Duke of Athens, and gave him the powers of dictatorship, but the experiment was not successful and was followed by more tumult than had preceded it. This episode led to a widening of the base of the electorate; "beginning with the autumn of 1343, shopkeepers and artisans actually sat in the seats of power and with varying fortune clung to them till 1382" [19]—although in cold fact the oligarchy continued to run things much as before. More alarming and dangerous to the established order was the so-called rebellion of the Ciompi which came much later in the century, indeed, after Petrarch's time. Historians can see in this civic uneasiness the pattern of preparation for despotism, and it would come to Florence as it came to all other city-states, but this was not to take place in the fourteenth century. Meanwhile, aside from preserving its independence, the city prospered. The banking and commercial families made money, and although there were serious bankruptcies in the middle of the century, the financial world recovered with remarkable resilience. Florence, as we have noted, was also very hard hit by the plague, but from this scourge its recovery was also rapid. It may be added that although the city was second to Milan in magnificence, it was still the artistic and cultural center of the peninsula. The Duomo was finished as was the Campanile, and in the first part of the century Andrea Pisano gave the Baptistry its first pair of bronze doors. In letters the supremacy of Florence remains indisputable. It is, during this century, the city of Boccaccio, Sacchetti, Pucci and the chroniclers Villani, champions of the vernacular, and of the humanist Coluccio Salutati, to mention only the outstanding names; save for Petrarch himself these have no rivals in any other Italian center.

The patrimony of Peter extending in a wide belt across Italy from Latium on the Tyrrhenian to the March of Ancona on the Adriatic was throughout the fourteenth century more of a geographical expression than a state in any sense of the word. In the absence of the popes Rome itself fell into endemic warfare, with the rival clans of Orsini and Colonna struggling for supremacy and with others of the predatory nobility contributing their own confusion. The comet-like trajectory of Cola di Rienzo in 1347 was a brief interval of truce, exciting in its implications but leaving no lasting effect on the conditions of the Eternal City. Bologna, as we have seen, fell into the hands of the Visconti. In the smaller cities or petty principalities (as Dante had reported to Guido da Montefeltro) the thought of war, if not its actual waging, was never absent from the hearts of the despots. "Tyrants like the Malatesta of Rimini in the March of Ancona, and the Ordelaffi of Forlì and the Manfredi of Faenza in Romagna, pursued their schemes in defiance of the papacy." [20] In 1353, however, Innocent VI sent as his legate to the abandoned patrimony the Spanish Cardinal Albornoz, who proved to be a first-class soldier and an excellent administrator. (Petrarch went to meet him on the occasion of his visit to Milan and seems to have had a rather indifferent opinion of him.) Although the fighting Cardinal was twice removed from his post as legate because of political maneuverings, he did manage to restore order to the region. In the nature of things, however, the patrimony, united in name only, played no very significant role in the politics of Italy save to provide recurrent opportunities for intervention on the part of the Visconti, the Venetians, and the Florentines. Finally we may note as a portent of things to come, though as yet so far removed as to be undistinguishable on the political horizon, that it is in this century that the Count of Savoy in the person of the great Amadeus VI acquires Piedmont and even comes into conflict with the Visconti. Indeed, in politics as in philosophy and in the area of thought and culture and in the arts, fourteenth-century Italy is full of portents of things to come, clearly visible to anyone who has good hindsight. For those who lived through those times, however, it was a period of uncertainty, frustrations, and uneasiness, lacking in a perceptible pattern. Perhaps Petrarch, making his own special kind of break with the past, groping without too much confidence into a future in which he did not always believe, wandering restlessly from city to city, putting his hopes of stability now in a melodramatic republic, now in a tyrant, and now in an emperor, may well be regarded as a symbol of his age. The political climate we have attempted to summarize is not merely the background of our poet's activity, it is a part of the fabric of his life. He was acquainted with most of the leading figures of his time; as we shall see, he could call himself an intimate of many. He was an eyewitness to many of the events; more than any man of his time, he was aware of the underlying forces which brought them to being. More often than not he expressed his opinion on political developments; he even occasionally made his own efforts to direct them. At the same time, with an art more instinctive than calculated, he managed to keep himself ultimately uncommitted. He could revile the papal court and remain friends with the Pope. He could live in Milan and be on good terms with the Doge of Venice. He could criticize the Emperor and yet be his welcome guest. Only to Cola did he make a really definite and passionate commitment, but Cola's regime was too short to carry the poet into an active political career, for which he would have been temperamentally unfit.

CHAPTER 2

The Young Exile

WHILE it is convenient to our approach to speak first of Petrarch's life and then of his works, it should be said at the outset that in his case such a division poses some problems. To a much greater extent than is true of most writers, Petrarch's life and works are inseparably entangled. We do not mean here simply to state the obvious truth that whatever a man produces in the field of art is bound to reflect his experience; we mean rather that the nature of Petrarch's inspiration is such that it is responsive to the events of his life on a day-by-day basis. He traveled, he played a role in many public affairs, every day he received news of happenings in the world and visits from friends; to all of these stimuli he responded as he did to any bit of reading he happened to be engaged in. The chronicle of his works is the chronicle of his life. This does not estop our critical intent, for the works may be examined on their own merits, but the circumstances of their composition are woven into the biographical fabric and as we trace the poet's career we shall repeatedly have need to take note of his literary endeavors; often indeed they are commentaries on contemporary problems and events.

There is another point that should be made in this connection. Such is the nature of our poet's production that we cannot, as with most authors, speak of the gestation of one work and then, after the proper biographical parenthesis, pass on to another. For all of the poet's major works, in which we include not only the *Rhymes* and the *Trionfi* but also the *Letters* and the *Africa* (for in his intention these were major works) are the labor not of any given time or period (though their immediate inspiration may be); as they come to us they are the finished products of years of retouching, revision, and polishing. It is possible, for example, to date many of the sonnets, but we know that if a certain sonnet sprang from a mood or an event in the early experience of the poet, it has yet been subjected to regular restudy, more often than not with revision, and may well bespeak the art of the writer twenty or thirty years later. One cannot speak truly of "development" in Petrarch; one must take his works *en bloc;* there is not a Petrarch of the *Canzoniere* and a Petrarch of the *Africa,* so far as any chronological criterion is concerned. And perhaps not in other respects either; although on that point we shall reserve further comment here. Almost all his works are made up of fragments, they are cumulative; some were left unfinished, and even the *Rhymes,* one feels, might have been added to had the poet lived another five years. All of which is another way of saying that life and letters, experience and art were concurrent and inseparable streams; Petrarch did not so much have a message to convey or a project to achieve as an attitude, a mood, perhaps one might say an obsession to share. Whatever it may be called, it was a lifelong condition, and the artistic expression of it could not, in the nature of the case, ever be finally stated. And even as his works suggest the tentative, the groping toward achievement rather than achievement itself, so too the course of his life shows us a restless spirit, chronically self-questioning, never entirely at peace with himself, never quite satisfied with his environment. Perhaps it is this condition which explains the affinity that we of today feel with him.

"My parents were honorable folk, Florentine in their origin, of medium fortune, or, as I may as well admit, in a condition verging upon poverty. They had been expelled from their native city, and consequently I was born in exile, at Arezzo, in the year 1304 of this latter age which begins with Christ's birth, July the twentieth, on a Monday at dawn." [1] So our poet tells us himself, in his *Letter to Posterity,* demonstrating in the precision of his details a scholar's scrupulousness and an autobiographical concern uncharacteristic of the Middle Ages. No biographer has contested the poet's statement as to the time and place of his birth; in fact, most of what he tells us of his origins, here and elsewhere, seems beyond question. His father, Petracco dell'Incisa, was indeed of ancient stock; he was the third in a succession of notaries in the family, which seems to have had a hereditary right to the surname dell'Incisa with its implication of landholding or at least stability. It seems likely that the poet's mother, Eletta Canigiani, was of somewhat higher social standing than his father. As for the siblings of our poet, he had an elder brother who died very young and a younger brother, Gherardo, born in 1307, for whom he cherished a lifelong affection, mingled, after Gherardo's entrance into the Carthusian order, with something like reverence. A shadowy sister hovers on the periphery of the Petrarch legend; if he had one he says nothing of her, and she may have been a half-sister.[2]

Petracco, a White Guelph as was Dante, had suffered the same fate as the author of the *Divine Comedy* and been banished from Florence; hence the poet's birth "in exile." Like Dante too, Petracco was destined never to return to his native city. He seems to have taken part in the effort of the Whites to fight their way back (on the same date as the poet's birth, as he tells us in a letter to Boccaccio);[3] we know little else of his activities for the years between 1304 and 1311, when the family was reunited at Pisa. Eletta and her sons had spent the intervening years at Incisa, situated between Florence and Arezzo. After a year at Pisa where the awesome Dante visited the family, leaving a lasting (and perhaps, Carducci suggests,[4] a not entirely favorable) impression on the seven-year-old Francesco, the family moved to Avignon, where the pope "held the Church of Christ in shameful exile"[5] and two years later settled down for a four-year sojourn in Carpentras, where the poet, put to school, found his delight in studies. The repeated moves of the anxious and uneasy little family left its mark on the poet; yet for all the uncertainties of an exiled and impoverished condition his childhood was neither "underprivileged," as we say nowadays, nor unhappy. Fifty years later he writes nostalgically to his lifelong friend, Guido Sette,[6] whom he had met in Genoa en route from Pisa to Avignon:

Do you remember those four years? What cheer reigned there, what happiness, what security, peace at home and liberty in public, what repose in the countryside, what silence! I am sure you agree; certainly I am grateful for those times, or rather I am grateful to the author of all times, who bestowed upon me those tranquil days, that, far from the world's uproar, in the time of the mind's weakness I might imbibe the bland milk of childish doctrine to strengthen me for the digestion of more solid food.

Although the phrase "those four years" is specific, there is some doubt about the actual dates of Petrarch's boyhood residence in Carpentras. According to Wilkins, Petracco moved his little family

in 1312 from Pisa to Provence and "unable to establish his family
in suddenly overpopulous Avignon . . . found a home for his wife
and their two sons in the town of Carpentras, about fifteen miles
to the northeast. There the two boys and their mother lived for
the next five years, visited often by Ser Petracco." [7] Whether the
residence in the little town was continuous or interrupted we cannot be sure; it is odd that Petrarch never mentions the memorable
Conclave, to which Dante addressed his eloquent letter to the
Italian cardinals and which broke up in an ugly riot between the
rival factions. (It was two years before a successor to Clement V
was elected; in spite of Dante's plea it was another Frenchman,
the aggressive John XXII, who continued to maintain the papal
residence in Avignon.) Certainly during the period of the Conclave, "Carpentras was no safe place for a peaceable Italian law-
yer with women and children to protect." [8]

In any event the residence in the small town remained a happy
memory for our poet. It was here that he had his first taste of
schooling under the direction of one Convenevole da Prato, whom
the poet remembers affectionately in later years,[9] and here too
that his friendship with his contemporary Guido Sette, was con-
firmed. The boys were to share their years of schooling from the
elementary to the university level; Petrarch, who always cherished
his friendships, counted Guido (later Bishop of Genoa) among
his intimates for the rest of his life. The years in Carpentras also
brought the prospective poet into contact with the land, the language, and the tradition of the poetry of the troubadours. Nor
should we overlook the fact that, as revealed in his *Secretum*,[10]
his home atmosphere, no doubt due to his mother, was one of
guided piety and devotion; it was perhaps at this time too that his
father directed his son's attention to the study of Cicero when
"other youngsters were yawning over . . . Aesop" [11] and the like.
It was also during the years in Carpentras that the boy made his
first expedition to Vaucluse (probably 1316) and resolved, if it
should ever be possible, to make his home by the source of the
Sorgue.[12]

In 1316 young Francesco was sent by his father to Montpellier
where he spent four years, studying civil law. His literary interests
were already becoming strong; he spent his textbook money on
the classics and was moved to tears when his father, on discover-
ing his cherished library, consigned it all to the flames, sparing only

Virgil and Cicero's *Rhetoric*.[13] It was during his sojourn in Montpellier too that the poet's mother died.[14] This was a great shock to the boy and the Latin lament that he wrote for her is still extant; it is the earliest verse of the poet that we have. It is a moving little poem, containing the half-pathetic, half-proud asseveration that his mother will share in his glory: "*Vivimus pariter, pariter memorabimur ambo*" (Together we live, and both of us shall be remembered together).[15]

On the plane of literary criticism we may observe that some of the devices that were to become conventionally Petrarchan can be found in this early composition. He plays on his mother's name "Electa" ("Elect of God as much in fact as name") as he will later play on Laura's, and he artfully calculates the lines in the poem to make their count equal the years of his mother's life; the one line we have quoted has a characteristically simple yet effective repetition and a chiasmic inversion of the verbs. (But one must not make too much of this—the poem, though written at the time, has no doubt suffered the usual revisions.)

In spite of the painful scene with his father and the shadow of his mother's death, Petrarch was happy in Montpellier and speaks of it in later years with the same nostalgia with which he recalls his days in Provence. In Montpellier his friend Guido Sette was with him, and Tatham speculates[16] that his course of study at this age might not have been limited to law, but may have included the arts, which, for a budding man of letters and one of Petrarch's already awakened interest, would be a pleasant and rewarding program.

The years from 1321 to 1326 were spent at the University of Bologna, although with several long interruptions. The first was a result of a student riot, with the consequent punishment of the leaders, which led to the removal of the whole university to Imola. Petrarch went with his colleagues, and during the time of dislocation of the university (well over a year) he found leisure with his friends to wander about Italy, *more studentum*, visiting such cities as Rimini and Venice. Finally, as the university showed no sign of reopening, he went back to Provence. He resumed his studies in the fall of 1362, staying two years in Bologna. After another interval in Avignon (from the fall of 1324 until the summer of 1325) he came back for his last "term." In April, 1326, on learning of the death of his father, he left the university behind him—and also abandoned forever the profession of law. In the letter from which we have quoted above the poet speaks of his student years as gay and carefree; he became "bolder" than before and perhaps more than he should have; he speaks of association with his fellow students and of rambles about the environs of the city and of returning late through gaps in the wall and goes on to deplore the changes brought about by warfare; now "grief has replaced light-hearted games, lamentations have taken the place of songs and gangs of outlaws that of girls dancing in chorus"—the items that have been replaced may indicate something of the nature of the life of the young undergraduate. Francesco had not been a poor student, nor even a reluctant one: he says with some complacency in his *Letter to Posterity* that many thought he might have had a distinguished career in law. But though the study interested him, the practice of law seemed to him to carry with it the need for dishonesty if it were to be successful; it was, he remarks in the *Letter*, "a profession that degraded those who practiced it." And with his father no longer alive to direct him, he was free to do as he liked.

During the years in Bologna where he was accompanied by his brother Gherardo and the faithful Guido, he made many friends, including Tommaso Caloiro (whom some suspect to be his mentor in the *Triumph of Love;* dead in 1341), the Florentine Mainardi Accursio and Luca Cristiani, who, with Accursio, was for a time to be a member of the household of Cardinal Colonna. It was in Bologna that the poet came to the attention of Giacomo Colonna, although it seems they did not actually meet. Surely the most important aspect of the years in Bologna was that Petrarch was brought again into contact with his native land, his native language, and, one can reasonably suspect, the Italian poetic school. Dante's master, Guido Guinizelli, had been a Bolognese, and the founder of "the sweet new style"; Cino da Pistoia was a member of the faculty of the university, though he was not present during Petrarch's sojourn. We may be sure that there were many practitioners of the art among Petrarch's fellow students and, perhaps, professors; Wilkins surmises that Petrarch may well have begun his exercises in the vulgar tongue at Bologna even though nothing has survived which can be with certainty identified as of that period.[17] But it is fairly certain that had young

Francesco continued his studies at Montpellier or gone on to Paris instead of Bologna, we should have had no *Canzoniere*.

Between 1326 and 1330, Francis and his brother seem to have led the somewhat carefree lives of men about town in the busy and elegant papal capital. Their style of life included flirtations, writing of verses, and great concern with dress:

You remember, I say, how strong and how foolish was our desire for fine clothes, which still amazes me, though less as time goes on. What endless boredom and bother of putting them on and putting them off, morning and evening! How we feared that a hair would be displaced, and that a breeze would upset the proper structure of our coiffure! How we had to dodge the animals coming every which way in the streets, so that our perfumed, spotless gowns wouldn't get a splash of mud or have their folds disarranged by jostling! . . .

And what shoes we wore! They were supposed to protect our feet, of which they were in fact the fierce and unrelenting enemies. They would have crippled me completely if, warned by extreme necessity, I hadn't preferred to shock other people rather than to squeeze my bones and sinews out of shape. And what of our curling-irons and our artful locks, which cost us labor and pain and robbed us of sleep! What pirate could have tortured us more than we did ourselves! How often in the morning we saw red wounds on our foreheads, so that when we wanted to show off our beautiful hair we had to hide our faces! [18]

He also refers to the trivial songs (*cantiunculae*) that he and his brother used to write for equally trivial women (*mulierculae*). Wallace Ferguson aptly describes him at this stage as a "young semi-clerical dandy." [19]

During the years of Petrarch's residence, Avignon must have provided an ideal setting for two personable young men of independent income. It had the dignity and elegance of a world capital and along with it something of the affluent exuberance of a boom town. The energetic John XXII, though now in his eighties, victorious over Emperor and anti-Pope, had brought, through an ingenious invention of new methods of taxation, a great deal of wealth into the city; it was he who laid down the plans for the great Palace of the Popes, implying the permanence of the papal residence; the dark days of the plague and the marauding mercenaries were still in the future; the city was growing fast and was

filled with dignitaries, magnates, and adventurers of all nations.
It had become "a cultural center for men of letters and
artists." [20] It must also have been very gay: a recent work on the
city of the exiled papacy contains an evocative paragraph:

> . . . There were feasts and tournaments and balls for the beautiful
> ladies . . . and the lords of Europe's most polished court. . . . Ele-
> gant priests and princes and pages and beauties, in a choice assortment
> of damasks, silks and velvets, embroideries in gold thread, peacock
> feather hats, long, pointed shoes, curls, jeweled crowns and ivory
> combs, ermine and that squirrel fur called vair . . .[21]

The writer is recalling the Palace of the Popes in the reign of
Clement VI, a few years later than the time we are dealing with
here. But Petrarch's own letters make it clear that something of
the same lighthearted splendor characterized the city even in his
youth.

Both brothers, during these years, passed from the flirtatious
stage to that of serious and ultimate commitment. Gherardo's
sweetheart, of whom Francesco speaks tenderly, was to die
young. It is likely that xci of the *Rhymes* (dated as of 1337?)
refers to her: the first quatrain suggests at least an acquaintance
with the lady who is the subject of the sonnet:

> The lady fair, whom thou didst love so well,
> Hath from amongst us suddenly withdrawn,
> And unto heav'n—that dare I hope—is gone;
> Such pleasantness and softness round her fell.[22]

Francesco met his destiny, as he tells us specifically and repeatedly, on April 6, 1327, when he first beheld the invincible Laura.
Perhaps, if we are willing to accept the chronology of the heart,
we may say that this meeting, following the old pattern but with
the principal actor that greatest of lyric poets, against the background of a triumphant church and a prosperous capital, in a region which still echoed the songs of the troubadours, was the
highwater mark of the medieval tradition, even as Laura's death,
caused by the plague, could be said to mark the end of the old
world, its gaiety and its aristocratic and refined security.

Of his first sight of Laura, a memorable date in the sentimental history of mankind as it was crucial for the life of the poet, Petrarch gives us very specific details. In the *Rhymes* (ccxi) he writes:

> Sixth day of April, at the hour of prime;
> Thousand, three hundred, twenty-seven; the maze
> I entered whence the issue is not seen.[23]

and this is supported by the note he wrote in his Virgil on the occasion of her death. In iii, iv, and v of the *Rhymes* he supplies further particulars, including the name, Laureta. But who was she? The most likely identification with any daughter of earth would make her one Laurette de Noves, married in 1325 to Hugues de Sade. This is, in the words of Bosco's cautious verdict, "the hypothesis most widely accepted,"[24] but there are other candidates. Cleaving to what the poet himself tells us and assuming it is the truth (and there is no reason why we should not): we know only that "Laureta" did capture the heart of the poet during the holy season of 1327, that she was married and had a number of children by 1342 when she was already well into middle age,[25] and that she died in 1348 on the anniversary of the poet's first sight of her.[26]

Laura's ensnaring glance, if it put an end to the carefree liberty of Francesco's youth, setting on his neck a heavy yoke of devotion which he was to bear for twenty-one years, at the same time released his genius. It is in his songs of her that the poet will find his deepest and most appealing expression—not in the Latin works over which he labored so long and with such industry. It is the poet who will endear to us the scholar-humanist.

CHAPTER 3

Lofty Column, Verdant Bay

A S the encounter with Laura marked a crisis in the emotional life of the poet, so a few years later another change occurred which was to alter the style of living to which Petrarch and his brother had become accustomed. They had been living, in some luxury as we have seen, on their inheritance; in 1330 their source of income dried up. The reasons for this are a little obscure: Petrarch seems to hint at malfeasance on the part of the executors,[1] but it is possible of course that his inheritance was not as ample as he had thought it. He was, after all, a young man with no great interest in financial matters. In any event, the young men about town found it necessary to secure employment. Petrarch, unwilling to corrupt himself by the practice of law, accepted the tonsure and probably minor orders. Then, with the good luck that was to characterize his career, he was taken under the protection of the young Giacomo Colonna (who had formed a good impression of him in Bologna), recently named Bishop of Lombez, in the Pyrenees. The Bishop was to leave Avignon that same year to take charge of his new assignment. He invited Petrarch to accompany him as part of his household. Two other young men also made the journey in the Bishop's train, both destined to be our poet's lifelong friends and favorite correspondents. One was the Fleming Ludwig Van Kempen, called "Socrates" by Petrarch, and the other the Roman Lello di Stefano dei Tosetti to whom in his letters Petrarch gave the name Laelius with its happy classical connotations, for Laelius was the name of the friend and confidant of the great Scipio Africanus, whose image was already beginning to haunt our poet.

On his return after a happy summer, Petrarch was recommended by the Bishop to the latter's brother, Cardinal Giovanni Colonna, who appointed him chaplain to his household. Petrarch was to remain in the Cardinal's service for seven years and to be a

friend and protégé of the Cardinal until the Black Death carried
his patron away. In 1333 the young chaplain, at the Cardinal's
expense, resumed his travels, going to Ghent, Aix-la-Chapelle,
Liége (where he discovered two manuscripts of Cicero), and Cologne, returning by way of Lyons to Avignon.

Of this tour he writes quite frankly in his *Letter to Posterity*
that "while I invented certain reasons to satisfy my elders of the
propriety of the journey, the real reason was a great inclination
and longing to see new sights." [2] And in fact the letters reveal the
enthusiastic delight in sight-seeing which characterizes the tourist
of today. Many of the observations will strike a familiar chord in
the hearts of twentieth-century travelers. In Paris the wayfarer
spent "considerable time, in open-mouth wonder" and when day-
light failed him "prolonged his investigations into the night"; and
after much "loitering" and sight-seeing he felt he had come to the
truth of Paris, the reputation of which was fabulous—but that
truth, he adds discreetly, would make "a long story, and not suited
for a letter." [3] At Aix-la-Chapelle he visited the tomb of Charlemagne and picked up some legends about the great Emperor, he
admired the industries of Flanders and, arriving at Cologne, was
amazed to find such a high level of culture in a land he had
thought of as "barbarous." "The appearance of the city, the dignity of the men, the attractiveness of the women, all surprised
me," he writes, and he adds a detailed account of a local custom
of lustration on midsummer night—again exclaiming on the remarkable beauty of the women who lived on the banks of the
Rhine. He returned through the forest of Ardennes "alone . . .
and in time of war." [4] Wilkins aptly remarks in this connection
that "Petrarch, a man of peace, scorned physical danger";[5] in fact,
throughout his life, over rough roads and uncultivated trails, beset
by mercenary troops or simply lawless bandits, often under fright-
ful weather conditions, in discomfort literally impossible for us to
conceive of nowadays, he remained a devoted traveler. He was
not unaware of his fortitude in this area, as is casually indicated in
the sonnet (*Rhymes* clxxvi) written at the end of his journey:

> Through savage woods I walk without demur
> Where men well-armed might hesitate to fare,
> What shall I fear who long since learned to bear
> Those love-charged glances that my pulses stir?

Boldly I tread and sing the praise of her
Whom Heaven could not from my bosom tear,
Nay, for I see her semblance everywhere
In fancied shape of looming beech or fir.
In the sweet melody by wood things chorus'd
I seem to hear her: in the quivering leaf,
The rippling brook, the thrush's plaintive note.
Ah, dear to me the wildness of the forest
And sweet its solitude past all belief—
Were not my only sun too far remote.

Perhaps it should also be noted that, as in the case of many
tourists who have come after him, journeys in foreign lands convinced Petrarch that home was best: "The more I travel," he
writes, "the more my admiration for Italy grows." [6]

In Paris he had made the acquaintance of the Chancellor of the
University, Roberto de' Bardi, a fellow Florentine; this contact
would prove to be useful to the young scholar's career. At some
time too in this period he met another cleric, destined not only to
be of value in the pursuit of his professional ambition, but also to
have a major influence on Petrarch's spiritual life and literary direction; this was the Augustinian monk Dionigi da Borgo San
Sepolcro; a copy of Augustine's *Confessions,* which Dionigi gave
him, the poet carried with him for many years after. In the following year, thanks to the influence of the Cardinal Colonna, Petrarch was appointed to a canonry in the cathedral of Lombez;
this appointment carried with it a certain income and no residen-
tial obligation. The appointment was made by Benedict XII, who
succeeded to the papacy on the death of John. Petrarch addressed
to him a verse-letter (*Ep. met.* I, 2) imploring him to restore the
papal seat to Rome: the Pope, another Frenchman, was, however,
quite content with Avignon; he enlarged the plans of his predecessor (and uncle) for the Palace of the Popes and carried the
massive fortress halfway to its completion before his death in
1342. He seems to have been, at least in intention, a good pope; he
labored hard for reforms long overdue in the behavior of the
clergy; he sought to mediate between England and France and to
bring the Greeks into the Catholic fold; he sent emissaries to the
Orient with intent to convert the Mongols and Chinese. But Petrarch, resentful of the continuing Babylonian captivity, thought

ill of him, and accused him of drunkenness, gluttony, and ineptitude.[7]

The year 1336 was memorable for two events in our poet's life: the ascent of Mt. Ventoux, which he undertook with his brother in April of that year, and his first trip to Rome, begun in late December. Much has been made of the ascent of Mt. Ventoux as a dramatic illustration of the poet's "modernity," and I believe with reason. It is true that when he reached the top he turned to St. Augustine and was struck by the passage that reads: "as men go about wondering at the heights of mountains and the great waves of the sea and wide flowing rivers and the girdle of the ocean and wheeling of the stars—and to themselves give no heed" [8] and having read it, felt ashamed of his impulse and descended wordless and reflective from the peak—yet for all that he had a good look at the view first, and he does indeed remain the first man of modern times who recorded a desire that others may have felt (but never voiced) to climb a mountain "because it was there." The episode in its combination of curiosity and nature worship with its bookish surrender to authority is a little parable of Petrarch's psyche and indeed of the course of his life.

The details of the journey to Rome are illuminating with respect to travel in the fourteenth century. Petrarch went by sea to Civitavecchia, thence overland to Capranica where he was a guest of Orso dell' Anguillara, brother-in-law of Giacomo Colonna, who had invited him, and, after waiting for an escort to come out from Rome to protect him, finally entered the Eternal City, with its feuding population severely reduced by the desertion of the popes. Sad as was its condition, Rome made a great impression on Petrarch, and he frequently refers to it in his letters.

His immediate response was, not unnaturally, brief: although Cardinal Colonna, to whom Petrarch wrote on "the Ides of March" (1337), must have been expecting a lengthy report of the poet's impression, he had to be content with a very short note, documenting Petrarch's admiration which had left him all but wordless: "You used to think I would write something in the grand style when I had reached Rome. I have found, it is true, a vast subject for future writing; at present there is nothing that I dare attempt, for I sink under the weight of so many marvels around me. . . . In truth Rome was greater and its remains are greater than I had imagined. I now only marvel not that the world was conquered by this city but that it was conquered so late." [9] It is only in later years that the poet records some of the events of his first visit, his archaeological walks with Paolo Annibaldi (kinsman of the Colonna and later Roman Senator) and with the old friar Giovanni Colonna di San Vito, to whom he wrote six years later (*Fam.* VI, 2), recalling their twilight colloquies on the roof of the Baths of Diocletian, where they climbed for a view of the city, even as today we ascend the Pincio or the Aventino. If Petrarch was awed by the grandeur of the ruins he was likewise infuriated by the depredations they suffered under the hands of the barons who systematically destroyed the old buildings in order to get material for their new fortresses. Petrarch's is one of the earliest voices to be raised against this kind of edificial cannibalism. (It is possible that during this sojourn he lived in the mausoleum of Augustus, which the Colonna had taken over as one of their town houses—or should we say strongholds?) Against both the chronic vandalism and the incessant brawling of the titled gangsters which was in part its cause Petrarch wrote (a few years later) an ode (*Rhymes* liii) to the Senator Bosone de' Raffaeli da Gubbio in which we can still hear the authentic accents of the antiquarian and the patriot:

> Her ancient wall, which still can stir mankind
> To love and hate, or fill their hearts with dread,
> If but her glorious deeds are told again;
> Her rocky tombs, which hide the mighty dead,
> Whose memory shall never pass from mind
> While the foundations of the world remain;
> And all who share with them the general bane
> Look for the healing of their wounds to thee.
> Great Scipios, faithful Brutus, could the voice
> Of rumor reach you, how you would rejoice
> At such a wisely placed authority;
> Nor will the tiding be
> Less welcome to Fabricius, which afford
> A glimpse of Rome's lost beauty now restored.[10]

As usual Petrarch got on well with everyone, including the formidable Stefano the Elder, warrior-leader of the Colonna clan.

He remained in Rome probably through Easter of 1337. We have no record of his return journey, and some biographers (beginning with de Sade) have postulated that he made a long, roundabout voyage, visiting Spain and even England; this notion is based on some rather vague references in his letters, but it seems probable that Tatham is right when he says that if the poet "had ever been in England or Spain there surely would have been some trace of it in his later writings." [11] If the reference indicates a visit to Lombez it may have taken him, as Morris Bishop suggests,[12] at least to Brittany on some business of the Cardinal Colonna but more likely in 1335 than in 1337; in any event, the journey, if it ever took place, is not documented with the usual detailed accuracy of our wayfarer.

By June of 1337 Petrarch was back in Avignon and very shortly after his return achieved his youthful ambition to settle in Vaucluse, by the springs of the Sorgue. He bought a small house (probably the Bishop advanced him the money) and for four years proceeded to enjoy the life of solitude—or more correctly, retirement, for he encouraged and received many visitors.

It was at this time (1336–37) that Petrarch prepared the first "collected edition" of his "trifles" as he somewhat coyly termed his vernacular poems; there were approximately a hundred ready for editing. In this occupation we may see the evidence of the poet's awareness of his status; in fact he had by now achieved a certain prominence. He had traveled widely, he had made friends everywhere, he was known as an intimate of the powerful Colonna tribe, and his devotion to Laura had spread his name among the poets of the day: Boccaccio, for example, had already read and admired the lyrics. He was, in Wilkins' phrase, "a marked man in Avignon" [13]—and well known far beyond the confines of the papal capital. The years in Vaucluse would confirm his position and afford the leisure for the planning of new projects and the furtherance of greater ambitions. He had also acquired a sizable library (we have a list of his "favorite books" made in 1333 and containing some fifty titles)[14] and was known everywhere as an avid collector of the works of Cicero.

At some time in this period Petrarch made his great decision henceforth to employ Latin rather than Italian in his major literary endeavors. In a letter to Boccaccio, written in his old age (*Sen.* V, 2), he confesses that he had at first thought that Latin had already been too well cultivated and that he would make use of Italian—indeed that he had begun "a great work" in the vernacular but had finally given up the idea lest his verses be "mangled by the public." Critics have speculated as to the identity of the "great work." Would it have been an *Africa* or something of like nature in the vernacular? Or do we, not improbably, have in the *Trionfi*, such an artifact, with its reminiscence of the *Divine Comedy*, and was it the inevitable comparison with that unique masterpiece that caused Petrarch to entrust his fame to Latin? [15]

Was his decision sound or otherwise? One can debate it. For Petrarch's immediate purposes the choice was wise. The Latin works gave him full citizenship in the world of scholars and intellectuals, and such compositions as the *De remediis* and the *De vita solitaria* kept his name fresh down to the sixteenth century. But in the long run he would have done better to stick to his original youthful intention; broadly speaking, from the Renaissance on, lovers of the Latin tongue have studied the classics and ignored the works of medieval Latin writers. There is hardly a single Latin work in the general category of strictly creative literature in the Middle Ages (as distinguished from works of philosophy, history, and the like) which the lettered classes of today esteem very highly, save perhaps for some Goliardic lyrics; Petrarch's survival as a poet is entirely due to the "trifles" which make up his *Canzoniere*.

Another noteworthy event in Petrarch's private life occurred at about this time. On his return from Rome to Avignon in the summer of 1337, "he found there," as Morris Bishop puts it, "either a baby boy or a mother big with child," adding somewhat gratuitously: "neither sight can have pleased him." [16] Bishop's version of the poet's sentiments may well be anachronistic; it is true that the only reference we have to the mother of his son, otherwise unknown, is somewhat disparaging, and an illegitimate child was hardly appropriate to his status and less so to his pose as Laura's devoted and faithful lover. Yet he acknowledged his paternity, provided for the child, and sought to find a place for him in the world. If he does not appear in his best light in the role of father, yet at least he did not attempt to avoid the responsibilities that fatherhood entails. The boy was called Giovanni, possibly after Cardinal Colonna.

We may not doubt Petrarch when he affirms (in the *Letter to Posterity*) that his retirement to Vaucluse sprang from his "deep-seated and innate repugnance to town life, especially in the disgusting city of Avignon"; nor may we question his more intimate reason, as set forth in detail in the rhymed letter to Giacomo Colonna, to escape from Laura and her irresistible temptation. We might, however, infer more positive reasons: he needed peace, a certain amount of solitude, and time to put into effect his decision to aim for high achievement in Latin poetry. If he was fleeing Laura he was also preparing to pursue Scipio. In the letter mentioned above he has given us a very pleasant picture of his life in scholarly retirement even though he was still haunted by his persistent temptress:

> Scanty my evening repast, with seasoning supplied by hunger,
> Labor and fasting throughout the long day. My servant's a peasant.
> As for companions I have myself and my dog, faithful creature.
> Others are moved to avoid this place from which idle pleasure,
> Armed with the darts of desire, has taken leave to go seeking
> Opulent cities to dwell in. Here in my hidden refuge
> Back from their exile the Muses stay with me, but seldom do other
> Visitors come—save only those drawn by the fame of the fountain.
> Though I have lived for a year in Vaucluse yet once or twice only
> Friends I would gladly welcome have come. Apparently distance
> Vanquishes friendship. However, they write; their letters are frequent.
> These speak of me when I sit at night alone by the fireside
> Or when I walk alone in summer under the shade trees;
> So that their daily talk is of me and I am their nightly discourse.
> See them in person I may not: the briars, the snows in the winter
> Frighten them off—and my diet as well; the cities have taught them
> Delicate habits. In short, both faithful friends and good servants
> Leave me bereft since I've chosen this savage manner of living.
> Nay, if perchance one comes, impelled by long-standing affection,
> Pity he offers as if to a jail-bird—then hastily leaves me.

But if visitors are few he has the consolation of the faithful comradeship of his "secret friends"—his beloved authors:

> Out of all ages they come, friends famous for wit and for learning,
> Eloquence, warfare and art, friends who are not too demanding,
> Asking a corner only of my little house, always granting
> Any request of mine, willing and eager to help me,
> Never giving me trouble, ready to leave at my signal,

Prompt to return when I ask them. I question now one, now an-
other:
Freely they give their reply and sing or speak at my bidding.
Secrets of nature some tell me, others offer good counsel
Touching on life or on death, still others narrate the stories
Handed down from of old, of their own deeds and their fathers'.
Some, with their light-hearted words make me forget my troubles,
Moving my lips to laughter with jests, and yet others teach me
Fortitude under ill, denial of desire and self-knowledge,
Masters of peace and of war, forensic art or of tillage,
Or of the charting of journeys on the wide ways of the ocean.
These are the friends that uplift me when I am cast down by mis-
fortune,
Tempering likewise my joy when prosperity makes me exultant,
Reminding me all things must end, that the days of our lives are
fleeting.
.   .   .   .

Often we spend whole days alone on deserted pathways,
Holding my pen in my right hand with the left hand clutching the
paper,
Cares beyond number flooding my heavy heart as I wander:
Often, all unsuspecting, we come on the beasts of the forest,
Often the cry of a bird breaks in on my quiet reflections,
Bidding me follow its song. On such strolls I resent interruptions,
Even so much as a greeting low-voiced by some passing stranger,
While I have thoughts fixed elsewhere and my mind intent on
grave matters.
Solace it is to me to drown in the leafy silence
And every sound is offensive save only the murmuring brooklet,
Trickling over the gravel or the breeze that ruffles my papers,
Causing my songs to give out a soft and gentle susurrus.[17]

Those were indeed fruitful years. Petrarch only slightly exag-
gerates when he writes years later (*Letter to Posterity*) that "almost every bit of writing I have published was either accomplished or begun or at least conceived there." Before the end of
1337 he had started on the *De viris illustribus*, on which he was to
toil for many years to come; and on Good Friday of the following
year (or possibly 1339), as he was strolling over the hills of
Vaucluse, he conceived the notion of writing a great epic, dealing
with the victory of Scipio over Hannibal. This work too was
destined to occupy him for many years and was left unfinished at

his death. The source of the *Africa* was probably in the Roman sojourn and more immediately in the *De viris* itself, which also contains a life of Scipio; in fact, it seems likely, in the phrase of Aldo Bernardo, that "the two works evolved simultaneously." [18] In any event, in the *Africa* Petrarch felt that at last he had found a subject worthy of him, one in which he could at once depict a great and epic personality and, like Virgil, sing the grandeur of Rome and its destiny.

Yet the Latin did not entirely displace the Tuscan. If in addition to the *De viris* and the *Africa* a number of Latin *epistolae metricae* may be assigned to the Vaucluse retirement, it was also the time of the conception of the *Triumphs* and the composition of some forty more items ultimately destined for the *Canzoniere,* including the beautiful "*Solo e pensoso i più deserti campi*" (xxxv), the deeply religious "*Padre del ciel, dopo i perduti giorni*" (lxii), and the memorable political *canzone* from which we have quoted, "*Spirto gentil, che quelle membra regge*" (liii). As Wilkins remarks, the poems composed in this period "show an advance in maturity of thought, of feeling, and of artistry." [19] We may properly quote sonnet 28 (xxxv of the *Rhymes*) as representative of the compositions of this season of the poet's life and as a kind of sentimental "candid" of the state of mind—or at least one recurrent state of mind—of the self-exiled scholar-bard:

> Alone and ever weary with dark care
> I seek the solitude of desert ways,
> Casting about the while a timid gaze
> Lest alien steps my refuge seek to share.
> No other shield I find against the stare
> Of prying eyes: too well my face displays
> In ashen cheerlessness how cruel the blaze
> That burns within, and lays my secret bare.
> 'Tis only hills, I think, and silent streams
> And meadows and deep thickets that can know
> The tenor of my life, from men concealed.
> Yet not so wide I wander in my dreams
> But Love comes with me, following where I go,
> And long we parley on the lonely weald.

Petrarch's gift for making friends was in evidence during his sojourn in Vaucluse. Topography made him a neighbor of

Philippe de Cabassoles, Bishop of Cavaillon, in whose diocese
Vaucluse lay, and the two men became fast friends; Petrarch later
dedicated to the Bishop his long letter-essay, *On the Life of Solitude* (although, like most of his works, it was to have a lengthy
gestation).

Here too, it seems likely, he began his labors on the *Triumphs,*
possibly writing as much as the first three *capitoli* of the first
Triumph, that of Love.

September 1, 1340 was a memorable day for our poet. He received two invitations to accept the poetic crown; one from the
Chancellor of the University of Paris and one from the Roman
Senate. "Who, I ask you," he wrote that same day (*Fam.* IV, 4) to
Cardinal Colonna, "could ever have guessed that such a thing
could have happened among our crags?" To which all biographers
have answered: Who but Petrarch himself, who had connived to
get both invitations (as he confesses, in his indirect way, in the
Secretum)? He fondly believed that the crown for which he
yearned had been regularly bestowed on the supreme poets of
antiquity. It is true, too, that local coronations had taken place in
his day; Dante seems to have had an actual crowning in mind in
his wistful reference in the *Paradiso* (xxv, 8–9) and had later been
offered a coronation in Bologna by Giovanni del Virgilio. Alber-
tino Mussato had been crowned in Padua in 1315. But Petrarch
wanted a crown of international significance and after some false
hesitation he chose to accept the Roman invitation. At this distance in time it may seem to us an empty and rather absurd ceremony; it did not seem so to Petrarch nor apparently to the world
of letters of his time. At any event, it put an end to his life of
meditative retirement in Vaucluse. In mid-February he sailed for
Naples to undergo his examination (he seems to have thought of
the laurel as a kind of Ph.D. and insisted on being examined for
it) at the hands of Robert of Naples, with whom he spent most of
March in friendly discourse. He was accompanied by Azzo da
Correggio, who was seeking Robert's aid in his plan to dislodge
his nephew Mastino della Scala from Parma. Petrarch's friend
Dionigi da Borgo San Sepolcro, now in the service of the king, had
taken care of the preliminary planning. When Robert had been
satisfied as to the poet's worthiness, the latter pressed on to Rome
where, in the Palace of the Senate on the Capitoline, after an

address on the nature and uses of poetry, he was crowned by Orso dell' Anguillara, representing the authority of the Senate. The conferring of the crown carried also with it the status of Roman citizenship. This ceremony, which Körting with some exaggeration called "epoch-making in the fullest sense of the word," [20] made of Petrarch "the most famous private citizen then living." [21] On sheer performance he hardly deserved the honor; none of his great works had yet been written, and he got the award more because of the people he knew than for what he had done. But, as time would show, the award was to be justified. Petrarch was to be the most enduring poet of his age and certainly the most able scholar as well—and with a social presence to match both of those qualities. Many years later (*Sen.* XVII, 2; 1373) he wrote Boccaccio that "the laurel came to me with its leaves immature, when I was not ripe for it in age or mind; if I had been older I shouldn't have wanted it." Perhaps, if we find his youthful calculation unbecoming we should also note, to his credit, that Petrarch seems to have felt under an obligation to deserve the honor bestowed upon him.

The road back to Avignon was longer than the poet might have expected. He left Rome shortly after his coronation (which had taken place on Easter Sunday, April 8) and after one false start (being captured by bandits in the Campagna and compelled to return to Rome and seek an escort) he arrived in Pisa toward the end of the month. Here he received an invitation from Azzo, who was on the point of executing his *coup de main* and recovering Parma from his uncle. Petrarch accepted and rejoined his friend in Parma the day after the city had been liberated (May 21) from the tyranny of its Veronese governor, an event that the poet celebrated in an ode (*"Quel c'ha nostra natura in sè più degno"*)— "Fairest of all things that our nature owns"—which he excluded from the *Canzoniere*. It contains, however, some very fine lines, notably the passage praising liberty, which Carducci six centuries later admired.[22] Azzo and his brothers treated Petrarch very handsomely, giving him a country residence some fourteen miles to the south for the summer months and a house in the city where he stayed during the winter until February or March of 1342. His rustic retreat near a wooded hill called the Selvapiana must have proved an adequate substitute for Vaucluse; it was here he wrote the *canzone* (*Rhymes* cxxix) *"Di pensier in pensier, di monte in monte*"—"From thought to thought, from mountain peak to mountain," which Bishop has rightly described as "one of the most beautiful and famous" [23] of his odes: in content it is quite similar to the sonnet we quoted on p. 53. During his sojourn in Parma, the poet also added a fourth chapter to his *Trionfi,* and finished the *Africa*—or at least the first draft of it. Here too he was saddened by news of the death of three of his dearest friends: the Bishop Giacomo Colonna, his first patron; Tommaso Caloiro da Messina, his college chum; and his confessor Dionigi da Borgo San Sepolcro, who had been so helpful in getting the laureate conferred upon him.

In the spring of 1342 he resumed his journey toward Provence. In Avignon he joined a delegation of Roman nobles who were waiting on the new Pope, Clement VI, to petition him to return to Rome. The Pope, another Frenchman, listened courteously to Petrarch; indeed, he not only gave him a private audience but appointed him to a canonry in Pisa—but he said the time was not ripe for the return of the papal court to Rome. The Pontiff did, however, accede to the other requests of the delegation, that he accept appointment as Roman senator for life and that he proclaim 1350 a jubilee year. (These requests were also on the agenda of Cola di Rienzo who arrived on January 11, 1343—and of this meteoric figure we shall have more to say.)

Petrarch seems to have spent most of his time in Avignon during these years, no doubt busy with his diplomatic charges; he may well have made brief visits to Vaucluse, but we have no record of a long sojourn there. The period of 1342–43 is, however, a very meaningful time for our poet. In April, 1343 his brother Gherardo entered a Carthusian monastery; this event must have had an even more sobering influence on Petrarch than the trio of deaths we have noted above. In the same year, possibly at about the same time, Petrarch's illegitimate daughter, Francesca, was born; we do not know whether of the same mother as Giovanni or not. Since Petrarch always regarded sexual relationships as "disgusting" he must have been overcome by a sense of guilt. (He was later to be grateful to Francesca who was a constant comfort to him in his old age.) His writings show the effect of these disturbing episodes; the *Secretum,* his secret confession, is of these years as are the Penitential Psalms. Eloquent of the spiritual stresses of this period is the sonnet *"Passa la nave mia"* (*Rhymes* clxxxix):

Charged with oblivion my ship careers
Through stormy combers in the depth of night;
Left lies Charybdis, Scylla to the right;
My master,—nay, my foe, sits aft and steers.
Wild fancies ply the oars, mad mutineers,
Reckless of journey's end or tempest's might;
The canvas splits 'gainst the relentless spite
Of blasts of hopes and sighs and anxious fears.
A rain of tears, a blinding mist of wrath
Drench and undo the cordage, long since worn
And fouled in knots of ignorance and error;
The two sweet lights are lost that showed my path,
Reason and art lie 'neath the waves, forlorn:
What hope of harbor now?—I cry in terror.

Some biographers have seen in such writings evidence of a "conversion" in the poet. Perhaps it is true that the strain of Christian melancholy becomes more pronounced from this time forth, although it had been already evident both in the *Canzoniere* and the *Letters*. One cannot say, however, that the change in the poet's worldly interest or daily life is very noticeable. This is, in fact, the beginning of his ardent championship of Cola, of his first steps in learning Greek (under the instruction of the apostate Greek monk Bernard Balaam), and of a rather busy diplomatic career. Nor can one see any great change in his attitude toward Laura; it should be said, however, that in his *Letter to Posterity* he says he renounced all carnal relationships with women shortly before reaching his fortieth year. So much of a conversion there may have been.

In September, 1343 Petrarch was entrusted with a mission to the court of Naples; the Pope, supporting Cardinal Colonna in his efforts to get certain protégés of the latter liberated from prison where they were languishing for rebellion, sent Petrarch as his ambassador. As it happened, the mission was unsuccessful, but the journey itself was certainly not without interest. Going by sea when the weather permitted, with stages made by land when the continuous warfare and brigandage permitted, Petrarch made his way to Rome and renewed his acquaintance with the Roman Colonna, who cordially welcomed him. Pressing on to Naples, he was appalled at the chaotic state of affairs which had come about after the death of his much-mourned Robert (occurring in 1343);

the young Queen Joan was beset by her own kin and her Hungarian in-laws, and the realm was in a parlous state. Petrarch has
left us many notes on this sojourn; most of them are "touristic" in
nature. He visited the environs of the city, marveling at the Solfa-
tara, Baia and Pozzuoli, where he saw the famous "Amazon"
Maria, a portent in her times. (His companions were his good
friends Barbato da Sulmona and Giovanni Barrili, who pressed
him to settle down in Naples.) One of his letters (*Fam.* V, 5)
contains a thrilling description of a combined earthquake, storm,
and tidal wave the night of November 25; such was the violence
of the sea as the poet beheld it that he vowed he would never travel
by ship again. He had his usual social success; the Queen made
him an honorary chaplain of her household as her grandfather
had done before her, and he was everywhere treated with respect.
But he found Naples depressing, he had a sense of imminent
doom, and he felt even the influence of his friend Philippe de
Cabassoles, Bishop of Cavaillon, now a member of the Regency
acting for the young Queen, could hardly hope to prevail against
so many scheming enemies of the troubled state. He left Naples in
December to make his way back not to Provence but to Parma
where he seems to have contemplated permanent residence. He
went so far as to buy the town house he had occupied on his first
visit and to have it thoroughly repaired. He sent for his son, Giovanni, now seven years old, and put him into school under the
direction of the able master Moggio dei Moggi who was the tutor
also of Azzo's children. And in a metrical letter (II, 10) written in
answer to Socrates, who urged him to return to Provence, he stated
frankly that he did not intend to leave Italy again. Meanwhile he
wrote a number of letters, continued work on the *Rerum memorandarum* and on his revision of the *Africa,* and added another
chapter, the *Triumph of Chastity,* to the *Trionfi.* Two of his most
noteworthy odes are also of this period; one is the ode "I' vo pensando" (*Rhymes* cclxiv), which Wilkins considers "the poetic
equivalent of the third book of the *Secretum*":[24] the first stanza
will give some indication of its burden and its dignity:

> As thought succeeding thought within me springs,
> Such keen self-sorrow in my mind is bred
> That I am moved to shed
> Far other tears than those I wept before;

Till every day drawn nearer to the dead,
From God a thousand times I seek the wings
Whereon to heavenly things
The spirit, freed from earthly bonds, can soar;
Yet strive in vain, for in the end my store
Of sighs and tears and prayers must fruitless prove,
And justly so, for if we let our feet
Stumble when we have strength to stand, 'tis meet
We sink, howe'er we long to rise above.
The outstretched arms of Love
Are open still, on which my trust is fixed,
And yet I pause perplexed,
Fearful to see my own in others' fate,
A prey to sins I may repent too late.[25]

The second is the celebrated patriotic *canzone,* "*All'Italia*" (cxxviii) which was to inspire Leopardi and the heroes of the Risorgimento period. In this poem Petrarch, observing the war-ravaged condition of Italy, deplores the fall of his country from the greatness and unity that had prevailed under Rome, reproaches the princes for their use of mercenaries, as short-sighted as it is immoral, and finally lays the responsibility for the unhappy state of affairs on the shoulders of these same princes to whom he says:

Ah! is not this the soil my foot first press'd?
And here, in cradled rest,
Was I not softly hush'd?—here fondly rear'd?
Ah! is not this my country?—so endear'd
By every filial tie?
On whose lap shrouded both my parents lie!
Oh, by this tender thought,
Your torpid bosoms to compassion wrought,
Look on the people's grief!
Who, after God, of you expect relief;
And if ye but relent,
Virtue shall rouse her in embattled might,
Against blind fury bent,
Nor long shall doubtful hang the unequal fight;
For no,—the ancient flame
Is not extinguish'd yet, that raised the Italian name! [26]

If the ode is of this period (1344–45), it may well have been inspired by the poet's own experiences, for in late 1344 Azzo, finding he could not administer the city of Parma, sold the lordship to the

Marquis of Ferrara. This meant war with Mastino della Scala from whom Azzo had taken the city and, what was worse, also with the powerful Visconti, to whom, it would seem, he had secretly promised it. Both armies, complete with mercenaries, moved on Parma in December, 1344 and by February of the following year life had become so uncomfortable that Petrarch fled the besieged city. After some harrowing experiences, he took refuge in Verona, where he remained until the following autumn; then by a roundabout way through the Alps he returned, at long last, to Provence, some two years after he had set out on the mission to Naples. The letter written to Barbato da Sulmona describing his flight from Parma is one of Petrarch's most vivid reportorial dispatches. It is worthy of quotation here, at least in part:

Leaving the city with a few companions at sunset on February 23rd, I picked my way between the enemy outposts. At midnight a body of brigands sprang from an ambush, loudly threatening us with death. There was no time to deliberate; our position, the dead of night and the encircling foe made every course full of peril. What could our little band, unarmed and unprepared, do against a superior force of armed men, bent on mischief? Our one hope lay in darkness and in flight.

> "My comrades scatter far and wide
> Well pleased in thickest night to hide."

For my own part, I admit, I snatched myself from death and from the clang of arms that rang all round me. And when I thought I had escaped every hazard (where can a man ever be sure of safety?) — whether from the obstacle of a ditch or a stone or some fallen timber, for in that cloudy and pitchdark night we could see nothing — the trusty steed which carried me fell headlong with such violence that I felt broken and almost lifeless. I rose without losing my presence of mind and — though now for many days I have not been able to lift my hand to my mouth — then, gaining strength from my terror, I remounted my horse. Of my companions some had returned home; others, though wandering vaguely round, had not abandoned their attempt. Our two guides, weary and panic-stricken, could find no sign of our whereabouts and compelled us to halt in a trackless spot whence, to add to our alarm, we could hear the calls of the enemy sentries on some neighbouring walls. Besides this, a storm had come on with savage hail; and the constant claps of thunder renewed the insistent dread of a more awful death.

It would be a long story if I were to tell you all. We passed that truly infernal night in the open, lying on the ground; and meanwhile the swelling and pain from my injured arm grew steadily worse. No grassy turf, no shelter of over-arching leaves, no rift in a hollow rock invited us to sleep; we had but the bare ground, a stormy wind, an angry sky, the fear both of man and beast and—an additional trial in my case—an injured frame. In such extremities we had one source of comfort which may arouse your astonishment and pity. We used the backs of our horses, which were drawn up crossways, as a kind of tent and shelter against the storm; though just before champing and excited, they now became quiet and still, as if from a sense of their own misery, and so performed a double service for us that night. Thus, weary and trembling, we waited for the dawn. As soon as a doubtful glimmer of light showed us a path among the briars, we left the perilous spot with all speed. Entering the walls of a friendly town, called Scandiano, we learned that a large force of horse and foot had been lying in wait for us the whole night near the walls, and shortly before our coming had been forced by the storm to retreat.[27]

Petrarch did not waste his time in his few months in Verona. It was there that he discovered, in the library of the cathedral, a book long overlooked, containing the letters of Cicero to Atticus. He immediately set about making a copy of these letters along with other Ciceronian letters; the resultant tome was so large that it could not fit on a bookshelf but had to stand on the floor. Since Petrarch's right arm was still suffering from the fall from his horse, the copying of such a vast work is impressive evidence of his devotion to learning and his love for Cicero. The find suggested a new audience for his letters; he wrote a letter to Cicero in mid-June of that year, another somewhat later, and in due course added such names as Virgil, Livy, and Homer to his list of correspondents. This may strike us as an odd and somewhat pretentious exercise; it may also I think be fairly regarded as a manifestation, as significant as it may seem childish, of the true humanistic spirit. Such correspondence, even though one-sided, is a recognition of common citizenship, an acknowledgment and even an assertion of the humanity of the classics and, at the same time, an affirmation of our kinship with them. For the rest, in Verona he worked a little more on the *Rerum memorandarum* but did not get far with it and apparently decided to give it up, for he never returned to this composition. And here too, he met Pietro, the son of Dante, to whom he later wrote a metrical epistle (*Ep. met.* III,

7), the rather obscure wording of which can be interpreted to suggest that Pietro had indicated to Petrarch that there was some hope that the poet would be welcomed back to Florence. It may well be; certainly more open approaches from the city of the lily were soon to come.

What we may call the second Vaucluse period was a happy one for Petrarch. He was glad to get back to the tranquillity of his country retreat after the trials of the road and the brush with violence. He wrote to his friend Philippe de Cabassoles, whom he had left in Naples struggling with the problems of the regency, a letter in rhymed hexameters:

> By civic broils from Italy exiled
> Hither I fled. Though almost reconciled
> To gain my groves, my streams, my rural bliss,
> Yet most of all my faithful friends I miss.
> Glad though I be to reach the well-known spot,
> No pleasure's quite the same where they are not.
> Yet, unless fate has some surprise in store,
> My youth's sweet haunts I vow to leave no more,
> Resolved to pass the short remains of life
> In thy retreat, secure from war and strife.
> Here, revered Philip, shall my country be,
> Here my Mount Helicon, my Castalie;
> Here am I fain to rest my weary Muse;
> Here, too, I count on thee; make no excuse.
> If books can give thee some respite from care
> And free my sleep from dreams of horrid war,
> Here shalt thou Naples, I my Parma find,
> Where no drums beat, where lurks no ambush blind.
> Let Wealth her votaries take, I choose repose;
> A poet's bliss none but a poet knows.
> (I need not blush so high a role to claim,
> For crowds, unblushing, arrogate the name.)
> Wilt thou ne'er rest from honour's panting race,
> Hastening forth, soon to return apace?
> While your worn keel furrows the ocean's foam,
> Think'st thou not death may part thee from thy home? . . .
> Here we have raiment, but no curtains fine,
> Nourishing food, not pampering courses nine;
> No couch with ivory steps we here prepare,
> But rest for limbs wearied with daily care;
> No purple coverings our apartments deck,

Nor floors of snow-white marble without speck;
Here wilt thou find no pearls, nor costly dyes,
But fresh, green turf, gemmed by the river's rise;
Here thou, so richly gifted by heaven's hand,
May bring, I trust, thy frail bark safe to land.
Death's sure approach bids me not aim too high,
Content with what my gardens small supply.
In these some old shrubs, set in the grassy lea,
Now need replacing—so in time shall we;
Till that time comes, which is youth's utmost dread,
Here may I rest, here lay my whitening head.
Now, while fruit-boughs o'erarch with grateful shade,
With hook and line we ply the fisher's trade.
Such plenty on the board Vaucluse can place—
Peaches and pears the second course to grace.
Bid thy attendants—man-at-arms and page—
Supply such dainties to thy green old age!
This woodland note, great Sir, thy friend erstwhile
Writes, who is Sorga's pilgrim or exile.[28]

In due course the Bishop did come, and Petrarch had other visitors as well; his young kinsman Franceschino degli Albizzi was his house guest for most of his sojourn; Giovanni had also apparently accompanied his father on the long and difficult journey from Parma. The letters either written at this time of the poet's life or referring to it are full of the same kind of contentment he voices in the letter quoted above: he took great interest in his garden, trying to reclaim some of the land from the "nymphs" of the Sorgue, enjoying the society of his steward and his wife, and delighting in the company of a big dog that the Cardinal had given him. He made frequent but brief excursions to Avignon, either on business or to meet friends, and he also called on his brother who was living in the Carthusian monastery of Montrieux. Petrarch took a lively interest, one might say almost a participant interest, in the lives of the peasants: one letter contains a sympathetic description of their life of toil, and two others display our poet as a protector of rustic virtue against the wickedness of the aristocracy. For it happened that during his time in Vaucluse a local *signore* had jailed the fiancé of a young woman on whom he had cast lustful eyes for no other reason than that the swain had claimed his legitimate rights. By feudal custom the lord had the right to put the peasant-lover to death and would have done so but for Petrarch's intervention. Writing to Laelius for his support, the worshiper of Laura argues, with a democracy not too common in those days: "We ought not to imagine that country-folk are less given to love than we are: the boy with the unerring bow has like power over all classes."

These were good years too for his poetic production. Here he began the *De vita solitaria,* which he dedicated to Philippe de Cabassoles and began and even finished the *De otio religioso,* dedicated to the monks of Montrieux but written, he tells them, for his own need rather than theirs. He wrote at least four of the "eclogues" that go to make up the *Bucolicum carmen;* of the *Canzoniere* the most notable items written here are the three sonnets of invective against the papal court, unusually violent in language, as one example in the outspoken English of the sixteenth-century translation will suffice to show:

> Vengeance must fall on thee, thow filthie whore
> Of Babilon, thow breaker of Christ's fold,
> That from achorns, and from the water colde,
> Art riche become with making many poore.
> Thow treason's neste that in thie harte dost holde
> Of cankard malice, and of myschief more
> Than pen can wryte, or may with tongue be tolde,
> Slave to delights that chastitie hath solde;
> For wyne and ease which settith all thie store
> Uppon whoredome and none other lore,
> In thye pallais of strompetts younge and olde
> Theare walks Plentie, and Belzebub thye Lorde
> Guydes thee and them, and doth thye raigne upholde:
> It is but late, as wryting will recorde,
> That poore thow weart withouten lande or goolde;
> Yet how hath golde and pryde, by one accorde,
> In wichedness so apreadd thie lyf abrode,
> That it dothe stincke before the face of God. (*Rhymes* cxxxvi)[29]

Whether conditions were really as corrupt as they are here portrayed or merely seemed so to the virtuous poet is a matter of opinion. But what is surprising about this sonnet and the two that accompany it is the time of their composition. For in these years Petrarch received many favors from the Pope. Clement acceded graciously to the poet's petition for the legitimization of Giovanni

(1347), and he gave him, again on request, a canonry in Parma and later a deaconry in Pisa. He offered to make him a papal secretary and even hinted at a bishop's miter. Petrarch refused the secretaryship, and we may believe him when he indicates that he likewise had no desire to be a bishop. In the nature of life in the Middle Ages he had to have the benefices of canonries and the like if he was to support himself; he did not seek and never desired any appointment that would cramp his liberty. He wanted time for his own literary labors; he wanted also to be free from responsibility. He served many masters in the course of his life and served them well and faithfully, but he never accepted any charge with fixed and regularized duties. This is understandable and one can only congratulate him on having managed to arrange, from the day he won the favor of Giacomo Colonna, just the pattern of life that suited him best. He does seem, however, a little ungrateful to the Pope and the Avignon bureaucracy who so indulgently collaborated in his purpose.

History did not stand still during this interval of rustication. When the smoke of war had cleared away, the affair of Parma was settled by the transfer of the lordship—for money—from Mastino della Scala to Luchino Visconti, another step in the vigorous growth of the Lombard state. In Naples the woes that Petrarch had predicted came to pass; on September 18, 1346, the consort of Queen Joan, Andrew of Hungary, was murdered, some said with the complicity of his young bride. The factionalism of Naples was thereby intensified; the vindictive Hungarians and the two branches of the royal house, Taranto and Durazzo, fell to brawling and, as we have noted, Joan was obliged to flee to Provence, where she sold Avignon to the popes (1348). And most important of all for Petrarch, the comet known as Cola di Rienzo came sweeping through the Roman sky.

It may have been Cola's appearance on the scene that led Petrarch to leave Provence. The reason given was the necessity of taking up or at least taking over his canonry in Parma; some have suggested that he was anxious to place his newly legitimized son in a position of advantage in Verona. Perhaps it was simply his temperamental restlessness. (For in truth, the account of Petrarch's life is as much a travelogue as a biography.) But what is certain is that when he did leave Provence in the fall of 1347 he had Rome in mind as his destination. It was also at this time that

he decided to leave the service of the Colonna. If he was to aid
Cola as he hoped to, he was bound to find himself working
against the interests of his old patron, for the Colonna, like all the
Roman noble houses, were of necessity hostile to the Tribune. But
it may be that his decision was made before Cola took power; in
which case we can only assume, to put it coarsely, that Petrarch,
with the various other powerful connections he had now formed
and with the relative independence he had gained by reason of
his various benefices, no longer needed the Colonna patronage. In
his eighth eclogue, entitled "Separation" he gives his reasons for
the break; speaking as "Amyclas" to the "Ganymede" who represents Cardinal Colonna, he lectures his old patron as follows:

> The wise man alters his course, only the fool is stubborn;
> Often the hour, the occasion, reasons of place or of time
> Bring about change in our plans. Mark you my flocks sad condition,
> Backs worn thin by scant diet, with the cruel briars and thorns
> Tearing their tangled fleeces! What shall I do? Nay, drinking
> Out of the springs is unsafe, the grass they must crop is pernicious,
> Even the very air makes me afraid to draw breath.
> Pity the need that drives me and suffer a just separation,
> As truly you may in peace. For poor did I come to your pastures,
> Poorer still I go home, for I am surely no richer
> In milk or in kids but only in harvest of years and envy.
> Grave too is your frown, overbearing, in menacing sternness
>   surpassing
> Etna the craggy and ice-crested Ossa and haughty Olympus.
> There was a time I could bear it with heart unheeding, but age
> Knows not the patience of youth; wrinkles give strength to
>   resentment.
> Slavery is sad in old age; I would spend my last years in freedom.
> Bondage of youth is behind me, I beg that a lifetime of service
> End with the death of a freeman. Farewell, remember me always.
> Let me depart and in fields round about find what fortune awaits
>   me.   (lines 12–30)

He adds to these veiled suggestions of Colonna arrogance and
the hostile atmosphere of Avignon the pretext of patriotism: "Gil-
lias" (perhaps Azzo da Correggio is meant) has offered to be his
guide and companion and Italy beckons:

Well do I feel the deep love of my country, calling me homewards;
Fairer by far than here the shy violet blooms on the dewy
Lea and the rose on the bush more sweetly blushes, more fragrant;
Clearer the rills of my homeland wind through the flowery
    meadows,
Sweeter than elsewhere on earth grows the very grass of Ausonia.
(lines 56–60)

Whether timing or tact be the cause, the eclogue says nothing of Cola. But it was with Rome in mind and thoughts of his new role as counselor to the Tribune of the Eternal City that Petrarch left Provence for Italy in September, 1347. He got as far as Genoa before news came that cut short these high hopes and altered the course not only of his journey but of his career.

CHAPTER 4

The Days of the Tribune

WE may profitably discard chronology for a moment and survey the involvement of Petrarch with the affairs of the self-styled Tribune of the Romans, Cola di Rienzo. In the lawless and unstable political context of fourteenth-century Italy, waxing like weeds among the relatively well-established centers of power, rootless but temporarily very vigorous growths inevitably sprang up. The case of Castruccio Castrocane comes to mind; between 1316 and 1328 his well-organized followers threatened the older states of Florence and Genoa; there was a brief cluster of strength in Lombardy and Emilia (1331–33) around the person of the King of Bohemia, and of course in the later years of the century the wandering companies of mercenaries carried with them a kind of nomadic despotism. Of the same impromptu nature was the emergence of Cola.

We may see him too as exemplifying, as did other popular leaders in the century, a growing restlessness on the part of the lower classes, coming gradually to a resentful realization that their betters were not administering the affairs of the world with either justice or efficiency. Cola's semi-literate biographer, justifying his seizure of power, paints a picture of anarchy in the Eternal City that Petrarch must have witnessed at firsthand: "There were no rulers," he writes; "every day there were fights. Wherever there were virgins they were assaulted. There was no protection. Little girls were seized and carried off to dishonor. A wife could be snatched from the very bed of her husband. When the workers went out to work they were robbed. Where? Right at the gates of Rome. Pilgrims, coming for the good of their souls to visit the holy Churches, were not protected; they were robbed and left with their throats cut. The priests were up to mischief. Every kind of evil and wickedness, no justice, no restraint." [1] In short, the times were ripe for the Strong Man, with or without appeals to the tradition of sturdy Roman virtue. Cola seemed to combine the zeal of the reformer with a reverence for the discipline of the ancient Republic of Cincinnatus, Fabius, and Scipio.

His origins were humble enough. "In a quarter of the city which was inhabited only by mechanics and Jews," as Gibbon puts it, "the marriage of an innkeeper and a washerwoman produced the future deliverer of Rome. From such parents Nicholas Rienzi Gabrini could inherit neither dignity nor fortune; and the gift of a liberal education, which they painfully bestowed, was the cause of his glory and untimely end. The study of history and eloquence, the writings of Cicero, Seneca, Livy, Caesar, and Valerius Maximus elevated above his equals and contemporaries the genius of the young plebeian; he perused with indefatigable diligence the manuscripts and marbles of antiquity, loved to dispense his knowledge in familiar language; and was often provoked to exclaim: 'Where are now these Romans? Their virtue, their justice, their power? Why was I not born in those happy times?' " [2] The quotation will suffice to indicate how strongly Petrarch must have been attracted to this eloquent champion of liberty and ancient Romanism. We may add only that Cola, born in 1313, sometimes claimed to be the illegitimate son of Henry VII as if to add the sanctions of an imperial connection to his honest republicanism.

Since Petrarch too deplored the anarchy of his times, worshiped the Roman tradition, and revered Cicero, his enthusiasm for the Tribune was predictable. It is possible that the men had met on the occasion of the poet's coronation; their first recorded contact occurred in 1343 when, as we have noted, Cola came to Avignon to report on conditions in the Holy City and to get papal sanction for the administration he represented. Although Clement rejected the new administrative plan proposed by Cola, he treated the young man with courtesy: Petrarch was delighted with the promise that Cola's intentions seemed to hold out for the restoration of Rome's dignity. Four years later, in defiance of the Pope, Cola struck and, by a carefully plotted coup, made himself master of the city. (The nobles and the barons were not in Rome: "My lord Stefano Colonna had gone with his soldiers to Corneto for grain," says our chronicler.[3]) Very wisely Cola had the Pope's vicar along with himself invested as Rector of the city, and only after these ap-

pointments together with the new constitution had been ratified
by the assembled populace did he go on to name himself Tribune,
a term which turned out to mean dictator.

Within a month after hearing the news (June, 1347) Petrarch
wrote two letters to Cola; the first[4] was addressed also to the
Roman people, congratulating them on their newly found liberty
and urging them to be prepared to defend it. Cola is compared to
both of the heroic Brutuses of republican Rome. In the other,[5]
more intimate note, Petrarch thanks Cola for the letters he has
received from him, congratulates him on their style and discretion, and goes so far as to say that "people are uncertain as to
whether your deeds or your words are more to be admired; for
your devotion to liberty they believe you deserve to be called a
Brutus, for your eloquence a Cicero." Shortly afterward he eulo-
gized the Tribune in the high style of an eclogue, which may
merit partial translation here.

In these stylized verses Festinus (the Roman people) breaks in
on a conversation between Apicius (the Orsini) and Martius (the
Colonna) with news of the great accomplishment of their third
brother (Cola). The allegory is easy to read: the animals represent the various noble families of Rome which have preyed on the
flocks (the people), and the songs sung by the shepherd youth are
the laws, promulgated by Cola, which, Petrarch clearly hopes, will
unite all Italy under one effective government; the trusting
mother is Rome itself. Festinus speaks:

> Squander no more in vain discourse the moments that pass swiftly
>   flying;
> He you are wont to despise, this youngest brother of yours
> Master is now of the forest. At home he is laying foundations
> For mansions yet to arise. To him his mother has given
> Pastures and flocks, and reposes secure on his trusted bosom.
> Each and all things obey him. This boy with drawn sword in hand
> Bears the burden of foresighted age; under a tree he is laying
> Snares for the claws of birds and their beaks and the feet of
>   marauders.
> Walls have been raised to protect the sheep, fattened and tender,
> Against the ravenous wolves. No longer the surly bear growls,
> Boars in their savage forays ravage the thickets no longer,
> Snakes hardly venture to hiss and the swift-footed lions have
>   ceased

To harry their prey. Lambs no more fear the cunning talons of
  eagles.
Seated serene on a hillock the shepherd with his sweet singing
Holds all the pastures in silence, his song reaches far to both
  frontiers,
Charming remote Calabria and the Northern Ligurian valleys,
Even Pelorus whose cliffs shatter the breakers can hear it.
Let him but uplift his voice, he will stir the Moors and the Indies,
Northern ice fields will harken and the burning sands of the desert.
Heed what he tells you: be silent, go back to your folds and your
  shearing.
Changelings are you, says his mother, denying her womb ever
  bore you;
You, Apicius, come from the folds of a neighboring valley
There where the heavy kine and the hardy sheep of Spoleto
Crop the wide pastures that lie high in the Apennine forests.
Martius, you come from afar, from the fields on the shores of the
  Rhineland.[6]

For a few months all went well, and indeed Cola did give Rome
a decent administration. Petrarch left Provence with the intention
of joining him. But by the end of the year the predictable end had
come. Cola had alarmed the Pope by his arrogation of all temporal authority to Rome and the Roman people and by his dismissal
of the papal vicar; he had mismanaged the Roman nobles, who
would probably have opposed him anyway, by humiliating them
(he had not learned the maxim, well known before Machiavelli
set it down, that one must either court or destroy one's enemies),
and he seems to have become a prey to a paranoiac megalomania.
He retired from the scene in November, even as Petrarch was
starting for Italy. The poet wrote him a last letter of sad reproach
from Genoa, warning him of the dangers of his excesses and
pointing out that Cola's misconduct would damage Petrarch's
prestige.

But this was not the end of Cola. After two years of retirement
in the Abruzzi he re-emerged, this time to attempt to enlist the
support of Charles IV, the new Emperor, whom he visited in
Prague. But Charles first incarcerated him and later (1352)
turned him over to the Pope, who had every intention of trying
him for heresy. Although he did not call on the wretched former
Tribune, Petrarch could not fail to be touched by his plight: he
wrote his friend Nelli:[7]

Cola di Rienzo has recently come, or rather been brought, a prisoner, to the papal curia. He who was once the Tribune of the city of Rome, inspiring terror far and wide, is now the most miserable of men, and, what is worst of all, I fear that, miserable as he undoubtedly is, he ought scarcely to arouse our pity, since he who might have died with glory upon the Capitol has submitted to be imprisoned, first by a Bohemian and then by a native of Limoges, thus bringing derision upon himself and upon the Roman name and state. How active my pen was in praising and admonishing this man is perhaps better known than I should wish. I was enamoured of his virtues; I applauded his design, and admired his spirit; I congratulated Italy, and anticipated a restoration of dominion to the mother city, and peace for the whole world. I could not disguise the joy that such hopes engendered, and it seemed to me that I should become a participant in all this glory if I could but urge him on in his course. That he keenly felt that incentive of my words his letters and messages amply testified. This aroused me the more, and incited me to discover what would serve to inflame further his fervid spirit; and, as I well know that nothing causes a generous heart to glow like praise and renown, I disseminated enthusiastic eulogies, which may have seemed exaggerated to some, but which were in my opinion perfectly justified. I commended his past actions, and exhorted him to persevere in the future. Some of my letters to him are still preserved, and I am not altogether ashamed of them. I am not addicted to prophecy; would that he, too, had refrained from it! Moreover, at the time when I wrote, what he had done and what he seemed about to do was worthy not only of admiration but of that of the whole human race. I doubt whether these letters should be destroyed for the single reason that he preferred to live a coward rather than die with dignity. But it is useless to discuss the impossible; however anxious I might be to destroy them I cannot, for they are now in the hands of the public, and so have escaped from my control.

At the same time Petrarch also wrote an open letter to the Roman people, which deserves quotation because of the mixture of stylized elegance and shrewd political perception.

Your former Tribune is now captive in the power of strangers, and—sad spectacle indeed—like a nocturnal thief or a traitor to his country, he pleads his cause in chains. He is refused the opportunity of a legitimate defence by the highest of earthly tribunals. The magistrates of justice themselves reject the claims of justice, and deny him what has never been denied to even the most impious offenders. It is true that he may perhaps deserve to suffer in this manner, for, after he had planted the Republic by his skill, with his own hands so to speak, after it had taken root and flowered, in the very bloom of glorious success he left it. But Rome assuredly does not merit such treatment. Her citizens, who were formerly inviolable by law and exempt from punishment, are now indiscriminately maltreated as anyone's savage caprice may dictate, and this is done not only without the guilt that attaches to a crime, but even with the high praise of virtue.

But that you may not be ignorant, most illustrious sirs, why he who was formerly your head and guide and is still your fellow-citizen—or shall I say your exile?—is thus persecuted, I must dwell upon a circumstance of which you may already be aware, but which is none the less astounding and intolerable. He is accused not of betraying but of defending liberty; he is guilty not of surrendering but of holding the Capitol. The supreme crime with which he is charged, and which merits expiation on the scaffold, is that he dared affirm that the Roman Empire is still at Rome, and in possession of the Roman people. Oh impious age! Oh preposterous jealousy, malevolence unprecedented! [8]

Cola was saved not, however, by the intervention of the Roman people, but by the death of the Pope, whose successor, Innocent VI, not only released Cola, but sent him back to Rome with senatorial powers, probably hoping to raise trouble for the nobles. Cola had learned little, however, and his provocative acts of extortion and violence brought him into disfavor; a Roman mob killed him in October, 1354. By now Petrarch had come to believe that if Rome were to be restored, it would have to be through the old trusted agency of the savior Emperor and he turned his guns on Charles IV—but he never forgot the Tribune.

CHAPTER 5

Year of Death

IT must have seemed to Petrarch and his contemporaries that the tormented years of the century were mounting to a crescendo of catastrophes. The fifth decade, seen even from the safe distance of our times, seems to contain an all but unique catalogue of woes. The French monarchy, the symbol of feudal stability, was dealt a fearful blow at Crécy (1346); the prince consort of Naples was murdered (1345); the conservative-minded must have been shaken by the emergence of the broader democracy in Florence that followed on the expulsion of Walter of Brienne, and hardly reassured by the activities of Cola. In 1345 the great banking houses of the Bardi, the Peruzzi, and the Acciaiuoli all failed. Harvests of the late 1340's were bad. Within the decade the year 1348 has a gruesome primacy. In January of that year an earthquake rocked Germany and Italy, wreaking enormous destruction in Rome and elsewhere; a few months later the Black Death, which had come to Sicily in the last months of 1347, spread to the mainland, devastating every nation in Europe.

Petrarch, in the face of these calamities, fared better than most. He had left Provence in November, 1347 and paused in Genoa on learning of Cola's downfall. From there he proceeded, possibly with a stop at Parma, to Verona; he was there when the earthquake shook the peninsula; in Verona, however, it was not severe, and its chief manifestation as far as Petrarch was concerned was to bring all his books tumbling out of their shelves. By March he was in Parma to take up his duties as canon in the cathedral: he was there when the plague struck—not, it would seem, as violently as elsewhere in Italy. But if his body was spared his heart was not. Many of his dearest friends fell victim, including the young Franceschino degli Albizzi who had been his companion during his recent sojourn in Vaucluse. But harder to bear was the loss of Cardinal Colonna, with whom he had continued to maintain friendly and respectful relations. And hardest of all, Laura was taken. This sad event he records faithfully in his Virgil; it has almost the form of a letter written to himself:

Laura, illustrious through her own virtues, and long famed through my verses, first appeared to my eyes in my youth, in the year of our Lord 1327, on the sixth day of April, in the church of St. Clare in Avignon, at matins; and in the same city, also on the sixth day of April, at the same first hour, but in the year 1348, the light of her life was withdrawn from the light of day, while I, as it chanced, was in Verona unaware of my fate. The sad tiding reached me in Parma, in the same year, on the morning of the 19th day of May, in a letter from my Ludovicus. Her chaste and lovely form was laid to rest at vesper time, on the same day on which she died, in the burial place of the Brothers Minor. I am persuaded that her soul returned to the heaven from which it came, as Seneca says of Africanus. I have thought to write this, in bitter memory, yet with a certain bitter sweetness, here in this place that is often before my eyes, so that I may be admonished, by the sight of these words and by the consideration of the swift flight of time, that there is nothing in this life in which I should find pleasure, and that it is time, now that the strongest tie is broken, to flee from Babylon; and this, by the prevenient grace of God, should be easy for me, if I meditate deeply and manfully on the futile cares, the empty hopes, and the unforeseen events of my past years.[1]

(This would seem to prove once and for all that there was in fact a Laura; not necessarily that she was Laurette, wife of Hugues de Sade.) Another letter to himself, this time so denominated, is the metrical epistle (I, 14), a kind of elegy for all his friends:

Why must I be so tormented? Whither would destiny drive me
Cruelly against my course? The years of a world fast decaying
Pass in swift flight before me. Hosts of the dead and dying,
Youthful and old surround me. I seek in vain and find nowhere
Promise of surcease nor any solacing haven of refuge
Over the whole wide world, nor hope of longed for salvation.
Funerals meet my terrified eyes, wherever I turn them,
Horror piles upon horror, the churches crowded with coffins
Echo to loud lamentations, while countless bodies unburied,
Noble and peasant alike, lie in the open unhonored.
Life's final hour oppresses my soul and memory moves me
Sadly to think on my past, recalling departed companions,

Colloquies never forgotten, dear faces that I once cherished:
Churchyards no longer have scope to contain their daily increase.
Italy sheds bitter tears, overcome by death's ghastly surfeit;
Gaul is also in mourning, bereft of so much of her manhood.
Nations of every region, all races under the heavens
Groan with their woes, not knowing whether their cause is God's
    anger
Merited by our own evil deeds, as I could well credit,
Or in malevolent nature, or some dire conjunction of planets.
                                 (lines 1–20)

The *Rhymes* contain a sonnet (cclxix) of mourning for Laura
and the Cardinal:

Down fallen lofty column, verdant bay
That once gave shade and solace to my care;
Forever lost, these treasures past compare,
Though I should search from Tagus to Cathay.
Death the despoiler strikes and strips away
All that could once make life seem sweet and fair;
No wealth there is, no jewel however rare,
No royal writ to banish my dismay.
Nay, since our mortal lot is resignation
Nought may I do but bear my soul in mourning,
Eyes charged with tears, head bowed in meditation.
Cruel pattern of our lives, with hope adorning
Our dawning skies,—then, without preparation,
Blighting a yield of years in one brief morning.

It is hardly surprising that the *Triumph of Death*, at least the
first two *capitoli*, can also be dated as of this year. It seems likely
too that three of the eclogues (ix, x, and xi) are of the same period; all of them contain echoes of the Black Death.

Parma remained Petrarch's base throughout the following three
years, 1349–51, but it was hardly more than a base. He made two
expeditions to Padua, the first in April, 1349, where he was invested
with a canonry which carried with it the possession of a house in
the cathedral close; he returned for a longer visit later in the year.
He was also frequently in Mantua and Verona and long enough in
Ferrara (perhaps in the fall of 1349) to feel the stirrings of love for
a lady of the town—his last and inconclusive brush with Cupid. It

might have been an even more consuming passion than that he had cherished for Laura, for he, "being of less green wood" was now the more inflammable. Happily, as he records (*Rhymes* cclxxi) with a rather unappealing egocentricity:

> Death came to liberate me once again
> Breaking the knot, extinguishing the fire
> Against which strength and wisdom strive in vain.

In 1350, like 2,000,000 other good Christians he made his pilgrimage to Rome seeking the indulgence granted by the jubilee year. On his way he stopped in Florence where Boccaccio met him and offered him hospitality. The poet's Roman sojourn was not as profitable as he could have wished, for on the journey he was kicked by a horse belonging to another member of the entourage and had to spend two weeks in bed on his arrival in the Holy City. On his return he stopped at Arezzo (where he was shown the house in which he was born) and once more, briefly, in Florence. He was back in Parma by Christmas and off to Padua again early in 1351, after learning of the assassination of his friend and patron Jacopo da Carrara, Lord of Padua. Aside from the normal business of life, which included watching over the education of young Giovanni, entrusted to a schoolmaster of Parma, he was concerned in these years with preparing his collection of letters: those in prose he dedicated to Socrates, to whom he wrote in 1350 to tell him of this plan and inform him that the *Metrical Letters* would be dedicated to Barbato da Sulmona. But he found time too to speak up on the political events of the time; he wrote a letter to the Doge of Venice (*Fam.* XI, 8) urging him to refrain from war with Genoa, which again was in the offing in 1351, and to the Emperor, (*Fam.* X, 1), pleading with him (as had Dante with other emperors) to return to Italy. Needless to say he suggested the young Emperor might imitate the virtues of his beloved Scipio who at the same age had achieved great triumphs. Neither ruler paid the least attention to Petrarch's requests, but they both treated him with respect and in due course sought to make his acquaintance.

In 1351, after four years in Italy, he returned to Provence. He had accepted the pressing invitations of his old friend Philippe de Cabassole and others and he had reason to believe that his prospects there would be good. In order to return to the papal court,

however, he was obliged to refuse a tempting offer, brought
him from Boccaccio, asking him to take up residence in Florence
and accept a professorship; along with this flattering overture
came the promise of the Florentine government to return to Petrarch the family property that had been sequestered at the time
of his father's exile.

The offer must have been appealing, but Petrarch did not take
it up and instead turned his steps back to Provence. No doubt
there were practical reasons for his decision. The Pope, it was
clear, intended to offer some office to Petrarch;[2] it may be that our
poet was hoping to be made a cardinal. (Wilkins believes that he
"never actually sought" such an appointment but would have accepted it had it been offered, adding that it would have been good
for the Church but "unfortunate for the development of humanistic culture.")[3] Possibly too Petrarch had in mind to ask a benefice
for Giovanni, who had now reached the eligible age. But, to do
him justice, heart as well as head must have urged him to return
once more to Provence. It could signify not only Avignon but also
Vaucluse, where in fact the bereaved lover spent the summer of
1351, happy to reclaim his old house and renew his memories.

He must have been frequently haunted by the ghost of Laura
during that summer, as he walked the old familiar paths and
looked upon the landscape that she had once adorned. There are a
number of sonnets of that period which give evidence of his mood
of melancholy reminiscence, of which the following (ccci) may
serve as an example:

> Fair valley, echoing with my weary sighs,
> And gentle river, with my tears full swelling,
> And tiny fish, within its waters dwelling.
> And forest creatures, birds that cheer the skies,
> Soft air, whereon my sad complaints arise,
> Beloved trail, its own sweet story telling,
> Remembered hill on whose fair slope upswelling
> I follow Love's old path with faithful eyes—
> Unchanged they stand, the old familiar places;
> Not so am I, alas, a heart forlorn
> That once gave harborage to joy and mirth.
> Here I saw love—but now these cherished traces
> Serve but to mark whence her pure soul was borne
> Leaving its fragile vestment here on earth.

And here he composed the much-admired *"Zefiro torna"* (cccx),
perhaps the best-known sonnet of the *Rhymes:*

> Zephyr returns, with his sweet season bearing
> Blossoms and shrubs and all his household train,
> Garrulous Procne, Philomel despairing,
> Spring showing white and red on hill and plain,
> And cloudless skies their fairest aspect wearing.
> Jove blesses with his smile his daughter's reign,
> Whose bounty air and sea and earth are sharing:
> All living things are stirred to love again.
> But to my heart return the heaviest
> Of sighs, remembering her who bore its keys
> To Heaven long since, to rack my grieving breast;
> For me songbirds and sweetly flowered leas
> And graces of fair women, the loveliest,
> Are wastelands, savage beasts and stunted trees.

Dear as these treasured spots were to him, Petrarch did not
settle down in Vaucluse. The prospects held out for him in Avignon turned out to be merely a papal secretaryship, a kind of
elevated drudgery which had no appeal for him. (He tells the
amusing story of how he disqualified himself by proving he could
not write the low-grade officialese Latin the post would call for.)
Having no good reason to stay, he found the air of Avignon more
unpleasant than ever. And perhaps he truly wanted to die in Italy.
In any event in 1353 he returned to his native land; in May of that
year he consigned the keys of his little house to the sons of Ray-
mond Monet, his faithful steward, whose recent death he had
mourned,[4] with orders to make it available to any friends who
might come by, and after a last visit to his brother in the monastery of Montrieux set off for Milan; he was never to see the fair
valley again. On crossing the Alps he saluted his fatherland in a
charming Latin poem (*Ep. met.* III, 24):

> Hail, holiest of countries, dear to God,
> Harbour of good men, terror of the proud,.
> Above all other lands more bountiful,
> More fertile and more fair to look upon,
> Girt by twin seas, adorned by famous mountains,
> And venerable for arms and sacred laws,
> Home of the muses, rich in gold and men,

On whom both art and nature have bestowed
Rare gifts to make thee mistress of the world!
Long absent now I eagerly return
To thee, to stay forever. Thou wilt give
Welcome repose, and when the end has come
Some of thy earth to cover these poor limbs.
Now from the summit of green-leafed Gebenna
On thee I feast my eyes, my Italy,
The clouds lie far behind, while a serene
Zephyr caresses me and the mild air
With gentle touch gives me a welcome home.
I know my country and with joy I cry:
Hail fairest mother, glory of the world!

CHAPTER 6

Guest of Princes, Friend of Caesar

IF Petrarch's departure from Vaucluse is understandable, his choice of an Italian residence is less so. His decision to accept the invitation of the Archbishop of Milan, Giovanni Visconti, and to settle in the Lombard capital dismayed his friends and has put all of his biographers on the defensive. Our poet was a Florentine by blood and spoke of Florence as his *"patria"*; he was a professed lover of liberty and a scorner of dictators; furthermore he had widely advertised his love of solitude and retirement. But the largest city in Italy seemed a rather inappropriate residence for a hermit, the Visconti were despots (even Petrarch had said so), and their southward drive had already made them the enemies of the Florentine Republic. It had indeed created a tension that would not be resolved until the foreign invasions of the late fifteenth century submerged both states. All these considerations made the choice of Milan surprising and disconcerting. Boccaccio expressed himself freely on the matter, wondering openly what had become not only of his friend's virtue but even his sanity.[1] How could Petrarch have permitted himself to become a friend of one that should be called Polyphemus or Cyclops, he inquired, adding that it would be easier for him to believe that deer should kill tigers and lambs hunt wolves. Boccaccio spoke for many others; one may say that he spoke for the world of letters both of his own and later centuries.

Petrarch's answer was evasive if not disingenuous. In fact, he never did answer Boccaccio's charges directly. He planned, he said, to write an explanation in some detail of this move (some think that the *Letter to Posterity* was meant to be such a defense),[2] and meanwhile he contented himself with stating that his action had no political or, as we should say nowadays, ideological significance. He thought of himself as a guest and not a servant of the Visconti; he admired the Archbishop, whom he regarded as a friend and he was sure that the Archbishop reciprocated his sentiments. These assertions were certainly sincere, but one must accept them with some reservations. No doubt Petrarch did regard the Archbishop as his friend (and the record also shows that the prelate treated his celebrated guest with affection and even a certain amount of deference), but the poet was not as free as he claimed to be—at least not always. When the Visconti needed his services as ambassador or orator, they requested them and Petrarch never refused, even though some of the missions undertaken must have been physically uncomfortable considering the war-infested routes, the dreadful weather that usually prevailed and, at least on one occasion, the envoy's state of health. Probably Petrarch was happy enough to oblige since these embassies brought him into contact with the great and enabled him to play his part in the public life of politics and diplomacy, but some of the letters written on behalf of his patrons are a little harder to understand. What are we to make of the letter (*Misc.* 17) sent in 1357 to Aldobrandino d'Este, Lord of Ferrara, warning him against Pandolfo Malatesta, who had quarreled with the Visconti? Only a few years earlier Petrarch had been on the friendliest terms with Pandolfo, who has his place even in the *Rhymes* (civ). If, as Wilkins puts it, "the content . . . is entirely due to Bernabò," [3] it was nevertheless penned by Petrarch. And one reads with uneasy distaste the letter (*Misc.* 7), written two years later, also at his master's bidding, to the heroic Friar Bussolari who was defending Pavia (which had temporarily recovered its independence) against the Visconti, taxing that beleaguered cleric, who was after all only defending in practice the sacred liberty which Petrarch so often praised in theory, with contumacy and inhumanity, with particular reference to his callousness in condemning the dogs of the town to death. This was a necessary measure in view of the unhappy plight of the besieged city; Petrarch makes it seem wanton cruelty. He suggests that the dogs be delivered to the besieging Visconti instead; readers who recall that Bernabò quartered a pack of five thousand hounds on his subjects, severely punishing those among them who did not take proper care of his pets, may wonder about the poet's good taste in this reference. It is indeed odd to read Petrarch's description of the brothers Galeazzo and Bernabò as "his young men," [4] protesting that they are not tyrants, when he was in a position to see more clearly than most their government in action. As for their character, although Galeazzo seems to have been a decent man, Bernabò had a vein of unpredictable ferocity in his nature and had fathered some forty recognized bastards. To be sure the brothers and the Visconti in general administered their power with the best interest of their subjects at heart, at least as they saw it, but theirs could hardly have been called anything but a despotic state. Concerning the solitude so dear to his heart, Petrarch may have been right when he said that he could get that in Milan as well as anywhere else; he did indeed enjoy long periods of leisure under the protection of the Archbishop and his nephews. In any case, his protestations of love for rural simplicity were taken more seriously than they deserved to be by his contemporaries; most of his life he lived in cities, and even the true retirement at Vaucluse and later Arquà were to spots from which a metropolis was easily accessible. Petrarch never considered the mountains of the Abruzzi nor even the Tuscan hills.

In fact, if we may digress a little on the subject of our poet's residences, we may note that they were not only for the most part cities but also despotisms. One would have thought a lover of liberty, given freedom of choice in fourteenth-century Italy, would have opted for Florence, where a true if limited, imperfect, and frequently turbulent democracy maintained itself throughout Petrarch's lifetime. Petrarch had had his invitations there as we have seen, and many of his dearest friends including Boccaccio would have welcomed him and made him feel, one would have thought, truly at home. It may be that he was still resentful of his father's exile and the confiscation of his patrimony. Wilkins thinks this is very probable, but such long-harbored rancor does not seem really characteristic of Petrarch. Possibly whatever he may have thought about freedom in the abstract, a republic did not seem to him quite safe, and perhaps his disillusionment with Cola's enterprise may have affected his views. I do not think that one can dismiss, either, the possibility that he might have felt a little ill at ease in the company of his compatriots. The Florentine intellectuals were well read, acute and, as Petrarch writes later to Boccaccio (*Sen.* II, 1), malicious. The achievements of Dante and his circle had already given the Tuscan tongue and Florentine culture in general a pre-eminence in Italy and even beyond the Alps. A Florentine man of letters could expect to meet almost automatic deference in every city of Italy—except of course Florence itself. Petrarch's only true rivals in either of the tongues he practiced were his fellow citizens; as Latinists one could cite Zanobi da Strada, Francesco Bruni, and Bruno Casini, while the day of Coluccio Salutati was about to dawn. In Italian there was Boccaccio himself whose language has, if the truth be told, a much wider range and a more genuine ring than Petrarch's, although to be sure the sector in which Petrarch labored in the vernacular did not afford much linguistic scope. One could cite also the names of Sacchetti and Pucci. Indeed as regards the vernacular it is legitimate to ask whether or not Petrarch felt truly at home in his native tongue. When in fact did he get a chance to practice it? Most of his conversations were either in Latin (even his memoranda to himself were written in Latin) or with non-Tuscan Italians. It is a well-known fact that distance from the source has a way of desiccating the flow of any speech; it is equally well known that the Florentines are purists, alert to note any lapse from the genuine Tuscan and not always charitable to those who fail to meet their linguistic standards.

If Petrarch opted for Milan in 1353, there were no doubt positive as well as negative reasons, the most persuasive and the most honorable of which would seem to be that the poet saw in residence in this power center a real opportunity to play a part in the affairs of his country. Such is Bosco's view, and Wilkins is of the same mind. Petrarch, of course, does not say this himself. For the rest he was given a comfortable house near Sant'Ambrogio and was treated with every consideration by the Archbishop. One may say he became virtually a member of the family. In November, 1353 he stood godfather to Bernabò's child. It is interesting to note that the eight years in Milan add up to a longer period of residence than Petrarch ever spent anywhere else; the lover of the Alpine glen seems to have felt very much at home in what was at that time the largest city in Italy and the capital of its most vigorous and populous state.

His hopes, if he had them, of what Wilkins calls "beneficial participation in world affairs" [5] were almost immediately fulfilled. In the fall of 1353 the Genoese, who had been badly defeated in the Battle of Alghero by the Venetians, sought the protection of the Visconti in terms that amounted to the annexation of their state by Milan with the consequent intervention of the Visconti in the

war. In early 1354 the Archbishop sent a peace mission to Venice
with Petrarch in the role of orator. By all accounts his oration,
delivered before the ducal council, was a masterpiece of eloquence; however, it was ineffectual, as the Venetians were deter-
mined to pursue the war. Later in the year, Charles IV, passing
through Lombardy en route to his coronation at Rome invited
Petrarch to call on him. Our poet's original patron, the Archbishop, had died in October of that year, and power had passed to
his three nephews, Matteo, Galeazzo, and Bernabò. This made no
difference in Petrarch's status, as "his young men" continued to
treat him with the same respect and confidence that he had previously enjoyed. Matteo was not long on the scene; worn out by his
excesses, he died in 1355. Both Galeazzo and Bernabò were able
administrators although they differed greatly in character. It was
thus under their administration that Petrarch visited the Emperor.
The fact that Caesar himself had sent for Petrarch is a spectacular
illustration of the poet's prestige in the world. Petrarch has given
us a full account of his journey from Milan to Mantua and of his
conversation with the Emperor (*Fam.* XIX, 2, 3; XXI, 7). The
winter of 1354/55 was one of the coldest on record; Petrarch said
it was *"sine exemplo"* and that the oldest men had no memory
of anything similar. Even the Germans in the Emperor's train
were astonished at its severity. The journey was a nightmare. The
poet tells us:

I set forth, on December 11th. I have never better appreciated Augustine's mention of "the icy soil of Italy." The road was not so much earth
as steel and diamonds, the snow was welcome, relieving us of our fear
of the ice, which was so exceptional as to be actually terrifying. We had
to take the utmost care where our horses would tread, although they
were surefooted; our constant fear of falling made us oblivious to the
toils of the journey. Add to this a clammy mist, such as had not been
seen within human memory; and add to the weather's rigors the dev-
astation and the dismal solitude of the countryside, not the solitude of
Apollo but that of Mars and Bellona. Everywhere stood destroyed, un-
inhabited houses, smoking ruins, neglected, weed-grown fields with
here and there soldiers emerging from their coverts. They did us no
harm, for they were on our side; but we could not but shudder at this
evidence of the present war's result.

. . . I was received by the successor of our Caesars with more than
Caesarean familiarity, a more than imperial graciousness . . . several

times from the torch lighting hour until late silent night we conversed together without regard for time. In sum, no one could be more cordial, more human than that prince, his majesty . . . The imperial conversation descended to an everyday level, he even asked me about some small works of my own, especially about the one I have entitled *De viris illustribus*. I told him that it was unfinished and that I needed more leisure time to complete it. When he asked me to send him a copy later, I answered with that frankness I commonly use towards eminent men. (It is natural but it seems to be increasing with time, and will be gigantic when old age arrives.) "I promise you a copy" I said, "if your virtue persists and my life too." He was surprised and asked my meaning. "As far as I am concerned," I said, "I need a lifetime to write such a big work, for it is very hard to treat great matters in a small space. And as for you, Emperor, you will be worthy to receive a book with such a title if you are to be numbered among the illustrious men not by wide reputation or any meaningless diadems, but by your deeds and by nobility of spirit, and if you so live that posterity may read of you as you read of the great ancients."

On this note of reciprocal understanding the conversation progressed. The still youthful Emperor (Charles was under forty at the time) was indulgent and at moments jovial; the venerable sage spoke frankly and freely. He made the Emperor a present of some ancient coins, one of which bore the image of Augustus, suggesting that Charles should imitate the example of the Roman. Charles wanted to hear from Petrarch's lips the story of the poet's life and "paid close attention as I told the tale at considerable length; and when I omitted something, from forgetfulness or from a desire to cut the story short, he would immediately supply it. Often he seemed to know my own record better than I did myself. How amazing that some wind had blown such trifles across the Alps, to catch the attention of one occupied in watching the world's predicaments!" Asked by Caesar about his plans for the future, Petrarch proclaimed his intention of leading the solitary life, on which he said he had written a book. The Emperor said, "If that book ever falls into my hands, I shall throw it into the fire." To which Petrarch replied that he would take care that it never might fall into the imperial hands. The Emperor invited Petrarch to accompany him to Rome, saying "he wanted to see the great city not with his own eyes but with mine. . . . He needed my presence, he said, in certain Tuscan cities." Petrarch adds, with considerable satisfaction, at the end in his letter, "I don't know that any Italian has been more honored in this particular way—to be requested and summoned by Caesar, to joke and dispute with Caesar." [6]

The friendship continued. Charles came in early January to Milan to be crowned King of the Italians, and Petrarch accompanied him some fifty miles on his subsequent journey to Rome, where he was crowned Emperor the following April. It is sad to report that this intimacy produced no very positive results. Indeed, the Emperor, before leaving Italy in late June, bestowed some unusual favors on the house of Montferrat, the Visconti's rivals, and crowned Zanobi da Strada with the laurel in a ceremony which must have seemed to Petrarch either a poor imitation or a mockery of the one arranged for him in Rome. But the Emperor's worst sin, in Petrarch's eyes, was simply his departure from Italy, for which the poet bitterly reproached him (*Fam.* XIX, 12), saying among other things, "You may be called Emperor; you are in truth King of Bohemia and nothing more."

It will be convenient to pursue here the theme of Petrarch's diplomatic missions. In late May of 1356 he again visited the Emperor; this time sent by the Visconti who had need of the imperial aid in their struggles against the alliance forming against them. The journey to the Emperor's court in Prague and back covered some three months; there was a brief stop at Basel on the way. This, too, was an arduous journey. Writing years later to Sagremor de Pommiers, the courier who had accompanied him, Petrarch says, "Recall to the eyes of your mind, I pray you, that time when we covered many miles a day through German forests attended by a band of armed men—footmen with their bows ready, riders with their swords drawn—doubtful even of our own guides, and in great danger from roving robbers." [7] In another letter (*Fam.* XIX, 15), he expresses a sentiment which he had felt many years ago during his first visit to the "barbarous regions" of the north. "It was in Germany that I learned how beautiful Italy is." However, in Prague he had his usual social success. The Emperor, overlooking his letter of reproach, made him a Count Palatine and a counselor and many members of the court circle became friends of his, including the young Empress who two years later wrote to tell the poet of the birth of her child. The diplomatic results seem as usual to have been somewhat less impressive than the social impact of Petrarch's presence. In June 1358 Petrarch accompanied his master Galeazzo to Novara. The city had just been retaken from the Marquis of Montferrat, and Galeazzo was anxious to reassure the citizens and conciliate them with the Visconti regime. Petrarch delivered an oration along the lines indicated by the Visconti policy. Finally we must speak of the memorable mission to Paris. In September, 1356, John, King of France, had been made prisoner by the Black Prince and subsequently carried off to England. The misfortune of the King was the opportunity of the Visconti. In effect, Galeazzo undertook to pay the King's ransom in the form of a dowry for the French princess, Isabelle, who would marry his son Gian Galeazzo. The French King accepted the bargain and, in the opinion of scandalized Europe, "sold" his daughter to the Visconti; the marriage took place in October of 1360 in Milan; more than a thousand ambassadors and guests came from the various cities and courts of Italy. In December, hearing that the King would soon be returning to Paris, Galeazzo resolved to send Petrarch, again with the title of orator, to the French capital bearing a message of congratulation. Petrarch delivered his oration, which was much admired, on January 13, 1361; he remained in Paris for another fortnight. In two of his letters he speaks of his impression of the war-ravaged country. He writes:

It was hard to believe that this was the same realm that I had once beheld, such were now the solitude, the gloom, and the desolation on every hand, so rough and untilled were the fields, so shattered and deserted were the dwellings—save those that had been protected by the walls of cities or fortresses—so visible everywhere were the sad traces of the English invasion and the fresh and ugly scars of combat. . . . Paris itself, the capital, defaced up to its very gates by fire and ruin, seemed to be shuddering in dismay at the fate that had befallen it.[8]

And in another letter he reports with melancholy:

I recognized hardly anything, seeing a once opulent kingdom turned to ashes. . . . Where now is that Paris that was once so great, where are the throngs of students, where is the fervid life of the University, where the wealth of citizens, where the general happiness? One hears now not the voices of disputation but the din of warfare, one sees piles not of books but of weapons. The sound of syllogisms and lectures has given way to those of soldiers on guard and of battering rams.[9]

It is unnecessary to say that Petrarch was very popular with the court. The King and Prince Charles listened with admiration to his oration and thoroughly enjoyed his conversation. As was predictable the King tried to detain him in Paris not only with fervid entreaties but actually taking him by the hand, as our orator notes with some complacency. The return journey over the Alps in wintertime was a very difficult one, and during the whole period of the French mission Petrarch was troubled by some undiagnosed affliction which he describes as being as painful as gout. As we have seen, the missions, although frequent and sometimes taxing, left long intervals between them so that Petrarch might indeed claim to enjoy the leisure which he had hoped to find in the Lombard capital. His letters give us accounts of his normal daily life and illuminate us on his habits of work. Writing in 1357 he tells his old friend Guido Sette:

By day and night I read and write, relieving each task by the solace of the other. . . . I know no pleasure and no sweetness save in such toil; and I am so absorbed and immersed in it that I am not aware of any other labor or of any other peace.

Further on he adds:

My body is still vigorous; so much so that I have not been able to subdue it by my increasing sobriety, by middle-aged placidity, by abstinence and the continual war I have declared against the rebellious, contumacious slave—or better, against that kicking ass. . . . In other matters such as I said to be dependent on circumstances, my way of life is very pleasant, being well removed from all extremes. Far from me are afflictions, wants, riches, envy; mine is sweet, secure, comfortable mediocrity . . . but in one way my state is not mediocre . . . I have been more conspicuous and more cherished than I deserve, not only by the greatest leader of the Italians but by his eminent staff and also by the general public. . . . I have been so captured by the benevolence not only of the city's rulers but also of the masses that I think I shall be bound forever by the worthy citizens, by the country, and its air, almost by the city's walls. It would take far too long to deal with my personal friends but I enjoy such general favor, regard, and applause, that I am certain that the people hold me dear. Why, I don't know, unless it is that fate works in mysterious ways or unless we are all so busy that they have not much occasion to see me nor have I much reason to appear in public. Thus they are mistaken about me and I hide from them. I am enabled to do so by the location of my home in the western corner of the great city. It is far from the urban tumult, except when, once a week, an ancient devotional practice brings worshipers to an early morning service. I am the guest of St. Ambrose. . . . You know my routine of food and sleep. No circumstances will ever lead me to indulgence. Rather I cut down little by little and now I have reached a point where I can hardly cut down further. If I should gain a King's wealth, it could hardly banish frugality from my table or bring longer slumbers to my couch. I never go to bed when wide awake and active-minded and I lie down only to sleep, unless I am sick. When sleep quits me, I spring up. I regard sleep as a kind of death, my bed as a tomb . . . I hate my bed; I never return to it except from urgent necessity; and when I feel that Nature's bonds are relaxed I cast them off immediately and repair to my adjoining library as to a castle keep. Sleep and I part company at midnight; and if sometimes the shorter night or some late vigils prolong my repose, still, never does the dawn find me abed. . . . As I always have, I still love solitude and silence, except when I am among friends. With them no one could be more loquacious than I. I think the reason is that my friends are fewer than they used to be; and rarity increases appreciation. Thus, often I compensate for a year's silence with a day's garrulity; and when my friends have gone I again fall mute. It is very tiresome to talk to the meaner folk, or especially to a man with whom you have no congeniality or common subject-matter.

He adds a word about his summer home from which he is writing:

I have obtained with the approach of summer, a very pleasant and healthy lodging. It is called Garegnano, and it is about three miles from the city. It is open country, elevated above the plain. It is surrounded on all sides by rivulets; they are not to be compared with our trans-alpine Sorgue but they are modest and limpid; they wind so gently, elaborately, doubtfully that one can hardly make out whence they come or whither they are bound. . . . They suggest the dance of nymphs by twining Meander, the sporting of virgin bands. . . . I follow my old habits, except that I have more liberty in the country.[10]

Some two years later Petrarch wrote to Francesco Nelli (*Fam. XXI, 12*) on the general theme of the best use of time but giving further particulars of his style of life. The passing of time haunts him; he writes:

I brood on time saving, I sigh for it and perhaps with firm purpose and with God's help I may achieve it. I shall try to waste no time; and if I don't succeed entirely I may do so partly. I shall assign a proper share to sleep and recreation and I shan't allow them to exceed their allotment. . . . I shall make a bargain with my eyes, that six hours of sleep must satisfy them; two hours must go to the other needs of existence; the rest must be mine. . . . In the matter of time saving, I follow Augustus, and while I'm being shaved or having my hair cut I commonly read or write or listen to a reader or dictate to a scribe. And it has been my habit to do the same while riding or dining. (I don't remember reading this about Augustus or anyone else.) You may be surprised to learn that sitting on my horse I have often finished a poem at the same time as my journey. And when I have been far from human society . . . the pen always stood among my rustic viands unless respect from a visitor from outside forbade it. Nor is my dinner table ever set without writing tablets. Often in the middle of the night I have wakened, in the dimmest light, and the first thing I did was to clutch the pen on my night-table, and for fear of losing an idea I would write in the dark something I could hardly read in the morning.

Such are my present concerns. To others I might seem vain and smug; but you will recognize my character and way of life in this familiar colloquy; and you will realize that I am rather ashamed than boastful because at my age I am busying myself at something other than the care of my soul. But that is the way that I am; and I persuade myself that my exertions will even be of benefit to my soul. So I keep going, the happier as I feel more secure, and as the fellow says, daily learning a little something and daily getting a little older. "And what do you think is still worth learning?" you say. Oh, a great deal. I am learning how to leave youth behind willingly, and—what I have always learned eagerly, but never enough,—I am learning how to grow old, I am learning how to die.[11]

Such, then, was the tenor of a poet's life between the affairs of state and the missions assigned him by his patrons. As he had in Vaucluse he cultivated his garden, and frequently records his plantings of fruits and shrubs. He had visits from friends; we may

mention particularly that of Boccaccio in 1359 who stayed a fortnight. The poets spoke of many things, among others, of the poetry of Dante, of which we shall have more to say. Boccaccio's visit
is sufficient evidence that he had at last forgiven Petrarch for his
residence with the Visconti. It seems that during their conversations Petrarch persuaded Boccaccio, or at least thought he did,
that his choice of residence was wise and indeed inevitable. A
memorandum of Petrarch's records the pleasant episode of his
planting olive trees on March 16 in the presence of Boccaccio
"*amicissimus.*" He made some sorties of his own, the most notable
being the trip to Padua and Venice which took up most of the
winter of 1358/59. He went to Padua to regulate the business of
his canonry which he had held there since 1349, and on to Venice,
as he says himself, for pleasure. In Padua he made the acquaintance of that pseudo-Byzantine Leontius Pilatus, later to be his in-
structor in Greek. The years in Milan add some items to the melancholy story of his son Giovanni. In 1354 Giovanni seems to have
been implicated, we are not quite sure how, in a family squabble
of the Lords of Verona; the result was that he lost the benefice the
Pope had given him and was obliged to flee the city. Finding his
son's company intolerable, Petrarch, two years later, sent him
back to Avignon. In 1359 he wrote the youth, who had apparently
pleaded to be allowed to return, a long letter concluding:

When you are assured that you have recovered health and spirit, as
I command—and in these pages you will see the aspect of your spirit
reflected as in a mirror—then only, and no sooner, may you hope to see
my face, which you scorned when it looked fondly on you. My attitude
will be properly adjusted to your needs. For I know what has ruined
you; it was my laxity. I shall make sure that my tenderness will no
longer make you wicked, my love will no longer destroy you. Imagine
these words to be spoken not "by the oracle of Pythian Apollo," as
Cicero says, but by the very lips of Christ. Nothing is more certain,
nothing is more true.[12]

But ready or not, the father was obliged to receive the prodigal.
In 1360 Giovanni returned without warning, and a painful scene
ensued, ending in a temporary reconciliation. Whether the years
would have made it permanent we cannot say. The troublesome,
vexatious, and somehow pitiable Giovanni had only a year to live;
he was carried off by the plague of 1361.

The whole story of Giovanni is a sad one, and one cannot help feel over the centuries a certain compassion for the unwanted boy. Petrarch described him as "fawning, deceitful and on occasion a violent, threatening person," [13] yet we are never quite sure precisely what the boy did that was so evil, for his father's charges are always the general ones of idleness, dissipation, and the like. Perhaps it was all true but on the record, even by his father's confession, the boy's schoolmaster and the poet's good friend Nelli found much worth in the lad. It has been suggested that Petrarch wished to imitate Cicero, who also had difficulties with his son, but this seems a rather far-fetched theory. It is more likely that the circumstances of Giovanni's birth made him forever a symbol of guilt in the eyes of his father. Perhaps it is the old story of the tension which frequently obtains between a prominent father and a son whose gifts are of a different nature. Petrarch speaks of Giovanni's lack of interest in reading, which must have been painful for him to contemplate. Hollway-Calthrop comments, it seems to me, very soundly on the relationship. He concedes that the lad was probably "slothful, undisciplined and prone to a disorderly life" and then adds "only by very judicious handling could his better qualities, of which Petrarch's friends discerned the rudiments, have a chance to win the day. Judicious handling was exactly what Petrarch could not give him. Sarcasm and sermonizing are the very worst tools for perfectioning the character of such a boy, and Petrarch, honestly anxious to train Giovanni into industry and instill into him a virtuous ambition, was at once sarcastic and didactic. The circumstances of their relationship [by which he means Giovanni's illegitimacy] probably aggravated the evil." [14]

With his daughter Francesca things went better; perhaps Petrarch did not expect as much of the girl as the boy (and the children may well have had different mothers). For whatever reason, the little we hear of Francesca is to her credit. She was married in 1362 to Francescuolo da Brossano, who had become a member of Petrarch's circle immediately after the latter's arrival in Milan. As we shall see, daughter and son-in-law became part of Petrarch's household as he grew older.

There were other personal and domestic miseries during these years. In an accident as painful as it was poetic Petrarch's leg was bruised as a result of his heavy volume of Cicero's *Letters* falling upon it, and the wound became infected. It healed, he tells us, only when he ceased to allow the doctors to treat it. In 1359 he had such trouble with his unruly servants that he was obliged to dismiss them all, and as a result of that he also left his house and took up residence just outside the walls near the church of San Simpliciano where he could be under the protection of the monks.

The house was much to his taste, providing him with at least the illusion of rural solitude, yet easily reached by his frequent visitors.

Literary activity went on apace during the residence in Milan. Here Petrarch composed the *De remediis utriusque fortunae,* one of the longest and, for many years, most widely read and highly esteemed of his works. It was begun in 1354 and was probably finished in 1360. It was here that he wrote the *Itinerarium syriacum* for his friend Giovannolo da Mandello, who was planning a pilgrimage to the Holy Land. Many of Petrarch's best letters were also written during the Milanese sojourn; we may mention two more here. In the early summer of 1359 he addressed to Boccaccio the celebrated letter (*Fam.* XXI, 15) setting forth his opinion of Dante and his poetic accomplishments. In it Petrarch protests that he had no envy of Dante; on the contrary, he is prepared to give him the palm for accomplishment in vernacular poetry. He goes on, however, to make the surprising confession that he does not own a copy of the *Divine Comedy;* and his remarks, for all the admiration they express, indicate that he was completely unaware of the scope, originality, or significance of Dante's masterpiece. In 1360 he wrote Nelli a letter (*Fam.* XXII, 10) in which he states that his interests are moving now from the classical reading of his youth to Christian authors more appropriate to his maturity. In the past he has loved Cicero and Virgil, but he is now turning to Ambrose, Augustine, and other Christian writers. Henceforth his philosopher will be Paul and his poet David. He is careful to say, however, that he is not renouncing the idols of his youth; he will continue to read them for instruction in literary matters and artistry, but for guidance in life he will henceforth rely on Christian authorities. Wilkins believes that "this letter records a significant literary and spiritual reorientation," [15] but it will seem to many simply an acknowledgment of an ambivalence that had long persisted in the poet's soul. For the younger Petrarch who had carried St. Augustine with him to the top of Mt. Ventoux was shortly to embark on his epic of classical theme and inspiration, and to the end of his life his letters will indicate how often he turned to the classics for moral guidance no less than for instruction in the techniques of art. Many readers will, however, see in this letter a statement in literary terms of the old Averrhoistic dichotomy, the basis of the "intellectual neutrality," as Olschki puts it, which would long characterize Italian civic and cultural life.

CHAPTER 7

Last Days

IN the spring of 1361 Petrarch left Milan and after a few months in Padua settled down (so far as the phrase is appropriate to his nomadic habits) in Venice. His immediate reason for leaving was the return of the plague; he had, however, with his characteristic restlessness, already been meditating a change. The Republic offered him a handsome house on the Riva degli Schiavoni; in return Petrarch engaged to leave his library, by now one of the largest in Europe, to the city: had this plan eventuated (and it was no fault of Petrarch's that it failed), his gift would have endowed the first public library in Europe. Needless to say, although he found his house much to his taste, he continued to move about; most summers of his Venetian sojourn were spent either in Padua or in Pavia, where Galeazzo Visconti, who, as we have seen, had recently (1359) triumphed over the misocynist Bussolari, put yet another residence at the disposal of the now venerable man of letters.

He was still involved in political matters and participated with vivid interest and sometimes with action in the world events of those years. Innocent VI died in 1362 and was succeeded by Urban V. Petrarch applauded the elevation of this sincere and virtuous Benedictine, assuring him that he had been chosen not by the cardinals but by God.[1] Among the numerous virtues of the new Pope, Petrarch and other Italians found a very special one—a willingness to consider the restoration of the papal court to Rome. And in fact Urban did move there but, finding the chaos too much to cope with, was obliged to return to Avignon. In 1368 Petrarch met the Emperor again, this time in Udine; he seems to have been useful in arranging the terms of peace between Caesar and the Visconti, in whose service the poet still labored intermittently. In the same year he was present at the marriage of Galeazzo's daughter to the Duke of Clarence, which took place at Milan.

In his personal life, as was to be expected, his circle of old friends grew smaller: the returning plague took not only Giovanni but also his cherished Socrates (1361); the old friend and sometime patron Azzo da Correggio died in 1362; Laelius and Barbato da Sulmona in the following year. Yet Petrarch's gift for making new friends did not fail him; Francesco Bruni came into his life at this period and gave the old scholar such affection and deference as to make up for many losses; and there were others. In 1363 his daughter Francesca with her husband and the poet's granddaughter (born probably in 1362) joined him; his grandson, little Francesco, was born in 1366, but lived only two years. To the lad's godfather Petrarch wrote one of the most moving of all his letters:

My own dear boy was your spiritual son, since you sponsored him in baptism. Let me join my own cruel, recent loss to yours, that we may both seek wholesome balm. Do not murmur that our wounds are not comparable, that you have lost a son and I a grandson. I swear by Christ and by your friendship that I loved him more than a son. What if I did not beget him? His parents were Francesco and Francesca, who, as you know, are both dearer to me than my own soul. Being born of two persons much dearer to me than myself, he was dearer than if he were my son. You gave an illustrious ancient name to your boy; we gave ours a humble family name, or rather you gave them both, since you christened my boy. Your Solon augured a great career, if only fate had been kind; our child received the name of both his parents and of myself. He was the fourth Francesco, the solace of our lives, our hope, the joy of our house. And to make our grief the keener, he chanced to possess unusual beauty and intelligence. You would have called him a princely child. He promised to equal his father in good looks and to surpass him in intellectual gifts. His only fault was to resemble me so much that one who did not know his mother would certainly have called me the father. So everyone alleged; and I remember that once, when he was hardly a year old, you wrote me that you could see my face in his, and that thus you had somehow conceived great hopes for him. This remarkable resemblance, despite the great discrepancy of age, made him the dearer to his parents and indeed to all; and it so impressed the great Lord of Liguria Galeazzo Visconti that he who had shortly before watched dry-eyed the passing of his only son could hardly hear of my loss without tears.[2]

But life still had its good moments. Apart from the important missions and the contacts with the great that meant so much to Petrarch, relationships with Boccaccio who stayed with him for

three months in the summer of 1363 became increasingly intimate. For a time the poets shared the burden of lodging with
them Leontius Pilatus, an unkempt, boorish character who was
priceless in the eyes of both these premature humanists, for he
knew Greek. He never managed to teach his language to Petrarch,
but he did a few years later complete a translation of the Homeric
poems into Latin, which Boccaccio sent on to Petrarch who received it with joy. (He had received in 1354 from a Byzantine
whom he had met in Verona, the manuscript of the Homeric
poems; he writes that he often embraced it, exclaiming: "Great
man, how gladly would I listen to you.")

During this period he completed the edition of his *Familiares,*
and the *De remediis utriusque fortunae;* he started to prepare the
section of his letters known as the *Seniles.* An "occasional" work is
De sui ipsius et multorum ignorantia, inspired or perhaps provoked is the better word, by the assertion of a group of young
Averrhoists (i.e. *Aristotelians*) in Venice that Petrarch, though well
intentioned, was ignorant. Petrarch's answer (composed partly on
a boat journey from Venice to Pavia in 1367 and finished later in
Pavia) did not arouse the enthusiastic response that he had hoped
for; Bosco speculates that his resentment at the young critics and
the apathy of the city in responding to them may have been at
least a contributing cause in his decision to leave Venice.[3] But the
true cause of all Petrarch's translocations are probably simply
temperamental. In any event, in 1369 he was again spending most
of his time in Padua.

In 1370 Petrarch removed from Venice to Padua; he probably
already had in mind a country retreat, a dream which was real-
ized a few months later when he built a little house in Arquà on
land given him by his patron Francesco da Carrara. The retirement to Arquà is a kind of reprise of the withdrawal to Vaucluse
so many years ago; inspired by the same yearning, in part self-
delusive, for solitude and detachment. The ensuing pattern was
similar, too; although the old poet did in fact establish his residence in his new hermitage and invite his daughter and her husband to join him, he remained continually on the move, passing
his time between Padua and his new home, even planning longer
journeys. He set out for Rome to visit Urban in 1371; but in Ferrara, he had a sudden attack of some illness that rendered him unconscious for thirty hours and was obliged to turn back. Again he

thought of making the trip to Avignon to see his old friend Philippe de Cabassoles and again was obliged to turn back. He was
able, however, to go to Venice and convey the surrender of the
Carrara family to the Venetians, victorious in the war between the
two states. That was to be his last excursion; he died on the vigil
of his seventieth birthday, appropriately while he was reading his
Virgil. (Or would he have preferred to be found with Augustine
on his desk?)

The last four years are amazingly full of literary activity. They
are, for one thing, the years of final editing: he put in order the
Rhymes adding (1373?) the hymn to the Virgin which crowns the
work. Likewise he revised the *Trionfi* and added the last two (and
perhaps the most appealing) chapters to the series. He rearranged
his letters for their final edition. And he found time not only to
write some of his best and longest letters but also to translate
Boccaccio's tale of "Griselda" (which deeply moved him) into
Latin. His translation was to a certain extent a recasting of the
story and, in Wilkins' opinion,[4] the most successful venture into
the narrative field that Petrarch ever made. It was this version
which Chaucer made use of. (Since Chaucer was in Italy in 1373
the possibility of his meeting with Petrarch has fascinated literary
historians; there is, however, no evidence that such a meeting ever
took place.)

Inevitably, the letters of this period are much concerned with
the poet's health, which grew continually worse. And, as old men
will and as he had good reason to, he grew increasingly pessimistic about the state of the world and its future. But his spirit still
glowed; he still found joy in conversation, in friendship, and above
all in writing. As late as April, 1373 he could write to Boccaccio,
enclosing the Latin version of "Griselda":

Continued work and application form my soul's nourishment. So soon
as I commenced to rest and relax I should cease to live. I know my
own powers. I am not fitted for other kinds of work, but my reading
and writing, which you would have me discontinue, are easy tasks, nay,
they are a delightful rest, and relieve the burden of heavier anxieties.
There is no lighter burden, nor more agreeable, than a pen. Other
pleasures fail us, or wound us while they charm; but the pen we take
up rejoicing and lay down with satisfaction, for it has the power to advantage not only its lord and master, but many others as well, even
though they be not born for thousands of years to come. I believe that

I speak but the strict truth when I claim that as there is none among earthly delights more noble than literature, so there is none so lasting, none gentler, or more faithful; there is none which accompanies its possessor through the vicissitudes of life at so small a cost of effort or anxiety.

Pardon me then, my brother, pardon me. I am disposed to believe anything that you say, but I cannot accept your opinion in this matter. However you may describe me (and nothing is impossible to the pen of a learned and eloquent writer), I must still endeavour, if I am a nullity, to become something; if already of some account, to become a little more worthy; and if I were really great, which I am not, I should strive, so far as in me lay, to become greater, even the greatest. May I not be allowed to appropriate the magnificent reply of that fierce barbarian who, when urged to spare himself continued exertions, since he already enjoyed sufficient renown, responded, "The greater I am, the greater shall be my efforts"? Words worthy of another than a barbarian! They are graven on my heart, and the letter which follows this will show you how far I am from following your exhortations to idleness. Not satisfied with gigantic enterprises, for which this brief life of ours does not suffice, and would not if doubled in length, I am always on the alert for new and uncalled-for undertakings,—so distasteful to me is sleep and dreary repose. Do you not know that passage from Ecclesiasticus, "When man has finished his researches, he is but at the beginning, and when he rests, then doth he labour"? I seem to myself to have but begun; whatever you and others may think, this is my verdict. If in the meanwhile the end, which certainly cannot be far off, should come, I would that it might find me still young. But as I cannot, in the nature of things, hope for that, I desire that death find me reading and writing, or, if it please Christ, praying and in tears.

Farewell, and remember me. May you be happy and persevere manfully.[5]

A year later Boccaccio was to join him "in yon third sphere" with "good master Cino, Guittone, Dante and the brotherhood/ that throngs around them. . . ." He would be at home at last.

He left behind him a testament, the provisions of which are characteristic of his thoughtful and considerate nature, while the style is of such quality that the *Testament* is included in his "Works" and is described by its editor as "a personal document" of the poet's old age.[6]

CHAPTER 8

Historical Works

THE distinction, dear to critics, between minor and major works in the canon of great writers is arbitrary. When they are sufficiently remote from us, however, we have at least the verdict of history based on the opinion of successive generations and, subject always to unpredictable revolutions of taste, we can commit ourselves with some assurance. In the case of Petrarch, though the *Letters* bulk large and the *Africa* is a substantial accomplishment and although he achieved in the *Secretum* a forceful presentation, at once formally integrated and emotionally convincing, of a true human dilemma, yet the *Canzoniere* remains in sheer truth his only major work. It is because we want to know more about the personality revealed and illuminated in the *Rhymes* that we find the other works worthy of our study. (This is of course not to deny them their importance in the history of Western thought, esthetics, and culture.) We may, I think, in clear conscience, classify every other product of our author as a minor work.

But this is not meant to suggest that such books are contemptible, or to be passed over with a mere mention. Quite aside from the fact that they help us better to understand the meaning of the *Canzoniere* and the character of its author, the denomination "minor" is a relative term, and many of these productions that pale before the *Canzoniere* shine with their own luminous splendor when they are studied for themselves.

In classifying them for our purposes here, I think we may say that, leaving aside the *Trionfi* and the *Rhymes* for special treatment, we could reasonably divide the products of Petrarch's versatile pen into three major categories of historical works, devotional works, and works of social commentary. Naturally, these are not water-tight compartments; for example, the *Letters*, taken *en bloc*, fall most easily into our third division but they are also frequently eloquent of devotional attitudes and as frequently

charged with historical references. Our division takes no account
either of the distinction between the creative and the critical. But
it may well be the simplest approach to the *"selva"* of Petrarch,
particularly since, as we remarked earlier, a chronological attack
would be meaningless.

We may well begin with the *Africa,* which the author for many
years thought of as his truly major accomplishment or at least
project, for he was never to finish it and never therefore truly to
accomplish the great task that he had set before him. Since he
labored so long over his cherished epic, we may well do him the
courtesy of expending a few pages on it here. As we have observed, the notion of such a work came to him after his first visit
to Rome and while he was wandering on the hills of Vaucluse
(1338 or 1339). But for the rest of the author's lifetime it was
worked on, put aside, reworked, revised—and somehow never finished. As we have noted too, it was a source of endless curiosity in
the poet's circle; on his Milanese visit Boccaccio pleaded with him
to share his great treasure with the public.[1] He would not; in
truth he had hardly been cheered by the reception (if we may call
it that) of the fragment which his friend Barbato da Sulmona had
injudiciously allowed to circulate.[2] But before proceeding to our
own commentary, let us see what the poem attempts to convey. It
begins with an invocation which is in itself indicative of the style
and direction of the work.

> The warrior Hero, whom the gods endowed
> so lavishly with virtues and on whom
> the Afric land, by Roman arms subdued,
> bestowed its noble name, sing me, O Muse!
> Sweet sisters, if I tell of wondrous deeds,
> allow your votary to quaff full deep
> of the pellucid fount of Helicon.
> Now that a favoring fortune has once more
> restored me to sweet springs and pleasant meads
> and to the shelter of the wooded hills
> and the soft stillness of the lonely fields,
> do you arouse the fire of poesy
> within my breast and stir my heart to song.
>
> And Thou, the firmest hope of all the world,
> and glory of the heavens, Whom our age

hails as the conqueror of the gods and victor
o'er Hell itself, Whose guiltless body bears
five gaping wounds, O Father of mankind,
I pray Thee, lend me Thy assistance here.
Full many a pious hymn I pledge to Thee
(If such may please immortal ears) when from
the peak of high Parnassus I descend.
Guerdon of tears I'll offer if my songs
be deemed unworthy, bitter tears that long
have pressed upon my lids, and had poured forth
long, long ago had blindness to my lot
and to man's destiny not checked their flow.

And you, Trinacria's puissant King and pride
of Italy, great glory of our world,
who on my brow have set the Laurel crown,
so ardently desired, and clept me bard,
deeming me worthy of the lofty name,
you I beseech, with heart magnanimous,
deign to accept the humble gift I bring,
for he who will but read mayhap shall find
some pleasant solace in an idle hour
and if with patience he begin the task,
it may be it will lighten as he reads.
Accept, O King, and with your gracious smile
assure my song of immortality,
for who would scorn what you are pleased to prize?
(*Africa* I, 1–29)

Without prejudice to further criticism we may pause to note
here in these brief lines the presence of certain elements which
will characterize the whole epic. The double invocation addressed
first to the traditional classical muses and second to the Christian
God reveals the dichotomy of a pagan tradition fitted to medieval
purposes; this to be sure is formally apparent also in the *Divine
Comedy* and even in *Paradise Lost,* but the synthesizing resolution eluded Petrarch, as we shall see. The fulsome eulogy of Robert of Naples strikes a discordant note. He is accorded more lines
than either the muses or God. Aside from the obvious practical
purpose of this dedication, the intrusion of the personal is, in simple truth, disproportionate in the opening lines. After a rather self-
consciously erudite reference to the epics of Homer, Virgil, Sta-

tius, and Lucan (thus establishing his line of progenitors), and hinting that some day he will undertake to deal in similar style with the *gesta* of Robert himself, the poet continues:

> Sweeter indeed it were to sing of them
> than of aught else, yet pondering my skill
> against the merits of your majesty
> I dare not treat of such. First would I try
> my timid art and if it fail me not
> then next essay the heights, and with stout heart,
> for you yourself shall bear me company.
> Then shall Parthenope throw wide her gates
> when I return, a poet newly crowned
> with Roman garland. Yet for the nonce I've plucked
> from lowly bush the tenderest of leaves
> and choose famed Scipio to share my path.
> One day I vow to gather sturdier boughs
> while you, a soul of courtesy, will aid
> my faltering pen. Then shall another wreath
> of laurel, fairest of our age, bedeck
> the worthy brow of one who loves you well.
>
> (I, 58–70)

After the invocation, which concludes by placing the blame for the Punic Wars on the Carthaginian envy of the Romans, we move immediately into the story with an account of the younger Scipio's prophetic dream. In this vision his father Publius Cornelius, who had died fighting the Carthaginians in Spain, reveals to young Scipio that he is destined to avenge his family and save Rome from destruction. By way of encouragement he is shown the great heroes of early Rome, from Romulus to the Horatii. It is significant that Tarquin is excluded from Heaven. Indeed, Scipio's uncle, who joins his father to welcome their young kinsman, lectures him on the nature of true immortality, for which this life is merely a preparation. Yet institutional piety is woven too, not without art, into the formula prescribed by the affectionate uncle:

> . . . Do you then hold faith sacred
> and justice cultivate. Let piety
> b⌣ cherished in your heart, a holy guest
> and comrade to your habits; great the debt
> of piety owed to your sire and greater

> to fatherland and greatest part of all
> is that which is the due of God supreme.
>
>   (I, 482–86)

In Book II Scipio, still dreaming, descends to earth in company
with his father, who en route assures him of his fated triumph
over Hannibal and the certainty of his lasting fame destined to be
celebrated by a poet in the remote future. Waking from his dream
(Book III), Scipio determines to press the war against Carthage
and dispatches his friend Laelius to Libya to make an alliance
with Syphax, king of that realm. Syphax asks for a meeting with
Scipio.

Laelius begins his reply with a survey of Roman accomplishments, finally proceeding to a description of Scipio, who (Book
IV) is painted as brave, wise, chaste, scornful of earthly honors,
and above all deeply religious. Book IV breaks off in the middle of
line 389—there is a lacuna in the text.

Book V is a digression from the main plot and tells of the love
of Massinissa, an ally of Scipio, for Sophonisba, the wife of
Syphax. It is necessary for Scipio to break up the affair, first of
course in order to restore his friend to the path of virtue, but also
because Massinissa's attachment to his mistress might be prejudi-
cial to the Roman cause, Sophonisba being anti-Roman. The story
of this passionate love, thwarted by the demands of duty, has
echoes of the Dido episode in the *Aeneid* (and in its voluptuous
coloring, points forward also to the affair of Rinaldo and Armida
in the *Gerusalemme Liberata*): as Aeneas yields to his destiny
and Rinaldo to the emissaries of Godfrey, so Massinissa yields to
the fatherly counsel of Scipio. He will not, however, allow his love
to become a Roman prisoner and so sends her a vial of poison,
which, in a scene an Italian critic compares to the death of Cleopatra,[3] she makes use of when her cause becomes desperate.
The episode, although imitative and contrived, yet contains passages of true feeling and some dramatic impact. Notable is the
description of Sophonisba, as beautiful as Laura and even more
seductive:

> Her eyes beneath her beauteous brow were such
> as, looking on them, the high gods would envy . . .
> and now, suffused with freshly flowing tears

they shone with greater sweetness than their wont,
like to twin stars in rival splendor gleaming
in evening skies, dew-drenched, when showers have fled
and all the heavens are serene again;
above their glow, two graceful arches curve.
Her cheeks were of the candor of the lily
blended with roses of a warm rich red;
and dazzling ivory flashed beneath her lips.
Her breast unbared stirred with such palpitation
as when her husband with his suppliant tears
has pressed her where she may resist no more.
See too those arms that Jove himself would wear
as a garland round his neck forever clasped;
the hands so long and slender and the fingers
tapering and tipped by shapely, lucent nails;
her softly yielding flank and other parts
all charged with grace down to the little foot
which did but brush the earth whereon she trod
with such discretion as to leave no trace,
and one would swear she walked upon the air.

                                                    (V, 35–57)

The meditations of Massinissa as he lies on his lonely bed, half-regretting his acquiescence to Scipio's persuasions, imagining the death of Sophonisba, have all the plausible charm of a *recitativo* of Metastasio:

Often, amidst his tears he dreams he holds
his darling in his arms and tightly clutches
the empty bed in vain embrace the while
he mutters words of madness. And when no
restraint avails against his pain, he seeks
solace in lamentation: "Dearest one,
sweet above all things that life has to give,
O Sophonisba mine, farewell! Henceforth
I shall no longer see your heavenly face
assume its soft expression, nevermore
shall I see you abandon to the breeze
your golden hair as you were wont to do,
nor hear those words that to the gods above
were once so precious . . . Nevermore to hear,
so softly falling from your fragrant lips
the secret syllables of love! Alone

and wretched I shall lie bereft, my limbs
abandoned on my cold deserted couch.
May it be Heaven's will that in one tomb
we may be placed together, dearest love,
and may the years that fate denies us now
at last be granted us beneath the earth
in union. Call our grave thrice blest if there
our ashes mingle and death makes us one,
with Scipio powerless to divide our hearts."

(V, 530–48)

Book VI disposes forever of the seductive and subversive Sophonisba, who descends to Tartarus, leaving behind a Massinissa
now concerned only with the prosecution of the war. Scipio's
speech of exhortation is followed by the account of Roman prepa-
rations and the resultant panic among the Carthaginians. They
feel obliged in their need to recall Hannibal (of whom we have
an unflattering description) and his brother Mago to the defense
of the fatherland (Mago dies at sea on his journey home). The
Carthaginians resort to various subterfuges including a pretense
of seeking a truce; Scipio recognizes their fraudulence but stoops
to no such deceits himself.

Book VI contains the moving soliloquy of Mago; it is a passage
that is as highly esteemed by critics as it was by the author himself. It was in fact this fragment that Petrarch incautiously gave to
Barbato da Sulmona to read and which the latter, breaking his
promise, allowed to circulate.[4] It is, for all Petrarch's defense of it,
out of character; it is not Mago who speaks, but Petrarch. Com-
menting on the Augustinian pessimism that characterizes the content and incidentally echoes one of the persistent themes of the
Rhymes, Tonelli calls it "one of the most beautiful pages of the
Petrarchan lyric." [5]

What a sad end to my once happy life
awaits me! And my mind, how blind it was,
duped by the facile promises of hope.
See now where the insensate craze for fame
may lead the credulous mighty, who believe
they mount up rapidly and do not know
they are exposed to countless raging blasts
and that it is the fate of every pride

to fall, struck down, to infamy. The glory
of lofty office, how it shakes and trembles,
how false is hope; how full of vanity
our honor though by flattering tongues extolled!
And how uncertain is our life, absorbed
in toil unending, and how sure the hour
fixed for our death that comes upon us always
unready, unsuspecting! Man is born
to sorry destiny on earth. The brutes
may know repose and quiet, we alone
are granted neither truce nor pause; we rush
through breathless years into the arms of death.
Thou truly, death, art of all things the best
and fairest; thou alone dost make amends
for our transgressions, liberating us
from the vain dreams of life that slips away.
How many things I struggled for in vain,
how many ills I suffered willingly,
how many labors that I should have shunned!
Doomed though he be to die, yet still man strives
to scale the highest heavens but grim death
points out the place that is reserved for us.
What did it profit me with fire and sword
to ravage mighty Latium or to trouble
the world's peace, or to lay waste bleeding cities?
To what end did I raise up palaces
of gold and marble, if an adverse fate
decrees my death upon the open sea?
Nay, thou too, dearest brother, art preparing
great enterprises, unaware the while
of grief to come, and knowest naught of me!
                                        (VI, 889–913)

In Book VII the confrontation of the two leaders emphasizes
the contrast between Roman (or at least Scipionian) virtue and
Punic wickedness. Scipio treats Carthaginian spies with courteous
hospitality, gives them the run of the camp, and merely suggests
they carry out their mission by reporting what they have seen. Of
course this, aside from being chivalrous, has magnificent propa-
ganda value. The episode is followed by the meeting of the two
chiefs.

Hannibal suggests peace terms. Scipio answers with a moralistic
discourse recalling the crimes of the Carthaginians and taxing

them with atheism. He is less a Roman champion here than a defender of the faith. Incidentally he rejects the peace terms proposed by Hannibal, and both sides prepare for battle.

The poet, after a special invocation, presents a scene in Heaven in which two matrons (Rome and Carthage) plead their cases before Jove himself. Carthage asks the protection of the gods; Rome only that the fight be fair, for she is confident of her youthful champion. God answers, without revealing who the victor will be, but stating that since He is despairing of mankind He plans to descend to earth in human form, and the winner of the battle will have the honor of providing His earthly home. After suitable harangues by the opposing generals the dreadful battle is joined, watched by God, Fortune, and Divine Providence. Fortune would leave the issue uncertain; it is Divine Providence who gives the victory to the Romans. The Carthaginians are routed; Hannibal flees to the sanctuary of a royal palace in a village in the environs of the battlefield.

Scipio enters Carthage (Book VIII), which he treats with clemency, even eulogizing Hannibal. The latter flees to seek shelter and aid from the King of Antioch. As Scipio leaves the conquered city he makes a speech to the citizens which seems to reflect as much Augustinian world-weariness as Roman pride. He bids the vanquished:

> Be satisfied with what is yours and live
> mindful of the immortals; let not envy
> blind you with fury, driving you to arms.
> A vast empire within your ancient confines
> is left to you and all your laws remain
> confirmed, your ancient liberty preserved.
> Though it be glorious to hold world empire
> obedience to the good is more secure.
> For a long time to come—believe my words—
> you are assured of peace, while on our shoulders
> a heavy burden of continuing toil
> must press and bring us many griefs and cares.
>
> (VIII, 1032–39)

Scipio then leaves Carthage for Rome, his departure suitably illuminated by the burning Carthaginian fleet. On shipboard (Book IX) the victorious leader discusses poetry with Ennius; the

latter gives a long lecture on the nature of poetry, stressing the
importance of truth as a basis of inspiration. He then tells Scipio
of a dream he had had just before the battle; in this dream Homer
had appeared to him and had enabled him to see into the future.
And his privileged glance had fallen upon a youth seated among
young laurels in an enclosed valley. Sensing that the young man
is extraordinarily gifted, he asks Homer who it is and the Greek
bard replies:

> The youth is known to me. In the last years
> of the world's age the land of Italy
> from a posterity afar remote
> will bring him forth. Etruscan Florence,
> daughter of Rome, wide-walled, as yet unknown
> but destined one day to be glorious
> and great, will give him to you . . .
> . . . .
> In the dying years his art, with lofty notes,
> will summon back the Muses fugitive
> and scattered far abroad; he will recall
> the errant sisters to the abandoned peak
> of Helicon, though sore beset the while
> by many cares and various concerns.
> Francis will be his name. In one design
> weaving the great deeds you have witnessed, he
> will sing the Spanish Wars, the Libyan
> campaign, your mighty Scipio, and call
> his poem: *Africa* . . .
> . . . .
> 'Tis he alone, O Rome, who will endear
> to you the seed of Florence, making you
> content to have established the new town
> beside the Tuscan stream.
>
> (IX, 222–56)

Homer, Ennius reports, had then gone on to speak of the other
works the fortunate youth would produce, mentioning specifically
the *De viris* and the *Rerum memorandarum libri* and adding that
it would not be possible to imagine all the enterprises contemplated by such a genius.

Scipio expresses his anticipatory gratitude to the singer as yet
unborn. We leave the hero of the poem in his triumph on the

Capitoline; Petrarch will follow him no further, for the misfortunes of his later years are not appropriate to the sacred Muses the poet has invoked.

In the final verses of the epic Petrarch mourns the death of Robert—in part because, in his opinion, there is now no one left in the world fit to appreciate his poem. He ends by putting his hopes in a happier future, although he tells his creation sadly (and more accurately than he may have believed):

> Few are the houses that will take you in
> and rare the shelter you may hope to find.
> (IX, 469–70)

So the poem ends as it had begun, with a reference to the "wise" King and a complacent advertisement of its own merits.

Critics and readers today contemplate the *Africa* with the same mixture of confusion, uneasiness, and dismay which characterized the immediate reactions of the late fourteenth century when the poet's disciples finally succeeded in getting it into circulation. Throughout the centuries the verdict on the epic has been consistently negative. The most recent opinion is indeed the harshest. Bishop writes of the book that "to this heedless generation it is balefully, cyclopeanly dull";[6] after allowing for a few merits, he calls it a "doomed exercise in scholar imitation." Other critics, Whitfield and Gerosa for example, have defended the poem but more for its illumination of the author's character and intention than on its merits as a work of art.

It is sad that the verdict should be so generally negative. The purpose of the author was laudable; Petrarch wished to write a work which would be, in the words of its editor, Festa, "the great national poem of Italy" rivaling Dante's *"poema sacro"* and, as even its critics can see, the poem is not without beauty. It is well planned; the various scenes are properly disposed; the proportions, except perhaps for the rather longish Book VII, do not get out of hand; and there is a reasonably successfully developed story line. The trouble is that its assets lie in the zone of the ornamental and the technical; its faults are of a more basic nature. Perhaps it is written in the wrong language. Not only will it be forever compared to Virgil and suffer by the comparison, it will also forever suffer from a lack of a reading public, for a reader of

Latin epics will want to read true Latin epics and not late medieval imitations. Ironically, this is in part the fault of Petrarch himself. He had a deep contempt for the whole range of medieval
Latin save for a few works of religious interest; he is indeed one
of the great breakers of the continuity which had characterized
the cultural and literary life of the Middle Ages. In his devotion to
Latin, he himself turned to the classical world and ignored everything that had come after the end of the Empire. For him the epic
is Virgil, Lucan, and Statius; he dismisses Alain de Lille as *"taedi-
osus."* Petrarch despised the Middle Ages; history has taken its
revenge on him by ignoring the medieval in Petrarch. One can
feel reasonably sure that had he written it in Italian, even in *terza
rima,* the poem would still have considerable life. But, of course,
no linguistic restatement would have obscured the even more
fatal flaw—the choice of hero.

In a way the poem suggests Tasso's *Jerusalem Delivered,* and a
comparison of those two epics may be useful in revealing what is
wrong with Petrarch's effort. The poets have much in common.
Tasso makes use of conventional allegory, he is at his best with
sentimental and lyrical moments, and above all his subject is identical with that of Petrarch; both recount the *gesta* of a great warrior fighting in a religious cause on behalf of the true faith. But
Tasso is successful because the elements of his epic are homoge-
neous, and of course these elements focus on a central character.
Tasso's Godfrey is a Christian soldier engaged in a Christian war.
He is, furthermore, the combination of three and a half centuries
of a legendary elaboration of a historical episode. Springing as he
did from what Vico calls the second barbarian times when the
outlines of events and personalities were shrouded by the relative
inarticulateness of contemporary records and even speech, he could
very easily take on the impressive and portentous aura of the truly
heroic. But Scipio is the product of a society already literate, he is
indeed the property of the historians not of the mythology of the
folk, and much as we may admire Petrarch's effort at syncretism
(the whole thrust of the *Divine Comedy* is in the same direction),
the secret of making it plausible somehow eludes Petrarch. Dante
could write "Oh mighty Jove, who wast crucified for us on
earth," [7] and the shock is startling but convincing because it is an
intuitional truth for the author. Petrarch's description of a pagan

Jove pompously plotting his own incarnation is simply absurd. And if Scipio is typologically wrong he also suffers from the defects of perfection. He is not a man of uncontrolled wrath like Achilles, a man doomed to die for his fatherland like Hector, a man subject to a fit of tempestuous passion such as even the pious Aeneas, who at least temporarily forgot his piety. He has no faults whatsoever and, what is equally bad, no real misfortunes. There is no irregularity either in his character or in the path of victory that he pursues. I am not sure that Petrarch has been successful in portraying the Scipio he had in mind. According to Olschki, who incidentally defines the *Africa* as "a medieval maze of allegories and parables, the Roman hero is no longer an historical prefiguration of chivalry or an instrument of divine providence. He is rather the poetical reincarnation of the old Roman *Virtutes*, the names of which were preserved by Christian ethics but with quite altered meanings. With Petrarch, for the first time since the classical age, *fides* no longer has a sense of belief in God but expresses the synthesis of fairness, loyalty, and mutual confidence for which modern languages have no equivalent word. Scipio's *pietas* is not compassion or devout belief but rather the devotion to parents, family, race and country glorified in Virgil's 'pious Aeneas'." [8] But this is not entirely true; we have seen in Book VII that fortune or rather Divine Providence specifically mentions Scipio as the instrument of its will, and it is precisely the belief in God that is the highest attribute of the Roman conqueror; it is indeed for the lack of such feeling that he castigates the Carthaginians. To be sure, the feudal concept is absent from the *Africa*, but the pure *pietas* of the Roman epic has suffered some contamination with pietism. The poem is, in fact, another affirmation, although in classical dress, of the old statement that Christians are right and pagans are wrong. Indeed, it is precisely this unsuccessful marriage of the two elements which distorts the image of Scipio and vitiates the action of the epic. Aldo Bernardo says shrewdly "that Petrarch discovered in the figure of Scipio a kind of catalyst that would give him the prototype of classical virtue, defined as natural excellence but mysteriously serving the end of Christian providence. Scipio has in him something of Aeneas, of Dante's Virgil, of David and of Godfrey of Bouillon," [9] and I would suggest much more of the last-named than any of the others; the Counter Reformation is adumbrated, it seems to me, at once in the stylized rhetoric, the self-conscious and almost calculated sense of mission, and even in the intervals of rather morbidly developed sensuality. But of course it lacks the sophistication of the Counter Reformation, which indeed would have had no use at all for Petrarch's plot. Lastly, the repeated intrusion of the poet's own role is out of keeping with the anonymity of the proper epic. The prevision of Ennius in Book IX is enough in itself to ruin the epic pretension of the poem. To be sure, both Dante and Milton brought in their own emotions and reactions, but Dante is the avowed hero of his own epic and Milton is much more discreet in his intrusions. Finally of course, Petrarch is simply not by nature a teller of tales. The action of the *Africa,* even in its most exciting moments, is submerged by the interminable discourses. Taken as a whole, the work is another reflection of Petrarch's persistent dilemma. The glorification of the Roman virtues is recurrently undercut by the melancholy acknowledgment that nothing in this world is of lasting importance. The ambivalence toward sensual beauty, alternatively admired and disparaged, wavering as one might put it, in terms of his other works, between St. Augustine and Cicero, does not strengthen the epic impact.

The literary sources are a rather intriguing miscellany: Cicero's *Somnium Scipionis* is clearly the point of departure of the first books; most of the history is straight from Livy; the style is by intent at least Virgilian; and Calcaterra has demonstrated a pervasive influence of Augustine's *City of God* not only in the emotional attitude of the author but in such basic themes as the recognition of Roman virtue and destiny and even the admiration of Scipio.

For all that, the poem does have a kind of appeal which lies, I think, in the very contradictions that contribute to its failure. Next to the *Canzoniere* itself, where these cross-currents do not trouble us, for they are consciously and purposefully elaborated, the *Africa* gives us the best self-portrait of the poet that we have, better I think than the *Secretum,* which is a little too self-conscious, and better, because of the *"fren dell'arte,"* than the *Letters.* And, to assess the work in less personal terms, it is fascinating as a kind of cultural artifact; it is a manifestation of the humanistic intent struggling to escape from the fetters of medieval commitments; it is also an assertion of individualism (even the embarrassing displays of the poet's vanity are significant here) in a sector previously reserved for the anonymous voice of the community.

The *Africa* is a poem and as such a creative work. But it is also meant to be history; the poet, Petrarch tells us, must build on truth. If, as we have noted, the *Africa* has its links with the *Canzoniere*, it is also from the point of view of its substance classifiable with other historical studies of the scholar Petrarch, of which the most significant—and the most ponderous—is the *De viris illustribus.*

This ambitious enterprise, highly esteemed by the writer's contemporaries, was begun in either 1338 or the following year, according to G. Martellotti, who is our leading authority for the work.[10] It seems likely that the notion of a series developed from the first "life," that of Scipio, was much on Petrarch's mind during this time. Subsequently, Petrarch rewrote the *Life* and put it in its proper chronological order in his first version of the work as a whole, which dealt with the following twenty-three "illustrious men" of Rome: the early kings, Romulus, Numa, Tullius Hostilius, and Ancus Martius; passing on then to the heroes of the early republic, Brutus, Horatius, Cincinnatus, Camillus, Manlius, Torquatus, Valerius Corvus, Decius, Papirius Cursor, Curius Dentatus, and Fabricius. There follows a trio of famous non-Romans: Alexander, Pyrrhus, and Hannibal, after which come Fabius Maximus, Marcellus, Claudius, Nero and Livius Salinator, treated together, Scipio and Cato the Censor. The series was meant to go as far as Titus, but the first version was laid aside. In the Vaucluse interval of 1351–53 Petrarch changed his plan, broadening his concept from the Roman to the universal (considering the subjects one is tempted to think the new direction may be associated with the penitential mood induced by the death of Laura and the plague; a triumph of the Augustinian over the Ciceronian Petrarch). In any event, after a preface outlining his new approach, he added the biographies of Adam, Noah, Nimrod, Ninus, and Semiramis; followed by those of the five patriarchs, Abraham, Isaac, Jacob, Joseph, and Moses; and concluding with a treatment of two Greek heroes, Jason and Hercules, the latter being left unfinished.

The gallery of names chosen is as interesting for the omissions as for the inclusions. Romans came first as might be expected, but even when the work takes on "universal" scope there is no room for anyone later than Caesar. For Petrarch no medieval figure, not even Charlemagne, was truly "illustrious," least of all, it would seem, any Christian saint.

At some later date, Petrarch wrote yet a third version of the life of Scipio and added a new biography: that of Caesar, by far the longest of them all and perhaps meant to stand apart as a separate work. Finally, toward the end of his life, he planned a definitive edition of thirty-six of the lives (to match the figures that Francesco da Carrara planned to have painted in a room of his palace) but got no further than a preface; after his death Lombardo della Seta carried out the poet's plan and also finished the *Compendium* to the work which Petrarch had undertaken at the bidding of Francesco da Carrara.

The work added much to Petrarch's prestige during his lifetime; it is interesting not only as revealing the interests of the poet (and his contemporaries) but also as an early exercise in historiography; the writer's approach has some touch of the critical attitude which we associate with modern historians and which was lacking in the Middle Ages. Hollway-Calthrop says very charitably and perhaps rightly, of the *De viris* that,

Considering the materials at Petrarch's disposal, this is a stupendous achievement; and the scale on which it is planned no less than the methods of its execution marks it as the first of modern histories. Its very excellence, indeed, probably hastened the day of its supersession; it must have kindled an interest in historical research fatal to its continued use as a textbook.[11]

The basic notion however of "history" as simply "lives of the great" remains medieval; the popularity of the book did not survive to the age of printing and there is even today no edition of the work as a whole, although the separate biographies of Scipio and Caesar are available.

The *Rerum memorandarum libri* as it stands appears to us thematically related to the *De viribus illustribus:* in fact, however, Petrarch had a very elaborate design in mind. The projected work was to illustrate by anecdotes from the lives of the great, all aspects of the seven cardinal virtues; it would have been a kind of moralized universal history, even as the *De viris* would have been a universal history told through biographies. If the plan seems to have about it something of the cumbersome medieval groping for all-inclusiveness, yet there is one aspect of it that is not without originality and may be seen as a reflection of the true humanistic spirit. His choice of Greek and Roman subjects reveals, as Bosco has put it,[12] a concealed but clearly apparent rivalry with Valerius Maximus, but what is peculiarly Petrarch's is the addition of anecdotes—and personalities—from the contemporary world. It is this element, as Martellotti remarks, that gives to the work a sure sense of perspective, almost a third dimension; he adds that "the desire to bring the modern close to the ancient implies at the same time the awareness of a distance to be overcome; the awareness of such a distance is the beginning and the source of a historical understanding." [13]

The project, like so many others of our poet, remained unfulfilled. He seems to have labored long over it in the years 1343–45 and then to have abandoned it to return only sporadically if at all. It is likely that the material he had in mind for the work found its outlet elsewhere, probably in the *Letters,* which, seen from one point of view, contain much of the same substance: Greek and Latin anecdotes and sketches, enlivened by and often juxtaposed with contemporary personalities and events. The following excerpt, dealing with the much-admired Robert of Naples, will serve to give an idea of the tone of the work and to indicate how close it is to that of the *Letters:*

Never was he ashamed to learn, old philosopher-King that he was; never was he reluctant to give information on things he knew; this phrase was ever on his lips and in his heart: that one becomes wise through learning and teaching. How deeply he burned with love for letters can be shown by a statement that I heard with my own ears. One day, during a lengthy conversation, he asked me why I had been so slow in coming to see him. And I, answering—as was the truth— that the dangers of land and sea travel and various impediments of fortune had frustrated my intentions, chanced, I do not remember how, to mention the King of the French. He then asked me if I had ever visited his court and I replied that I hadn't even thought of it. Smiling, he asked me why. I said, "Because I don't care to waste the time of a king who has no literary culture—and to waste my own time as well. I prefer to maintain the pact I have made with my poverty rather than try the halls of kings where I couldn't understand anything and wouldn't be understood."

He then said he had heard that the king's oldest son did not neglect the study of letters. I said I had heard the same but this was so annoying to his father that he regarded the prince's tutors as enemies. Whether it's true or not I don't know and I don't say that it is, but that's what I'd heard said and the rumor had done away with any slightest notion of mine of going to see him. Hearing this, that generous soul sprang up, quivering all over. He stood a moment in silence, eyes fixed on the floor. Then with an expression of indignation on his face (I recall these details as clearly as if I still had the scene before my eyes) he raised his head and said to me: "This is human life: inclinations, aspirations, tendencies vary greatly. But I swear to you that letters are dearer and sweeter to me than my kingdom; and if I had to choose I would rather lose the crown than my interest in letters." A sentence worthy of a philosopher, worthy of being venerated by all scholars. How greatly it pleased me, what courage it gave me in my studies, how firmly and deeply it remained fixed in my heart! [14]

CHAPTER 9

Devotional Works

ACCEPTING for purposes of discussion the validity of our categories and passing now to the second or devotional group, we must give first place to the *Secretum.* It was born of the crisis of 1342–43, which we have referred to in an earlier chapter. The birth of Petrarch's daughter, another living evidence of his carnal weakness, and quite possibly a reaction from the worldly triumph of the coronation, a general uneasiness about the purpose of his life; in these elements are its genesis. His brother's decision to enter a monastery and the death of his patron Robert of Sicily may also have contributed to the sense of unease and even despair which led, if not to a "conversion" (for in fact one cannot see much difference in the pattern of the poet's life after these trying years) at least to a thorough soul-searching, of which the *Secretum* is the record. Its literary source is in the reading of Augustine, to which he ardently turned during the period of trial. *Secretum meum* is the title given the work by the author himself; it was written, he said, only for his own eyes and to be kept with him always and never "published" (although the style and certain rhetorical ornaments bely this statement). In some manuscripts it is called *De secreto conflictu curarum mearum.*

The book is written in the form of three dialogues between Petrarch and St. Augustine, while Truth stands by as a silent arbiter. In the introduction Petrarch tells how in the midst of his reflections Truth, clothed in white, appeared to him (much as Lady Philosophy appeared to Boethius). By her side stood a figure recognizable at once by his African dress, his Roman style and his austere bearing, as St. Augustine. He looks upon Petrarch with affection. Truth asks him to come to the rescue of the poet, who, she says, has always been an admirer of the saint and whose troubles are similar to those Augustine had experienced when he was alive. Augustine expresses his willingness to help, and a three-day conversation begins. In the first book, Augustine compels Petrarch to admit that the happiness of man depends upon his will; peace of soul can be achieved by avoidance of sin, and the first step toward that goal is meditation on death and final judgment. Petarch replies that he has tried to follow that prescription but finds only terror in such contemplation. To which Augustine answers that in this case terror is salutary, for it shows that the poet is at least aware of his perilous state.

The second dialogue (Book II) takes place on the following day. It is, in effect, an examination of conscience. St. Augustine runs through the list of the seven mortal sins. He finds the poet free of the sins of envy, wrath, and gluttony but guilty of the rest; he stresses particularly pride (as evidenced by Petrarch's ambition), lust, and the kind of egocentric melancholia which the saint calls *accidia*. Petrarch defends himself as best he can but is obliged to concede the truth of the saint's charges, though "not entirely convinced."

In Book III, the liveliest as it is the most pointed and personal, Augustine returns to his attack. Petrarch's really dangerous diseases, he says, are love and desire for glory. Petrarch argues valiantly in defense of Laura, but the saint is merciless. Some of his descriptions of Laura are unflattering, to say the least. He reminds Petrarch that her beautiful body, worn out with illness and frequent parturitions, is mortal and corruptible; later on he urges the poet to meditate on the filthiness of the feminine body. When Petrarch argues that he loves only Laura's soul, Augustine asks him if he would love it were it found in an ugly body—and receives only a quibbling and evasive answer. When Petrarch says she is admirable because she has checked his base desires, Augustine points out that this is a confession that the poet's love was not truly pure. He compels the poet to recognize that the healthy piety of his boyhood (a result of his upbringing) left him just at the time when Laura appeared. At her very best she represents a distraction from what should be the true love of the poet—that of God. The love for the creature stands in the way of the love for the creator. Even her name has had an evil influence, leading the poet to worship the laurel "either of emperors or poets." The best remedies he can suggest (for by this time Petrarch's defenses have collapsed) are flight—he suggests to Italy—and meditation.

Petrarch's love of glory is of the same subversive stamp as his devotion to Laura, the saint points out. Earthly glory is in itself a transitory thing but dangerous too as being a diversion of the devotion due to things eternal. He will not urge Petrarch to be indifferent to glory but only to put first the quest for virtue. He urges Petrarch to put aside his *Africa* (on which at this time the poet was placing his highest hopes for fame) telling him sardonically that if completed, that work would add neither to Scipio's glory nor the poet's. And above all, he urges him to meditate on death. Petrarch, crushed by all these arguments, can only concur with the saint's counsel, yet even at the very end he admits he has other cares which he cannot bring himself to neglect.

All of Petrarch's biographers are unanimous in the admiration of the *Secretum.* Tonelli speaks of its "great and well-deserved fortune," [1] and Gerosa calls it a "precious document";[2] one could easily compose a litany of such adulatory phrases. Morris Bishop, whose enthusiastic approval is in accord with the views of older critics as far back as Körting, says of the work:

It is the revelation of an abnormally sensitive mind in an emotional crisis, frustrated in love, in ambition, and in self-esteem, and trying to be utterly honest with itself. It is the indispensable gloss to the *Rime;* it lays bare the reality underlying the poetic fiction. It is the first great example of literary introspection, as opposed to the professional introspection of literary seers. As such it has its importance not only in the history of literary psychology, but in the history of the European concept of human character. . . . Its picture of a tortured sensibility involved in a maze of doubts, struggling against its own impotence, is as modern as yesterday's best-seller.[3]

All of this is true up to a point, but one must make, I think, some reservations. Whitfield suspects that the connection with the *Rhymes* has given the *Secretum* "perhaps more than its fair share of attention," [4] and I am inclined to agree. Coming to it from the *Canzoniere* we are delighted to find confirmation in Latin prose for the lyric statement of the sonnets and odes. It is reassuring to learn that Laura really existed, and certain other biographical details cannot fail to interest us: we learn that Petrarch was at this point worried about the success of his *Africa,* that he had turned gray in early youth, that some ugly circumstances surrounded the loss of his patrimony. But that it is "indispensable" for an understanding of the *Rhymes* is, it seems to me, saying a little too much.

In truth the *Rhymes* need no key; they speak plainly and, I would say, more eloquently than the *Secretum*. Indeed one could regard the whole book as an elaboration of the ode *"Di pensier in pensier, di monte in monte,"* but not, I would say, as an indispensable gloss, for the ode says all the *Secretum* does and much more effectively.

It is true that the little book does document very clearly the dilemma of the soul, attracted by transient beauty, knowing its proper focus should be on the eternal; a dilemma quintessentially Augustinian and, as Bishop says, also universal. And the documentation is well set forth. But it is also a little too pretentious, too self-conscious. One may not doubt the sincerity of the writer, but one may find his exposition somewhat artificial. The imitation of Augustine is patent and may even be considered smug; it is not a humble man, however soul-shaken he may be, who asserts that his suffering may be paralleled with those of one of the great Church Fathers. The staging too is suspect; the three "acts" of the drama, with carefully plotted dialogue, bespeak a man who, however wracked by sobs, still has a pretty firm hand on the pen, with no perceptible trembling of the fingers. Of course, from a purely technical point of view the discipline is admirable. Which, I suspect, is another reason why readers think well of the *Secretum*. It is very well designed, with practically no irrelevant diversions, a minimum of erudition (though enough to be troublesome now and again) and a good deal of vivacity in the dialogue. It is a very well-made book, not too long, beautifully proportioned, and full of substance. But it is a crisis, it seems to me, chronicled in cold blood, heavily derivative, pleasantly artful. For the true *cri de coeur* we must look to the *Rhymes*, the indispensable justification of the *Secretum*.

It seems likely that the *Penitential Psalms* are of the same date of composition as the *Secretum*. They also reflect a mood of deep religious meditation, although by their nature they are less personal than the more confessional work. We may read the fourth psalm as characteristic of the little collection, and from a strictly literary point of view the most appealing of all of them:

1. I take pleasure in remembering Thy gifts, my God, in order that confusion may st and before my eyes and a blush may spring to my cheeks.

2. For perhaps then Thou wilt have compassion upon me, when Thou seest that I am not entirely unmindful of all that Thou hast given me, Thou best of benefactors.

3. For me Thou didst create the heavens and the stars—for what need didst Thou have of these things?—and for me likewise the alternation of the seasons.

4. It was Thou who didst set apart the sun and the moon, the days and the nights, the light and the darkness.

5. The air is a creation of Thy fingers; the clear sky and the clouds are Thy handiwork, and the winds and the rain.

6. Thou hast surrounded the land with waters; Thou hast created the mountains and the seas, the valleys and the plains, the fountains and the lakes and the rivers.

7. All this Thou hast made fertile, sowing different seeds within; all this Thou hast adorned with varied beauty.

8. Thou hast clothed the fields in green grasses; Thou hast adorned the hills with flowers, the woods with the blossoms on the boughs.

9. For the weary Thou hast prepared rest, for those who suffer heat, the shade of the trees, and pleasant shelter for our leisure.

10. Thou hast prepared clear fountains for the thirsty, for the hungry, berries of all sorts and divers refreshments for their restoration.

11. With what many horned animals hast Thou populated the land and the seas and the spaces of air which surround them! Who could enumerate them all?

12. And all of these things Thou hast put under the feet of man. Thou hast loved man so much as to give him various delights.

13. Thou hast loved me not less although I be but one among many. In truth some things Thou hast given to me for my own.

14. Thou hast embellished the body of man more than all Thy creatures; Thou hast disposed his members in a marvelous order.

15. Thou hast given him a serene and commanding face, and a spirit capable of knowing Thee and of contemplating celestial things.

16. Thou hast added thereto countless arts in order that this life might be more beautifully adorned; and Thou hast given also hope of eternal life.

17. Thou hast shown the way by which we must pass; Thou hast thrown wide the entrance to Thy tabernacles; Thou hast shown us from whom we should protect ourselves and where we may find refuge.

18. Thou hast given me an ever faithful guide and companion from a lofty peak. Thou hast surveyed all my steps and marked my errant course.

19. When I fell Thou didst raise me up; when I faltered Thou didst support me. When I strayed Thou didst show me the right path. When

I fell to earth Thou didst lift me up again; I was nigh unto death and
Thou didst bring me to life again.

20. Thou hast shown compassion for my tribulations, aye, when I
was not worthy of mercy but rather of scorn.

21. And for what merits of mine, gratuitously, undeservingly have
I received these gifts beyond price?

22. Thou seest what I have given Thee in return, yet even so do
Thou have pity upon me yet once again and save me, for without
Thee I die.

23. Remember no more my ingratitude, but make my soul safe for
it is already despairing of its strength.

24. Glory to the Father and to the Son and to the Holy Ghost. As it
was in the beginning so now and forever world without end. Amen.[5]

These religious verses, which are clearly written in imitation of
the Old Testament Psalms (although scholars have found in them
also traces of St. Augustine and even of Cicero), are appealing
and, for Wilkins and others, even "moving." There is no reason to
believe that they are not genuine expressions of the poet's emotions in his time of crisis, yet some may feel that they are too
perfect of their kind; if we did not have Petrarch's signature to
them, we could find nothing very personal in them and might
even suspect that they were the work of David himself. The pattern has been so well learned, the lesson so well absorbed that
these compositions might easily seem simply very successful exercises in imitation. It is not Petrarch who speaks in these lines but
The Sinner; from a religious point of view they may well be all the
more admirable on that account, but their imitative nature is so
patent that it must arouse some suspicion not necessarily of their
sincerity but of their spontaneity. The reader may have, I think,
the same reservation concerning the hymn to the Virgin, which
concludes the *Rhymes*. In such exercises personality is of necessity
submerged. The Muse, no doubt for the noblest of purposes, becomes, as it were, institutionalized. I have a feeling that Petrarch
may have felt this himself; it is, it seems to me, significant that we
have only seven psalms as against 366 items in the *Rhymes*.

A third work of strictly devotional nature is the *De otio religioso*.
This is a tractate in two books composed in 1347 but containing,
as we have it, certain revisions, some of which are as late as 1357.
It was dedicated to the Carthusians of Montrieux, where
Gherardo had taken refuge from the world. As the title indicates.

the book is a study of the religious life, written, as the author says, for his own benefit rather than that of those to whom it is dedicated. It paints the serenity of the tranquil spirit without ambitions or conflict, dedicated to the service of God and to contemplation of the eternal verities. It is a glorification of the life of religious retirement which Petrarch wistfully admired but was never quite willing to share. By its nature it is of course a very medieval book, somewhat rhetorical and static, and in all frankness not very interesting to readers of today. Needless to say St. Augustine is everpresent, especially his *De vera religione*. Nor is Cicero absent.

Although the works we have just discussed differ considerably in form and somewhat in character, it seems fair to regard them all as "devotional" so far as their basic motivation is concerned. There remain three other works in which the religious element is strong enough to warrant our designating them as in some sense devotional but wherein the main thrust is less religious than philosophical, or in one case, informational. Two of them are substantial compositions, on which Petrarch labored hard and long; they deserve, I think, somewhat more attention than is usually accorded them.

The *De vita solitaria* seems to have been composed in first draft in 1346, but the poet kept it with him and revised and enlarged it; it was not finished until 1356 and was released to Philippe de Cabassoles only ten years after that; a few years later another addition to it was made. As the dates of composition indicate, it is the fruit of the same harvest that brought forth the *De otio,* to which it may be regarded as a kind of companion piece. The work is divided into two books, the first dealing with the general aspect of the subject and the second presenting a long catalogue of practitioners and examples of the solitary life. Both books are subdivided into tractates, of which the first book contains six and the second, nine. The tractates in turn are subdivided into chapters. Now and again the author wanders from the main line of his argument; the fourth tractate of Book II, for example, is given over to an invective against the contemporary princes who "apply themselves to sleep, pleasure, disgraceful gain, plundering of their subjects, while none of them is moved by the loss of the Holy Land";[6] the third chapter of the third tractate of Book II contains a little excursus on the evils of the company of women, suggested by a quotation from St. Ambrose. "However you may be if you seek peace, keep away from women," Laura's lover instructs us, adding that "peace and a woman seldom live under the same roof." And the worshiper of Laura's magnetic glances even adds that "like a basilisk a woman slays with her eyes and infects you before she touches you." [7] Such digressions give the work an air of intimacy and informality that make it comparable to a letter, as his translator Zeitlin has observed, and Petrarch himself writes at the end of the work: "I had intended a letter and I have written a book." [8] On the other hand, the scrupulous subdivisions, even though their logical order is occasionally interrupted, are surely an echo of the scholastic method. This mingling of the personal and the traditional in form is characteristic of Petrarch. The life of solitude the poet has in mind is not the hermit life of the anchorites, although he quotes the habits of several of them with approval, but is nearer the Sabine farm concept of the classics; the ideal way of life is apparently in the country, close to nature but with plenty of books available and frequent visits from congenial friends. ("If I had to choose I would rather be deprived of solitude than of my friend.") [9] Although he cites examples of Christian withdrawals from the world in order to meditate and pray for the sake of mankind, the poet is really interested in the kind of retreat that will give him leisure to pursue his own studies; it is an aristocratic and in effect rather worldly rustication that he envisages. Aware of the latent egotism in it, he says that, much as he would like to labor for the salvation of others, "It is enough for me, yea, a cause of great happiness, if I do not perish myself." [10] On which Zeitlin comments: "This surely is the renunciation not of the ascetic but the egoist, an attitude forestalling Montaigne in all but outright candor." [11]

As a work of art *On the Life of Solitude* suffers from the defects that mar other works of Petrarch. It is verbose, discursive, and full of erudition, with appeals to all kinds of classical authorities and examples of notable classical figures and great Christian saints who have practiced the life he admires. Yet it contains some very fine passages. In his introduction to the work Petrarch lashes out against those who make a show of their learning and have constant need of the applause of the ignorant herd. "Store of learning does not always dwell in a modest breast, and often there is considerable strife between the tongue and the mind, between teaching and the conduct of life." [12] Such men he says, "scatter through the streets and arcades, counting the towers and horses and carriages . . . gazing in stupid admiration at the dresses of the women. . . . These are the men with whom it is proverbial to say that it is a splendid thing to visit other countries and to mingle with people." [13] (The reader familiar with Petrarch's tourist letters will read this diatribe with some inner amusement, for here certainly the author is attacking one of the most beguiling aspects of his own character.) And this leads him to the affirmation of a kind of misanthropy that throws us forward to the disillusioned outburst of Machiavelli; he goes on to say:

Surely it is much better to visit stones and trees and to mingle with tigers and bears. For man is not only a base and unclean animal, but furthermore—I say it unwillingly, and I only wish that experience had not made it and were not continuing to make it so well known to all—he is pernicious, unstable, faithless, fickle, fierce and bloody, unless by the rare grace of God he puts off his bestiality and puts on humanity . . .

And he adds, very perceptively and perhaps more so than he knew:

If you ask such people why they are ever seeking the company of others, they will answer, if they are moved to speak the truth, that it is only because they cannot endure being alone.[14]

We may also admire some passages of highly colorful description. For example, in the course of the first book, where he traces the contrasts between the life of the city man (always associated with luxury and vice) and that of the countryman (similarly linked with austerity and virtue), he pictures the state of each at various hours of the day, painting the horrors of urban life in particularly violent colors. Here, for example, is the man of business at dinner:

The roof resounds with a variety of noises while all about stand the dogs of the hall and the household mice. A crowded array of flatterers vie with one another in obsequiousness, and a troop of greedy menials sets the tables with bustling confusion. As the floor is swept of its dirt

everything is filled with vile dust. Silver vessels wrought with gold
flash through the room and goblets hollowed out of precious stones.
The benches are covered with silk and the walls with purple, and
carpets are spread over the floor, but the servants shiver in their naked-
ness. Once the line of battle is drawn up, the signal of the onset is delivered by a trumpet. The captains of the kitchen rush against the captains of the hall. A great clatter is set up; dishes conquered by land and
sea are dragged in, and wine trodden in ancient Cos. The vintages of
Italy and Greece glitter in the ruddy gold; in a single cup are blended
Gnosos and Meroe, Venusius and Falernus, the hills of Sorrento and
Calabria. . . . In another place may be seen an equal display of a
different sort—horrible beasts, unknown fishes, unheard-of birds, saturated in costly spices. . . . There are smoking dishes which are a
cause of amazement to the very banqueters, having been subjected to
every wanton trick of the cooks. . . . Amidst such an impure mixture
of divers and mutually hostile ingredients, amidst all these yellow and
black and blue condiments, the busy taster not without reason looks for
the suspected poison, though against hidden treachery another kind of
remedy has been found. Between the wine and the food there shoot
forth the livid crests of serpents cunningly twisted among golden
branches, and as though by a voluptuary device Death itself wonder-
fully stands on guard against the death of miserable man. But the
feaster sits with countenance overcast, eyes dull, forehead clouded,
nose wrinkled, and cheeks pale, parting his sticky lips with difficulty,
scarce lifting his head. Fairly overpowered by all the glitter and odors,
he knows not where he is, being still swollen with the excesses of the
previous night, dazed with the outcome of the morning's business, and
already cunningly plotting where to turn next and what mischief to
perform. He perspires, he sniffs, he belches, he gapes, nibbling at
everything and nauseated by all.[15]

Sturdy and eloquent invective, in fact, gives the book a good
deal of its vitality. Nor does the poet fear to name names; Chapter
iii of the fourth tractate of Book II is a blistering denunciation of
the princes of Christendom; it contains a kind of prose equivalent,
but with a wider scope of attention, of the famous *canzone* to
Italy, short enough to quote in full:

Germany has no other aim than to arm mercenary brigands for the
destruction of the state, and from her clouds she showers down a continuous rain of iron 'pon our lands. It is deserved, I do not deny, for it
falls upon an abject people. Italy ruins herself with her own laws, and
when she does draw breath, the love of gold, more potent than the

love of Christ, seizes on the minds of its people and scatters them over all the lands and seas. Greece, turned away by her own errors or our pride, despises the ancient fold and our pastures.[16]

Such a spectacle leads the poet to a consideration of the meaning of patriotism and to the expression of his somewhat original views of the subject.

Not for any country are all things to be dared, though those who have dared are exalted to the skies with many commendations. . . . If you ask my opinion about all of these, it is that our love should be for the celestial state, which is not disturbed by the agitations of tribunes, the uprisings of the populace, the arrogance of the senate, the envy of factions, or foreign and domestic wars; whoever sheds his blood for it is a good citizen and certain of his reward. Not that I think one's earthly country should on that account be forsaken, for which, if the situation requires it, we are even commanded to fight, yet only provided it is ruled by justice and lives under equitable laws, as was once the case with the Roman republic according to the writings of Sallust, Livy, and many besides.[17]

On the more affirmative side we may still read with admiration his remarks on literature. Speaking of the great benefactors of mankind, the "inventors" of agriculture and the arts, he goes on to say:

If in truth some honor is due to the discoverers of things of this sort— and I do not deny that great honor is due, provided it be human and reasonable—what glory shall be showered upon the inventors of literature and the noble arts, who have provided us not with a plow to make furrows, nor woven garments for our bodies, nor tinkling lyres for our ears, nor oil and wine for our gullets—though to be sure our ears and gullets take pleasure in the sounds and tastes—but have furnished us with nobler instruments wherewith to procure nourishment, raiment, instruction, and healing for the mind? Moreover, I ask, where can this debt most effectively be paid? Who doubts that this pursuit of literature, by means of which we consecrate our own name or that of another, carving statues of illustrious men much more enduring than bronze or marble, can be carried on nowhere more successfully or more freely than in solitude? Here at least I speak from experience, for I know what spurs it supplies to the mind, what wings for the spirit, what leisure time for work—things which I know not where to seek save in solitude.[18]

But most of all what appeals to the reader of today is the tone of civilized tolerance, which, apart from the special invectives, pervades the work. "In all things I ask for measure" [19] he says, in the course of distinguishing between the simplicity of the pastoral life and brutish primitivism. Furthermore he affirms repeatedly that he recognizes all men are not the same: "I am reluctant to set up what may be peculiar to myself as a truth for all," [20] he writes and again, even more categorically: "There is nothing more vital than independence of judgment; as I claim it for myself I would not deny it for others." [21] It is this serenity of outlook that has made many readers of the work think of Montaigne, and indeed if we have yet a long way to go to the open-minded urbanity of the great Frenchman yet it must be said that Petrarch's position is even further away from the doctrinaire assurance of the Middle Ages.

Mario Fubini affirms that in the *De vita solitaria* we recognize the author of the *Canzoniere*.[22] Perhaps this is to praise the book too highly; we miss the lyricism (and not merely the formal lyricism) of the *Rhymes,* the tenderness, even the persistent melancholy. But the mixture of motifs, the manner of treatment, the gentle and highly personal style are all here.

The book is not a work of art, but it is a kind of honest self-analyzing essay. For all its cumbrous arrangement and intrusions of pretentious learning, it is by no means unreadable and is surely as frank and revealing as the *Secretum*—and less self-consciously anguished.

The *De remediis utriusque fortunae,* over which the author toiled for some seven years (1354–60), has a Stoic-Christian intent and a medieval pattern, episodic in design and equipped with the usual didactic allegory. It was dedicated to Azzo da Correggio, possibly to console him for his political misfortune—he had been driven out of Verona in 1355. In Part I of the work the good things of life, presented by Joy and Hope, are unmasked as illusions by Reason; in Part II it falls to Reason to offer consolation for the miseries, equally illusory because transient, depicted by Grief and Fear. Since the arguments of Reason must be supported by case histories the work is filled with learning, and sometimes the encyclopedist seems to win out over the moralist. The intention of the work gives it something in common with the *Secretum,* revealing as it does Petrarch's ambivalence in his attitude toward earthly things; its anecdotal construction, while perhaps an artistic blemish, does lend it a certain intimacy of approach; indeed the work, though seldom read nowadays, was repeatedly reissued and translated down to the eighteenth century. "Under its medieval wrapping," in the opinion of Francesco Flora, "one can sense a modern taste that makes one think of Pascal or Montaigne." [23] One's first impression would be that such a statement is open to question. The medieval wrapping is very thick, and the intent to disparage the things of the world is firm and unshaken. But Whitfield, not denying the "fundamental aridity" of the *De remediis*, quotes the basically optimistic statement of the preface: "Life of itself would be assuredly happy and enjoyable above all other things if it were but guided by reason," and he points out how such an affirmation is completely opposed to the hopeless "contempt of the world" view of the true medieval ascetic.[24]

Yet this cannot be regarded as the final statement on this puzzling and contradictory book. Gerosa[25] points to the same aspect of the work as evidence of its ultimately Christian spirit, defending it against those who, like Körting, would see in it an early affirmation of systematic and skeptical pessimism.[26] On behalf of Körting it may be said that even if we grant the validity of Whitfield's reference, the continuous disparagement of life's joys and the easy dismissal of its cares seem to come very close to a negation of the value of life itself and to press the pessimistic attack somewhat beyond the Christian frontiers. When, for example, Petrarch argues in another part of the same preface that animals are happier than men because they are not conscious of the passage of time and take no care for the future, or in other words because they do not have reflective intelligence, one can almost detect the adumbrations of a Leopardian despair. However, probably Gerosa is right in affirming, with reference to the poet's stress on virtue as the road to happiness, that the work is, at least in intention, sincerely Christian.

It is unlikely that many nowadays will labor through the *De remediis*—it is in fact a little hard to come by. The following dialogue will give some idea of the tone of the work which now and again has a gleam of sardonic humor. It is from Chapter xcix of Book I and deals with armaments.[27]

JOY: I have war machines of every sort.

REASON: What you are saying fits in with other follies indicative of your delight in being able to do as much harm as you can to others, when on the other hand it is precisely princes who ought to behave best toward others. They were put at the head of kingdoms and called "kings" so that they might take care of the affairs of men and be loved and revered as fathers, indeed some of them have been called "Fathers of their Fatherland." But nowadays rulers do everything in just the opposite fashion so that they have become tormentors and rascals and public robbers and are hated and feared by everyone.

JOY: I have enough war machines to reduce cities.

REASON: How much better it would be to have machines to build them up and maintain them. Do you think it is more glorious to ruin cities than to preserve them? Do you wish to appear another Polycretus of this age? But I will tell you one thing: cities are not always taken with war machines. You must have something else as well. In the war which he was waging in Gaul against the people called the Avantici, Caesar had very high towers constructed. At first he was ridiculed by his enemies as if he were a man trying to do something impossible to human power. But when they saw the towers move and approach the wall their scorn was turned into fear and amazement and putting aside all defense they surrendered to Caesar as their last refuge. Similarly in the civil wars in Rome, Brutus, a captain of this same Caesar, had similar towers constructed against Marseilles and drawn toward the city. And it amazed the besieged folk of the town. But the effect of the fear was not quite the same because they came out at night and burned the towers and the machines.

JOY: I have many machines to destroy towers and I have catapults.

REASON: Almost all the things that you are so proud of are concerned with doing harm to others and not with what you ought to be doing. How much more decent, proper, and becoming to a man it would be to have facilities for sheltering your friends or the needy poor and to be kind to them rather than to have things which enable you to go about disturbing the peace of the country, eager to destroy cities against all reason and justice.

JOY: I have mangonels which throw great and heavy stones.

REASON: Fools like to throw stones.

JOY: I have catapults beyond number.

REASON: I'm only surprised that you do not yet have bombards with which you could throw balls of heavy iron with a thunderous sound which is generated by the fire. As if the wrath of God thundered from the sky were not enough, lo, vile mortal man, mingling cruelty with pride, wants to thunder over the earth and as Virgil says, "Human fury has chosen to continue to throw lightning on the earth," which is not suitable for mankind. What can we say when we see that which God used to send down from the Heavens discharged by man on earth with infernal instruments made of wood? This instrument some people think was invented by Archimedes at the time Marcellus was besieging Syracuse in Sicily but he invented this weapon to defend the liberty of his fellow citizens and to avoid the destruction of his fatherland, while you use it to conquer each other or to destroy free peoples. This damnable bombarding only a short time ago was little in use; now it has come into general use like every other machine or engine of war. This comes about because the spirits of men are so ready to learn how to do the worst.

JOY: I have catapults a-plenty.

REASON: It would be better to have hatred of warfare and solicitude of peace. The desire to use other kinds of weapons is an indication of a man who cannot stay quiet and at peace; the use of catapults not only points to this weakness but besides it is a sign of cowardice. It is displeasing to men of peace and it is hateful to magnanimous soldiers. In conclusion hear what I have to tell you. The man who first invented catapults was either cowardly or treacherous or desirous of doing evil but he was afraid to come face to face with his enemy. His thought was, as Lucan puts it "to stretch out the thongs of the cords from afar and give to the winds power to wound carrying the arrow where they would," and I would have you understand that this may be understood of everything which is meant to attack the enemy from a distance. The brave warrior wants to meet his enemy face to face but he who throws an arrow is fleeing from him.

Some historical interest attaches to this dialogue; it is the first reference in literature to gunpowder, which was gradually coming into use in the fourteenth century. But more arresting is the support it gives to Whitfield's argument. For Petrarch's implication suggests that a good life is possible and even admirable on earth; the building and preserving of cities is accounted a virtue and not an irrelevance to mankind's central concern for salvation. The subject of good princes calls to mind the close of the ode to Italy where after reminding the Lords of Italy, that time is passing and death and judgment await them, Petrarch goes on to urge them not to prayer and meditation but to some "work of hand or wit" more becoming than inflicting pain on others.

If one cannot call the dialogues vivacious, they are at least well planned and are characterized by a certain harmony of design and proportion which may explain their popularity in the following centuries. To read the book from end to end is more than we should have a right to expect of a twentieth-century man; monotony sets in and fairly soon. Yet the *Remedies* do contain in their approach a kind of astringent realism which is not out of keeping with our times; a judicious selection might make a very readable book.[28] Taken collectively, these dialogues make up one of the most ambitious of the author's works and one of the few that he carried to a conclusion. If Reason seems a little too erudite for our modern taste, it cannot be denied that she often speaks the language of common sense and in a crisp phraseology which must have been refreshing to Petrarch's contemporaries. It is not surprising that the book was so popular in its day and indeed for a century afterward; what is surprising perhaps is its fall from grace. The first Italian edition is of the mid-sixteenth century, and the book is now pretty much neglected among the Petrarch canon.

Lastly we may mention the little work called the *Itinerarium Syriacum;* it may serve as a bridge between our categories of devotional and informational. The devotional element is secondary and indeed vicarious: not for himself but for his Milanese friend Giovannolo da Mandello who was contemplating a pilgrimage to the Holy Land, Petrarch wrote this little guidebook. Wilkins dates the composition as of March, 1358.[29] Since Petrarch had never been to the Holy Land (and refused Giovannolo's invitation to accompany the party on this occasion), his information on that area is derived from his readings. But on the coast line of Italy (the route the pilgrims were to follow) he can speak as an expert, and his description of the bay of Naples in particular has a good deal of vivacity; it is interesting to note, now and then, the phraseology of a guidebook of today: "Do not omit," he says, a visit to the Royal Chapel of Naples to admire the frescoes of his fellow townsman (*conterraneus*), which is to say, Giotto.

CHAPTER 10

Personal Commentary

OUR third category, which we might for convenience label "personal commentary," bulks large; in sheer wordage larger than the other two groupings. Taken as a whole this area of his work gives us the best picture of the personality of Petrarch, neither submerged by his historical concerns nor distorted by his devotional attitudes. Which is not to say that either strain is missing in the category we are now discussing.

We shall speak first of the *Letters.* To begin with those in prose, in themselves "a literary document of primary importance in the history of European culture." [1] They were divided by the author himself into four major divisions. The first he called the *Familiares,* which Morris Bishop translates as "Letters on Familiar Affairs." [2] Of these there are twenty-four books and a total of 350 letters. For some reason Petrarch included two metrical letters in this collection. It was probably in 1349 (perhaps a little earlier) that the poet conceived the idea of making a collection of his letters: he set about the arrangement and editing quite seriously in 1351, returned to the charge in 1359 and again in 1363–64. The collection was dedicated to Socrates, who never lived to see the complete edition, for he died in 1361. Indeed the final version was prepared only in 1366. The earliest letter is of 1325; the latest of 1366. The first letter is that of dedication to Socrates written in 1350: the following letters follow, in a general way, the order of chronology. The *Seniles,* or, again to borrow a useful rubric from Bishop, "The Letters of Riper Years," [3] are cut of the same cloth but are, as the title indicates, of much later composition; they cover the years 1361 to 1374 and are dedicated to Francesco Nelli; they are 125 in number more or less, for they still await a proper critical edition. A smaller collection, called *Sine nomine* (*sine titulo*), or without specification of the addressee, are largely concerned with political matters; in dates they range from 1342 to

1348, but a very large number are of 1351–53. They are nineteen
in number, and many of them reflect Petrarch's hostility to the
papal court at Avignon. Yet a fourth collection is known as the
Varie, in a large part not published by Petrarch himself but collected by editors after his death; in the older collections these
number fifty-seven, a few others, called "miscellaneous," also await
definitive editing.[4] Finally there is the *Letter to Posterity* from
which we have frequently quoted; this was meant to be the poet's
autobiography but, in fact, carries him only to the year 1351. It
seems likely that the original draft was composed sometime before 1367: as we have it now, it indicates retouchings as late as
1371. It is not clear why Petrarch left unfinished this very interesting little work; one would have thought it would have been an
attractive labor for him. We have, in the course of our study, read
enough of it to have noted its sometimes slightly artificial tone and
a certain unself-conscious vanity; for all that, it is one of the most
human "autobiographies," for the most part convincing in its sincerity, which we have from any author before Cellini.

There is rich variety in the letters. Some are very brief; some
are almost little books. The range of subject matter is very wide:
perhaps the majority may be described as highly subjective in that
they deal with the events or circumstances of Petrarch's life. Some
are accounts of his travels and encounters. Many are concerned
with public matters: the list of correspondents or at least address-
ees contains the names of emperors, doges, and various princes.
Many, particularly those addressed to classical figures, deal with
history and social and literary criticism.

The chapter headings of the selection made by Robinson and
Rolfe for their volume *Petrarch: The First Modern Man of Letters* indicate the range of interest. The editors have grouped their
translations under the rubrics "Biographical," "Petrarch and His
Literary Contemporaries," "The Father of Humanism," "Travels,"
"Political Opinions," and "The Conflict of Monastic and Secular
Life." Morris Bishop, supplying each of his translations with a
subject title, offers even more impressive evidence of their variety,
ranging from "Walks in Rome," "Storm in Naples," and "His Dog"
to such philosophical matters as "On the Efficient Use of Time"
and "Praise of Old Age."

We have, with deliberate intent, quoted freely from the *Letters*
in the course of our study; sufficiently perhaps to give a fairly

good idea of their variety, their tone, and their scope. If, viewed strictly as works of art, they may be faulted for their discursiveness; but this defect serves to deepen our understanding of the author and to enhance our admiration for the breadth of his interests and the charm of his manner. As Foscolo put it: "His pen followed the incessant restlessness of his soul: every subject allured his thoughts and seldom were all his thoughts devoted to one alone." [5]

The *Epistolae metricae* of the same thematic stuff as those in prose consist of three books of sixty-six letters written in Latin hexameters; the books contain, respectively, fourteen, eighteen, and thirty-six letters. The earliest letter can be dated as of 1331; there is none assignable to a date later than 1355. The first two books follow chronological order in their disposition of the items; the last book does not; indeed in regard to its arrangements it suggests that the author never found time for a final editing. Petrarch began to put these letters in order sometime between 1350 and 1352; the letter dedicating the collection to Barbato da Sulmona is of 1358; he may have sent the volume to his friend two years later, but if so, Book III at least, was still in unfinished form.

The *Metrical Letters* contain some of the most attractive of Petrarch's writing. Like the letters in prose they cover a wide variety of subjects: personal and autobiographical reflections, observations on the state of the world, and discussions of literary matters. The style is almost uniformly straightforward, making allowance for the conventional rhetorical touches that would be inevitably applied by the pen of an intellectual. One might describe them, in general, as written with a tone of polished informality. Perhaps the best are those in which the poet speaks of his own tenor of life and of familiar objects in his background. Wilkins has translated some of these: the one written to the Cardinal Colonna, thanking him for the gift of a dog, is worth quoting for the picture it gives us, as much of the owner as of the dog himself (it is the fifth letter of Book III; its position may indicate that the poet had some doubts about including it, for it is probably of 1347). We quote a part of it:

> I live in freedom now,
> Since he and he alone is my protector,
> And my companion constantly. At night,
> When, wearied with the labors of the day,

I seek my couch and close my eyes in sleep,
He guards my house; and if I sleep too long
He whimpers, telling me the sun has risen,
And scratches at my door. When I go forth
He greets me joyously, and runs ahead
Toward places often visited, and turns
Around from time to time to see if I
Am following; and then, when I recline
Upon the verdant margin of the stream
And there begin again my wonted task,
He starts this way and that, tries all the paths,
And then lies down, white on the grassy ground,
Turning his back to me, his face to those
Who may pass by.
                    Continually
He gives amusement: with great bounds he goes
Through woods and waters: with his shrilly bark
He imitates the children when they sing;
His sudden twists and turns are laughable.
He is forever chasing the wild geese;
Over the shore and over the rocks he leaps:
They find no safety even in the stream;
He plunges in, catches them in his mouth,
And brings them out, offering them as a prize,
Whether or not one hungers for a feast.
Often he goes a-hunting, and brings back
His booty for my table. Yet for him
All this is play, not wrath, perhaps he likes
To catch the geese as he swims, or does not like
Their cackling. He is gentler than a lamb
With weaker creatures. Never would he attack
A sheep, a fleeing she-goat, or a kid.
If a timid hare appear in his way, he stands
As if in fear; yet he would rush upon
A breeding sow or a bullock, and would seize
And bite their ears.[6]

Or we may study III, 30, written in 1343 to Guido Gonzaga, as an interesting example of literary criticism and perhaps as an unconscious confession of literary influences; the time is also that of the composition of the *Triumph of Chastity* which shows tolerably clear traces of a recent reading—or rereading—of the work criticized here:

How far the eloquence of other tongues
Is by our Latin eloquence surpassed
(Greek I except, on Cicero's report
And that of Fame), you for yourself, my lord,
May see from the little book that I am sending—
A thing that Gaul, renowned in speech, exalts
To heav'n, and claims as equal to the best
That man has ever written. Now herein
The Gallic poet tells the common folk
The substance of his dreams: what love can do,
And zeal; what fire burns within the heart
Of untried youth; what the false hopes of age,
The craftiness of Venus' maddened lover,
And the dire peril lurking in a glance;
What grief and toil, what rest and toil commingled,
What laughter you should shun, and what laments:
How often tears must fall; how rare is joy!
Could there be richer field for eloquence?
And yet he dreams e'en as he tells his dreams,
And though he wake he is but dreaming still.
    How much more nobly, in the days of old
Your fellow citizen set forth the sorrow
Of passionate love, in his illustrious tale
Of Dido's death upon her Phrygian sword!
And thou, Verona, hadst thy bard; and thou,
Sulmona, fruitful home of amorous song,
Whose poet learned from him of Umbria.
Still others might I name, of ancient times,
Or sprung more lately from our Latin shores.
    And yet I pray you to receive my gift
With gladness, and despise it not. To one
Seeking a poem writ in the common speech
Of a foreign land nought better could be given,
Believe me—unless Gaul and Paris fail
In their esteem. So then, my lord, farewell.[7]

Or, in brief how vastly superior are Virgil, Catullus, Ovid, and Propertius to one of the masterpieces of the Middle Ages.

Finally, the letter (III, 33) written to Francesco Nelli during the poet's last sojourn at Vaucluse touches a theme that recurs in the *Canzoniere*. Perhaps we should observe that, melancholy though it be, it does not strike a note of ultimate despair or renunciation. Weary hope can be raised up; our destiny is in our hands.

Living I am but resentful of fate that, postponing my birthyear
Placed me on earth in these times, the sorriest season of mankind.
Better had it been before, or it may be in days yet to follow;
Happy the world was once, perhaps the future will be so;
Ours is an ugly age; and well you may witness how all things
Vicious and evil converge on the present. We live in a sewer
Running with every ill. All virtue, genius and glory,
Fleeing the world, have made room for blind chance and lust and low
    pleasures.
If we attempt not to lift ourselves up only ruin awaits us,
Reefs will soon shatter our bark, the current bear us away,
Cold earth will cover our bones, our graves lie neglected, forgotten:
And at one stroke the fame we have labored to win will be blotted.
Even the urn preserving our ashes will vanish, the winds
Bear off the ashes as well. The wayfarer years hence will vainly
Strive to distinguish our names on the scattered fragments of marble.
Time hurries everything on; if we intend to resist it
Hope long exhausted we must raise up from the ground; the anchor
Sunk in the shifting sands will be unable to hold us.
Read if you will, my friend, these verses I send to you now
Written in haste on my Helicon, where I sit on a verdant meadow
Under a lonely rock that hard by a murmuring brooklet
Sheltering stands between the laurels I planted for your sake.
How many times have I bid them to grow, in the hope that one day
You too would sit beside me in the shade of their sacred branches.[8]

In addition to the above-mentioned collections which are specifically called "letters" by the poet, there are a number of other
works which have the same characteristics, dealing with like matters of personal or poetic interest. I believe the eclogues that compose the *Bucolicum carmen,* for all the pretense of their title and
the poetic veil cast over them by the poet, fit very well into this
category. Since there is no indication that the poet planned to
write any more than the twelve items that have come down to us,
the *Carmen* may claim to be one of the few works that Petrarch
took in hand and really finished.

The *Bucolicum carmen* is a collective name given to a series of
pastoral allegories in Latin verse. As the French translator rather
archly informs us, we shall hardly find the *Carmen* or *Eclogues,* as
they are sometimes called, very instructive on the lives of shep-
herds. It is interesting to note the subjects they do cover. Three
deal with Laura (iii the living Laura and x and xi mourning her

death); two (vi and vii) with the wickedness of the papal court; it is in vi that Pamphilus (representing St. Peter), addressing Miton (Clement VI), speaks of the cardinals as "lascivious goats" and reproaches his interlocutor for his eyes "made heavy with drink." Eclogues i and iv are concerned with poetry: the opening poem is a debate between Petrarch and his brother on the relative merits of sacred and profane poetry; the fourth proclaims that poetry is a gift of nature and that, incidentally, Italians have been more favored by the Muses than have the French. Three are dedicated to political figures; ii is a eulogy of Robert of Naples, whose death was the occasion of so many woes to his realm; v is a panegyric to Cola, composed when the poet's hopes were still high. Eclogue ix deals with the ravages of the Black Death, sent, Petrarch suggests, to punish mankind for its sins; and the last of the eclogues is a lament for John of France captured by the English (1356). We have had occasion to refer to number viii, written when the poet left the service of the Colonna, and perhaps the passage we have translated there may give some idea of the style of the verses. They are in fact not without charm, although the allegorical veil is likely to be somewhat thick, and we can only be grateful to the poet for the clues elsewhere supplied which reveal the identity of his sylvan characters. Still, where it counts the message comes through and, as noted above with regard to the anticlerical (or perhaps more correctly anti-Avignon) chapters, real passion can be read in the rather stilted lines. But what is especially noteworthy I think is that they cover the same range of themes: amorous, personal, political, occasional, as we find in the *Letters*, whether metrical or in prose. At the same time, some of the subject matter and the lyric tone of the verses take us occasionally into the area of the *Rhymes*. There are many phrases in the "Laura eclogues" that recall the sonnets to us. The following might be a preliminary sketch (more likely it is an echo) of *"Chiare, fresche, e dolci acque"*:

Daphne, when first I beheld you alone upon the deserted
Shore of the stream, I knew not if you were woman or goddess,
Fragrance hovered around your mantle of purple and gold,
Filling the air about you, wafting a peregrine perfume.
Smiling, your face shed a glow like to the splendor of starlight,
Zephyr the while sent rippling your dazzling hair over your shoulders.

Astonished I stood while the sun fought an unequal fight with your
    glances,
All of your person glowing with a radiance unknown to mortals.
Fearful I was lest the gods might chance to look down and mark you;
Surely then, fired by passion, they would bear you away to Olympus,
Never to know of my wound and the flame you had kindled within me.[9]

    The idea of the *Eclogues* is of 1346; most of them were com-
posed between that year and 1348. In 1357 in Milan (and with
Boccaccio at hand to reread the verses to him so that his ear might
catch any imperfections) the poet prepared his definitive version.
The inspiration of the work is, as the name indicates, in the
Eclogues of Virgil, but the allegory is much heavier than that of
the Latin poet. It may be well be, as Tatham conjectures, that the
Eclogues of Dante and Giovanni del Virgilio were also known to
Petrarch and were not without their influence upon his manner.
These rather unusual ventures of Petrarch delighted Boccaccio
who states "that his famous teacher gave uncommon fluency to
this form of writing." But this unfortunately has not been the view
of posterity. Tatham, while speaking approvingly of certain passages and particularly of the three eclogues whose subject is
Laura, yet remarks "that the framework of his symbolical machinery is often clumsy; you feel that the poet is much more concerned
with the allegory than with the appropriateness of its pastoral setting," [10] and even our contemporary taste for the recondite and
oracular has not restored the *Carmen* to any high place in critical
approval. In fact, the allegory is not of a very high level; it has
nothing of the metaphysical about it. One might more accurately
call the *Carmen* a kind of *roman à clef*, for once one knows the
identity of the pseudo-shepherds the burden of their song becomes quite clear.
    The lines we have quoted from one of the "Laura" eclogues
and, earlier in our text, from those written to the Cardinal Colonna and to Cola will give a tolerably good notion of the quality
of the little work. I do not think it is to be despised. It had, to be
sure, very little influence unless we are prepared to accept
Tatham's rather tentative theory—that it may have in a certain
sense taken the place of the drama which was otherwise missing
in the fourteenth century and so prepared the way in a fashion for
the composition of later pastoral comedies, but it is interesting as

a kind of meeting place of elements of the *Canzoniere* and the *Trionfi* (the parade of poets in the tenth eclogue is a kind of "Triumph") and the mixture of personal, social, and political commentary that characterized the *Letters*. It must be added too, I think, that whether their inspiration be Virgilian or Dantean the poet has put his own stamp on his verses. If they are not as classical as he would have liked to think, and if they are not in fact very important, yet they deal with matters very close to his heart and say what they have to say with commendable economy.

If our category of commentary and instruction can include the lyric *Carmen* it can, at the other extreme, also take in the works of satiric or polemical intent: these too, I believe, had the author not given them different designations, we might fairly classify as letters. I have in mind the invectives in which I would include the curious little work called *De sui ipsius et multorum ignorantia*. Of the three that the author himself called "Invectives," the most amusing is perhaps the one written against "a certain doctor." Petrarch had advised Clement VI during an illness of that pontiff in the winter of 1351/52 to be on his guard against the flock of doctors in attendance. Not unnaturally one of the doctors took offense and wrote to the poet, objecting to his censures. The poet answered, the doctor replied again, and Petrarch closed the debate with a second letter and released his two letters in the form of a treatise, divided into four books, after some re-editing in 1355. Aside from the spirited tone of the diatribe, its chief interest perhaps lies in Petrarch's exaltation of poetry as against science and vocational disciplines. As far as medicine is concerned, one must concede that Petrarch practiced what he preached; he had little use for doctors and their prescriptions and, medicine being what it was in those days, one finds it hard to fault him.

The second invective, written it would seem also in 1355, is a response to a personal attack made by the cardinal Jean de Caraman who, among other things, criticized the poet's residence in Milan as a guest of the Visconti. The third is of somewhat the same nature, though a little less personal: it is a reply to the Cistercian Jean de Hesdin who argued for the residence of the popes at Avignon; in the course of his brief he had spoken ill of Italy. Petrarch seems to have got hold of this document rather late, for it sprang out of the discussion centering around Urban's premature return to Rome in 1368, while Petrarch's answer is of five years later. It is notable more for the vigor of the expression than the originality or even cogency of its argument. He does present an interesting ethnic theory: in the course of disparaging his antagonist's argument that many Italian cities have been founded by foreigners, implying that such cities could not truly be claimed as Italian, Petrarch answers:

Such changes of residence do not transform the land to which men migrate but rather the men who have migrated. So the Gauls who went to Asia became Asiatics, the Italians who departed for Phrygia became Phrygians and when they returned to Italy after the downfall of Troy they became once more Italians. So too our Romans moving to Gaul or Germany, absorbed the characteristics and the barbarian customs of those lands. The Milanese who sprang from the Gauls and who once were Gauls are now the most peaceful people in the world and preserve no trace of their ancient origin.[11]

The reference to the Milanese is a polemical thrust, but the theory is worthy of note: I do not know if Petrarch has a source for it; he does not quote one nor does his editor; if it is his own it does him credit.

As for the vigorous sally *On His Own Ignorance and That of Many*, we have spoken elsewhere of the circumstances that inspired its composition: the lèse majesté committed by a group of young Venetian Aristotelians, who had described Petrarch as well-meaning but ignorant, the wounded poet's reaction of indignation and his reply, written on a boat journey in 1367. The work, addressed to Donato Albanzani, a Venetian friend, makes lively reading.[12] It is a very significant little work for those who are interested in our poet's philosophical stance. He comes out strongly against formal logic, the worship of the syllogism, and the complete submission to Aristotle. This is an attitude that can be styled variously Augustinian, Franciscan, or perhaps simply anti-philosophical; the poet stresses the dehumanizing effect of rigid logic and its peril to the good Christian life. He does not deny the value of dialectic for training the mind, but insists that it is not an end in itself. The work is a revelation of the temperament of the poet, a defender of the life of the mind but opposed to the aridity of subtle intellectualism. The passage dealing with his devotion to Cicero is interesting as an indication of his inner resolution of the "humanistic" and Christian currents within him:

. . . I admit that I admire Cicero above all others who have written in any time or among any people. However to admire him does not mean to imitate him; I strive rather to do the opposite in order not to be an excessive imitator of anyone, lest what I disapprove of in others might happen to me. But if to admire Cicero means to be a Ciceronian, then I am one. I admire him so much indeed that I look with wonder on those who do not admire him. If this may seem to be another proof of my ignorance; yet such is my taste and I confess it. But when we come to consider religion, which is to say supreme truth and true happiness, and our eternal salvation, then certainly I am not a Ciceronian nor a Platonist but a Christian. The more so as I am sure that Cicero himself would have been a Christian if he had been able to see Christ and know the doctrine of Christ. With regard to Plato there can be no doubt, on the word of Augustine himself, that if he returned to life today or if in his life he had been able to foresee the future, he would then have been and would have become today a Christian. Augustine cites the example of several Platonists of his time who did precisely that and it may be believed that he himself was of their number. With that understood, in what way can Ciceronian eloquence be considered an obstacle to Christian dogma? What harm can there be in putting one's self in contact with the books of Cicero when it is not harmful to read the books of heretics—nay, may even be useful according to the apostle: "there must also be heresies among you, that they which are approved may be made manifest among you." (I Cor. 11:19) On the other hand in this matter I would have much greater faith in any devout Catholic, even if illiterate, than in Plato himself or Cicero.[13]

CHAPTER 11

The Triumphs

IT is an irony too often commented on to bear repetition here that the great Latinist of the fourteenth century is remembered chiefly for his works in the vernacular. Perhaps there is another irony in the consideration, which has a good deal of validity although susceptible of some reservations, that these same vernacular works which have ensured the poet's survival are less forward-looking in attitude than at least some of the works of Latin prose. In the *Letters,* for example, one can today feel a kinship with the writer that overleaps the intervening centuries, while the *Trionfi* are thoroughly medieval in concept and the *Rhymes* too are, at least formally, exercises in a traditional school of writing. To a certain extent, it is the vernacular which sets these works apart and has ensured their immortality; in the case of the *Rhymes,* as we shall see, there are other elements. And in both of them it is the poet who speaks and not merely the scholar or the commentator, and a poet too who, in contrast to his concern in the *Africa* and the *Bucolicum carmen,* looks first into his own heart, rather than to classical models, for his inspiration. There is, at least for the reader of today, a great gulf between the two works yet both stand apart from the Latin works and on a higher esthetic plane. We shall speak first and briefly of the *Trionfi.*

The framework of this ambitious work is modeled on that of the ecclesiastical processions, suggestive of the great symbolic parade at the end of *Purgatorio* (which Petrarch may well have had in mind). But the framework is very loose, and it is ignored whenever it suits the author's convenience. The first and longest of the *Triumphs* is that of Love, consisting of four cantos and running *in toto* to seven hundred lines. The first three *capitoli* were written in 1338 or shortly after; the fourth in 1342. The poet speaks of a vision which came to him just before the spring equinox as he wandered in Vaucluse: he beheld the great dominating figure of

146

Cupid, white but with long, multicolored wings, and leading a
long line of captives. A figure appears beside the poet, unidenti-
fied. (Some have daringly suggested Dante; Calcaterra gives convincing support for Giovanni Aghinolfi di Arezzo, Chancellor of
the Gonzaga family of Mantua and lifelong friend of the poet.)[1]
He explains that these are all prisoners of love and warns that Petrarch himself will soon be among their number. He then enumerates the classical personages who have been subjected to love;
all in summary fashion until he reaches the African lovers and
hears Massinissa's own story of his sacrifice of his wife under the
influence of Scipio's virtuous counsel. And at this point Laura appears to claim the poet as her own. The enumeration continues
through the Provençal troubadours and the poets of more recent
tradition, including Dante, who marches beside his Beatrice. At
the end of the *Trionfo* the unhappy prisoners are led off to the
island of Cytherea, described in sensual terms but with a note of
moral censure that is a kind of foretaste of Tasso and Spenser.

One does not have to read more than the first *capitolo* of this
division to be aware of the strong and persistent influence of
Dante. The *terza rima,* the syntax, even phrases that recall those
of the *Comedy* without quite being identical: these give us plenty
of formal evidence. The figure of the wandering poet-observer in-
structed by a guide, and the roll call of prominent names are also
of the stuff of the *Comedy.* The lack of proportion, a certain heav-
iness in the presentation of the material, and the intrusion of the
poet's own sentimental biography into the "plot"—these are
Petrarch's contributions.

The *Triumph of Chastity* (consisting of only one canto of 193
lines, written probably in 1344) resumes the narrative. Once arrived at Cyprus (Venus' island), Laura challenges the God of
Love and, flanked by the virtues Honor, Modesty, Prudence, and
their sisters, defeats him in combat.

A swarm of virtuous women from legend and history joins
Laura in her triumph. Chastity would seem to cover both virginity
and marital fidelity in the poet's concept; among the entourage of
Laura we find Judith, Penelope, Lucretia, Virginia, and (another
Dantean echo) Piccarda Donati. These heroic ladies with their
captive, Love, then make their way back from the languorous is-
land to Italy. At Linterno, near Naples, they are joined by
Scipio, who accompanies them to Rome where they leave their

trophies in the temple of chastity (the patrician one, Petrarch is careful to tell us) under the guard of several males also selected for their fortitude against the assaults of the tender passion; the poet is able to recognize among others Joseph and Hippolytus. In the battle between Laura and the Virtues on the one hand and Love on the other, the influence of the *Roman de la Rose* is noticeable;[2] allegory of the rather heavy, old-fashioned sort is perhaps more evident in this chapter than elsewhere, and its ponderous machinery seems at times a little inappropriate in its bearing on the human or autobiographical element; the picture of Laura and Love, heavily armored and clashing like "two lions roaring in their rage" seems, to a modern reader at least, more comic than impressive. And one might say the same for the inclusion of Scipio as a kind of venerable abbot in the procession of love-despising women. But Petrarch is concerned, and not only here, with bringing his two ideals together on the same plane of austere supremacy.

Chastity's triumph is short-lived. Even as the poet stands watching the triumphant train, a dark female figure appears and proclaims her dominion over all of them. She foretells the death of Laura, who professes her serene indifference. The procession suddenly vanishes, and the poet's eye sees nothing but ranks of the dead. There follows a lament for the death of Laura and a description of the ladies mourning over her dead body. The second canto of this division (*The Triumph of Death* contains two *capitoli*, totaling 362 lines and written in 1348–49) tells how, the day after Laura's death (we have stepped out of the poem and into the poet's memories), the shade of Laura visited him; on his questioning, she assures him that she had truly loved him in life but had, for his good and hers, never given him any indication of her love. She adds that she is grateful for the fame his songs have brought her and, predicting that he will survive her by many years, she departs. The second canto of this *Triumph* has its sentimental and psychological interest, and, presenting as it does, a not unpleasingly pathetic rationalization of Laura's coldness, touches us with a certain humanity. The theme, however, is treated much more successfully in the second half of the *Canzoniere*.

Death, though triumphant over Chastity, is itself defeated by Fame, the subject of the fourth *Triumph* (three *capitoli*, 413 lines; written in 1352). Here the poet's vision becomes purely that of

the encyclopedist, and the three cantos that make up this chapter
are nothing but lengthy catalogues of the great names of the past:
Latin and Greek heroes, Old Testament characters, philosophers,
and some chosen women. Some names we have seen in earlier
Triumphs recur here; Cleopatra, for instance, is eligible equally as
a captive of love and an example of fame. There is some interest
for the historian or the biographer of the poet in observing the
arrangement of the categories and the kind of names that appear
in this rhymed "Who's Who"; it is interesting to note that, like
Dante, Petrarch thinks Saladin worthy of inclusion: he mentions
also a few names out of medieval history, including Charlemagne
and Godfrey de Bouillon, but finds, in general, not many worthy of
mention after the fall of the Empire. He does enliven his catalogue by the selection of a few contemporaries; they include, as
well as his friends Robert of Naples and Stefano Colonna, the
Steward of England, Henry, first Duke of Lancaster. This valiant
soldier of Edward III visited Avignon in 1354; his name if not his
presence presumably impressed Petrarch. But such an inclusion
makes us wonder the more about the omissions. Not only are
greater soldiers than Henry missing but whole catalogues of medieval worthies are excluded. There are no great kings: one might
have expected St. Louis at least, or, given our poet's devotion
to the house of Sicily, Charles of Anjou; and if philosophers, why
not Christian saints? Perhaps this last category would have seemed
inappropriate; it is worth remarking, however (as Whitfield has),[3]
that Petrarch seems to have had no cult of saints—save of course
for his beloved Augustine.

That the question of inclusion and omission should pique our
curiosity is an indication of the nature of this *Triumph*, which is
not so much a poem as a compendium. It is certainly the least
appealing of all the *Trionfi;* the enumeration seems endless, and
the efforts of the poet to find phrases of individual definition or
distinction are painful to observe. There is one flash of true feeling, it seems to me. Petrarch, in the course of praising Godfrey
and deploring the failure of the Christians to hold Jerusalem,
speaks out with passion:

> O miserable Christians, go your way,
>   Consuming one another, caring not
>   That over Christ's own tomb dogs now hold sway.

But even as Death had triumphed over Chastity, Time must triumph over Fame; such is the subject and thesis of the fifth division of the *Trionfi*, shorter (145 lines) than any preceding division and composed in such a way as to suggest rapidity of movement and incessant change. It is not without a certain poetic appeal.

The encyclopedic interest of Fame yields here to the elegiac note, and the *Triumph* is, in effect, a long meditation on the erosive power of time. Time is like death but of course much more powerful, as even those who survive their earthly lives to live on in renown must eventually be obliterated by time—a kind of second death. The theme is a traditional medieval one (we have but to think of Oderisi's words to Dante in *Purgatory* xi on the vanity of all human accomplishment), but the phrasing seems at times to look forward as far as Leopardi:

> How many, once renowned, are so no more,
>> Beside the streams of Thrace or Thessaly
>> Or by the Xanthus or by Tiber's shore!
>
> . . . .
>
> Your glories fade, your captains and your kings
>> And all your pomp, while Time at its own will
>> Disposes of all fragile mortal things.
>
> . . . .
>
> Happy is he who dies in his first age
>> And wretched they who linger long in years;
>> "Blessed are those unborn," well says the sage.

The imagery is successful too: the *Triumph* begins with the appearance of the sun, whirling in haste through the heavens and demanding his rights over those singled out by Fame, who in fact are one by one summoned away from her. The greater polish and unity of this *capitolo*, as well as its tone, are evidence of the maturity of the poet, and the philosophical and acceptant melancholy are appropriate to the years of composition, for it is the work of the last years of the poet's life, no earlier it would seem than 1371.

The *Triumph of Eternity* consists of but one *capitolo* and that a short one (145 lines). It is a natural sequel and almost the true second part of the preceding *Triumph;* even as time washes away all earthly glories so, in turn, eternity will make time's triumphs seem vain. We are here in the area of the mystic vision; there are, in fact, elements in the last *Trionfo* that call to mind the final cantos of the *Paradiso*. For example, even as Dante draws a distinction between the empyrean and the physical universe, so Petrarch affirms that all the preceding triumphs may be seen on earth, but for the last we must wait for Heaven. And there are other points of similarity.

Petrarch too has a vision of the elect, but the only one mentioned is Laura, who in her transfiguration will surpass all others. Here the poet forgets the sensual side of Laura's attraction, no longer admitting, as he had in the *Secretum,* that love of her has distracted him from proper Christian concerns; he sees her precisely as Dante saw Beatrice; as an inspiration, a consolation, and a guide, ultimately indeed as a saint. In this last *Triumph* the encyclopedist and the scholar yield to the devout Christian—and the poet. For the intensity of the feeling is matched by felicity of expression, and this final work is to be counted among the highest accomplishments of the artist. It is neither as intellectual nor as dynamic as Dante's ultimate vision, but it is not unworthy of standing beside it, both for the purity of its emotion and the serenity of its exposition. The *Triumph* has been dated as of the poet's last year, even of his last months of life: if all passion is spent, art yet burns more brightly than ever. The last lines of the poem will give some notion of its beauty.

> And those who had achieved a high renown
>   Which time had dimmed, and all those faces bright
>   That years and bitter death had trampled down
> Will wax more fair in the eternal light:
>   Then shall cruel death and time both undergo
>   Defeat and sink into forgetful night.
> While they, renewed in fame and glory, show
>   In fair fresh faces all their youth restored,
>   And first and foremost of their train shall go
> She whose departure hence is still deplored,
>   As my sighs witness and my aging pen;
>   But flesh and soul were called to serve her Lord.
> My heart still stirs when I remember when
>   Love for her sake beset me hard and how
>   I warred with him in that spring-bathèd glen.
> Happy the stone that covers her fair brow

> And one whom sight of her on earth entranced
> Will call himself more blessed than ever now,
> Seeing her loveliness in Heaven enhanced.
>
> (lines 127–45)

If, as we have, we take the *Trionfi* one by one and weigh each on its own merits, we are doing justice to the method of their composition and also, I think, to the genius of their writer. We have followed Wilkins in the assignment of dates: other authorities differ; some would place the writing of the earlier chapters much later than Wilkins. But in any event, there were sizeable intervals between them, and they were written under varying circumstances and in varying states of mind. If we are to pass a judgment on the *Trionfi* as one work, we should hesitate to regard it as successful. Bishop speaks for the twentieth century (and probably for most readers since the Renaissance) when he writes, a little cruelly perhaps:

Today the *Triumphs* have sadly faded. The endless parade of classical figures bores us. How can we recognize Laodamia and Protesilaus and Argia and Polynices? Their gold and silver is tarnished; their ox-drawn floats pass all too slow. All that remains for the average modern reader are a few fine passages, and suddenly sonorous lines, and the long interlude . . . wherein Laura dies and returns to join the poet in a final duet on love confessed but misunderstood, on earthly happiness lost but heavenly beatitude gained.[4]

The basic flaw derives from a constitutional incapacity of Petrarch to handle the grand design. Not only a *Divine Comedy* but even a *Decameron* would have been beyond his technical scope. Even on such a simple level as the narrative plane, his work lacks consistency; the central figure is partly narrator, partly actor, partly a man with a vision, partly a commentator. There seems to be no good reason for the scene to shift from Vaucluse (after all it is only a vision) to the island of Cyprus and back to Rome; and in fact the realism of the narrative suffers by such odd translocations. It has been pointed out that the beatiful last *capitolo* of the *Triumph of Death* is a vision within a vision; Dante too had visions within a vision, but he had the equipment to persuade us that the enclosing vision was of a different nature. Dante, to put it sharply, convinced us of the existence of his main character as a

character, of the truth of his *"bella menzogna,"* whereas we
never lose sight of Petrarch, quite simply *qua* Petrarch, outside
the story, whether in the role of scholar or of melancholy lover.
His gift was for the purely lyric, for the expression of a moment of
intense feeling or illumination: indeed all of his longer works are
made up of fragments or episodes, very loosely united: thus he
could put them down and take them up as his leisure and mood
might dictate: this is true of such Latin works as the *De remediis*
and the *De vita solitaria* and is inherent in the *Epistolae* (which
the author regards as works of art); it is certainly true of the *Canzoniere*. Only the *Secretum* and the *Africa* are exceptions, and the
former is not very long and the latter hardly very successful.

Yet, as Wilkins reminds us[5] and as the number of early editions
attests, the *Trionfi* were very popular, widely read, and highly
esteemed for well over a hundred years after their composition;
they were in this early manhood of the poet's fame much more
admired than the *Rhymes.* And, one suspects, for the very reason
that they were later displaced: for the vast element of encyclopedic erudition. The interminable catalogues of names which we
hurry over nowadays with distaste were an asset in days when the
average reader did not have within easy reach his *Britannica* or
his *Americana* or his *Bullfinch.* Great writers, if they were serious,
were expected to provide a good deal of sheerly factual material;
they were the purveyors, the retail men whose proper task it was
to ransack the great storehouses of historical and legendary information and put the merchandise at the disposal of the hungry
customers. All the great works of the Middle Ages have this ingre-
dient if they aspire to anything more than the purely narrative
and in Italy, with the tradition of Brunetto Latini and Dante Ali-
ghieri, it was to be expected that Petrarch would follow the same
line. The trouble was he had more classical names at his tongue's
end than most writers and lacked the discretion (God's gift to
Dante) to keep the informational drive under control. Collectively, the *Trionfi* remain a monument to a kind of literary taste
which characterized the reading public for a long time: and as for
that of today, we may admire the fragments: the vision of the
transfigured Laura and the not-quite-mystic, wistful and tender
mood of the crowning pair, the *Triumphs* of Time and Eternity.

CHAPTER 12

The Rhymes

PETRARCH'S major work is known by various names. He himself refers to it as the *Rerum vulgarium fragmenta,* and in the opening sonnet he speaks in the vernacular of his *"rime sparse";* in Italian the collection is commonly called the *Canzoniere* or *Rime.* English authorities usually use either the Italian *Canzoniere* or call the work simply the *Rhymes.* Perhaps this variation of nomenclature would have pleased the author; he speaks with satisfaction of their "varied" style and our uncertainty as to their title would reinforce his own professed casualness about them. Whatever we may call them, they are the result of a lifetime of work. The "final edition" approved by Petrarch himself consists of 366 items (266 for the living Laura and 100 after her death, although some editors begin Part II with cclxiv, *"I' vo pensando").* The time of their composition as individual pieces covers the poet's youth, maturity and age; the final revision is the work of the last year of his life. If it is true that the deprecatory attitude the poet affected toward his *Rhymes* is belied by the record of assiduous revision, it is also true that a collection seems not to have developed from an original design which the poet had in mind from the beginning, but simply grew; having grown, it was given form and pattern by the author; the plan was rearranged as revisions and further inclusions suggested themselves. Wilkins, who is the leading historian of the composition of the *Canzoniere,* puts it with his usual cogency. The work, he says "is not a collection made toward the end of Petrarch's life in a single editorial effort, nor is it a mere gradual accumulation of poems: it is a selective and ordered collection, the fashioning of which, begun in his youth, continued to the day of his death." [1] It is fair to add that although the collection as we have it may have satisfied the poet's notions regarding its arrangement and its unity (although Ruth Shepherd Phelps suggests that some groupings are tentative and even casual),[2] we should probably have had another arrangement if the poet had lived for another five years. The writing of the *Canzoniere* was a continuous process with Petrarch.

The original nucleus of the *Rhymes* is to be found in what Wilkins called a "reference collection" brought together in the years 1336–37; this contains seventeen poems which ultimately found their place in the final draft.[3] A few years later (1342) Petrarch began a systematic arrangement of his vernacular poems of which Wilkins speculates there were now 100;[4] this may be called the first form of the *Canzoniere* and it may have had as an introductory sonnet the one numbered xxxiv, beginning "O Phoebus, if that fond desire remains . . ."; it has undeniably the air of an invocation. (It does not follow of course that it was the first written by the poet; that is a matter much more difficult to determine.) This is what we may call the first formal arrangement. In the years 1347 to 1350 and again in the years between 1356 and about 1360 Petrarch returned to his *Rhymes* and prepared the first "edition" (i.e., a draft meant for circulation), a copy of which he sent to his friend and patron, Azzo da Correggio; this, taking its name from the manuscript which contains it, is called the Chigi version. Further revisions were made between 1366 and January of 1373, at which time the poet prepared a new version which he was working on until the day before his death; this is the authoritative text of the *Rhymes* as we have them and is to be found in the Vatican manuscript 3195.[5] We have given here the more important dates in the outline of the development of the *Canzoniere;* even these are sufficient to show that the preparation of the work was a matter of lifelong attention on the part of the writer.

The genesis of the work from one point of view is quite simply in the poet's own experience, by which we mean not only his encounter with Laura but the education which had prepared him to channel his thoughts and emotions springing from that encounter in a particular way. Petrarch followed a conventional path; we may say that the *Rhymes,* formally and in a broad sense thematically, are directly in the steps of his Tuscan predecessors, particularly Dante. This is a book—another book—consisting of a series of short poems all of which are distinguished by rhyme and fixed metrical pattern, telling of a desperate love for an unattainable woman. Such a tradition leads back through Dante and Guido Guinizelli to the Provençal troubadours. The ode "Alas, I know not whither hope may turn" (lxx) is an overt acknowledgment of influences. We may remark in this connection that, if Petrarch does not seem to have the high opinion of the *Comedy* we wish he had, he has great respect for Dante as a lyric poet. In the letter (*Fam.* XXI, 15) of which he speaks in a rather off-hand way about Dante's masterpiece, Petrarch writes to Boccaccio that in his youth he was working in the very same vein as his great predecessor's. We may recall too that Dante and Beatrice have their place in the procession of lovers in the *Triumph of Love*. It would not be hard to find in the *Rhymes* sonnets of which the cadence and tone are very suggestive of some of the lyrics of Dante and his circle. It would be if anything even easier to find traces of the Provençal poets. Just how widely read Petrarch was in the literature of the troubadours is hard to determine. It is true that the great period of Provençal production was over by the time he was born, although there was a rather significant revival during the years of his sojourn in Montpellier, but the works of the poets must have circulated in many manuscripts and these manuscripts must have been readily available to Petrarch during his formative years, particularly but not exclusively those spent in Montpellier. The roll call of the great names in the Provençal canon which we find in the *Triumph of Love* is lengthy; this is sufficient evidence to show at least that the poet knew a lot about the tradition even if he had not read the works of the writers he enumerates. Since, however, in the manuscripts the biographies of the poets are always accompanied by a selection of their works, it is very reasonable to assume that he was familiar with many of their poems. Definite echoes can be found in the *Canzonieri* of Arnaut Daniel and Folquet de Marselha; in the sector of the formal we may note that the *sestina,* of which the *Canzoniere* contains nine examples, is a Provençal pattern and that two of the odes of our poet are cast in the Provençal mold; that is to say with rhymes not within the stanzas but repeated in a fixed pattern from one stanza to the other. A recent critic[6] goes so far as to define items that suggest if they do not precisely imitate all of the various forms used by the Provençal poets: the *canso,* the *sirventes,* the *planh,* the *tenso,* and for that matter the *crusade* song and even the *enueg.* All of these influences which are very much alive in the *Rhymes* would justify our calling it a work in a recognized medieval tradition.

There are, however, notable differences between the *Canzo-*

niere and the various anthologies that had preceded it in the
chronicle of the love lyric, quite aside from the major differences
of purpose, direction, and attitude of which we shall say more
later. Other more superficial but perhaps no less important aspects
spring immediately to our attention if we compare any group of
Petrarch's poems with those of his predecessors. The *Canzoniere*
is, for one thing, saturated in classicism. The Middle Ages is of
course in great debt to Ovid whose works, possibly misunderstood
and certainly reinterpreted, contributed greatly to the formation
of the rules of love. Ovid specifically, as Calcaterra has eloquently
shown,[7] serves a different purpose for Petrarch. The myths of the
Metamorphoses are employed by Petrarch without either the dis-
tortion wrought on them by the moralistic commentators or the
utilitarian eroticism for which they had served some of the poets
who had gone before him. It is quite possible, particularly if we
may assume that the above-cited sonnet xxxiv was meant to be the
opening sonnet of the collection, that the cult of Laura, who is
after all the center of the *Rhymes,* had its inception in the evocative and suggestive legend of Daphne. This sonnet and many
others of like stamp, as well as the celebrated ode of the transfor-
mations (xxiii), bespeak an ease and familiarity with the classics
—and one may say the intent of the classics—which adds a new
element to the traditional love lyric. In addition to Ovid, Virgil,
Horace, Catullus and possibly Propertius are remembered in the
Rhymes—although scholars differ in their estimates of specific
and recognizable allusions. Perhaps we may remark in this connection that the scholar Petrarch of the Latin works intervenes in
the vernacular poems more often and more visibly than the lover
of the *Rhymes* is permitted to thrust into the Latin works. The
Canzoniere, particularly the first part, is not only embellished
with classical adornment but infused, one might say, almost with
a pagan coloration. Another novelty of the *Rhymes* is their self-
conscious (if occasionally puzzling) arrangement. The poems of
Dante's *Vita Nuova* are very strictly arranged chronologically, but
this is rather exceptional; most of the collections that had preceded the *Rhymes,* whether they be the work of Provençal poets
or Petrarch's Italian predecessors, come to us simply as collections
arranged as often as not by the hazards of manuscript tradition
rather than by the careful editing of the author. This leads us to a
further consideration of Petrarch's criteria of arrangement. It has

been said that he had in mind three guiding principles; first, the poems were to follow a chronological order but second, this could be broken by appropriate thematic sequences and third, both of these considerations could and did yield to the writer's intuitive sense of the need for variety. We may not quarrel with the justness of such criteria, although we cannot always perceive their successful application. The chronological notion is at once upset when we look at the first poem, which was written, it would seem most likely, in 1349[8] and therefore can be in no way considered the chronological beginning of the *Rhymes*. There are many other items out of order, in obedience to the second principle. There are some striking examples of the operation of the second rule, most noticeably perhaps the sonnets of invective against the papal court (cxxxvi–cxxxviii), the little trio describing in very classical terms the effects of Laura's departure and return (xli–xliii), the three odes on Laura's eyes (lxxi–lxxiii). Yet it is equally true, as we shall see better later on when we examine the substance of the *Rhymes,* that certain thematic elements are taken up, put down, and returned to; for example, all the sonnets of despair are not in one group, nor are all the sonnets of playful courtship, nor for that matter are all the sonnets having nothing to do with Laura at all (of which there are a substantial number). This would seem to be in line with the third principle, but this too is subject to exception.

Perhaps here we may go somewhat more into detail on the matter of the variety and disposition of the poems. A census of the types of verses employed by our poet reveals that there are in the *Rhyme*s 317 sonnets and 29 *canzoni;* the remaining score is made up by nine *sestine,* seven *ballate* and four *madrigali.* All the *madrigali,* six of the seven *ballate,* and eight of the nine *sestine* appear in Part I, written in the lifetime of Laura; this is an element in the somewhat lighter and more experimental character of the first part of the work. We should add that the *sestina* allowed to intrude into Part II is no ordinary *sestina;* it is in fact a double *sestina* and so has if not weight at least the bulk to justify its inclusion in the more serious part of the *Canzoniere.* Actually it is a very fine poem. In any event what the foregoing brief census establishes is that when Petrarch speaks of his *vario stile* he is not deceiving his public. Even within the sonnet category there is considerable variety. There are ten different kinds of rhyme patterns employed by the poet, though there is a marked difference in frequency of occurrence. The quite straightforward pattern that we find in the opening sonnet (*abba abba cde cde*) is found 113 times, the next favorite scheme is *abba abba cdc dcd;* of this type there are 103 examples. Alternating rhymes in the octet are very rare; I count only ten: most of the variations are in the arrangement of the last six lines. Between parts I and II, I think it worth noting that although there is ample variety in both, the sonnets after Laura's death do seem to be a little less capricious and experimental in arrangement. Two of my ten lesser types are absent from Part II, and the proportion of the two favorite types is much higher; 72 per cent are of that traditional duo as against only 52 per cent in Part I. The only sonnet made up of equivocal rhymes is in Part I as is also the only sonnet based on a kind of coy acrostic wherein the poet puns on the three syllables of Laura's name. Added to what we have said above of the disposition of the other forms, I think this gives statistical support to Croce's assertion that the second part is less full of artifice and virtuosity than the first.[9] The intention to preserve a collection apparently assembled more or less by chance is clear in both parts; one could call the arrangement willfully casual—but after Laura's death the element of playfulness or exhibitionism, if you want to call it such, is I would say, absent.

All of which is mere statistical detail, probably not vitally significant. The point to be stressed, I think, is that the poet does indeed offer a *"vario stile,"* and if this is true in the formal sense it is equally so thematically. One thinks of the *Canzoniere* as all Laura's, but this, on investigation, turns out to be rather far from the truth. I find that 37 of the 266 poems in Part I may be thought of as non-Laura poems, although in one or two she is, as it were, adumbrated. These break down into the political, the moralizing, the occasional sonnets to friends, and a few, like the lament for Cino da Pistoia, which are rather special cases. In all, something more than 1 in 7; not very many perhaps but some loom large: the *Rhymes* would be very different without *"Italia mia"* or *"Spirto gentil"* or the trio of anti-papal sonnets, to cite but a few. Part II is, however, almost completely dominated by Laura. From this point of view the two parts of the *Canzoniere* stand in contrast; *vario* indeed is the thematic nature of the first part; less so, and with a smaller though deeper range in the second.

Readers who approach the *Canzoniere* with the architectonics of the *Vita Nuova* in mind will be disappointed to find no obvious pattern in the disposition of the various forms. Morris Bishop, in the course of analyzing the early items of the first part, notes that after the seventh number the poet moves from the sonnet form to the *ballata*, "as the sound of the sonnet begins to thump in the sensitive ear";[10] and it is true that for the first fifty poems or so the variation is fairly constant although the sonnet is allowed to thump consistently from number xxxviii to l. Later the breaks are fewer, and indeed numbers cl through ccv are all sonnets and the thumping seems to be inaudible to the poet, whatever the reader may think about it. Furthermore, he wastes his chances for symmetrical variation, lumping potential punctuation marks, the odes and the shorter poems, close together. Numbers cxxv–cxxix are all odes, and they are at once so important and so diverse in content (they include *"Chiare, fresche, e dolci acque," "Italia mia,"* and *"Di pensier in pensier"*) that they might very well have stood apart, like lofty church spires each over its own parish. But instead we have a concentration of skyscrapers—and at the other extreme unrelieved suburbs of sonnets. There is no visible plan in the arrangement of the sonnet forms we have noted either. There will be a run of one type, two or three of another, perhaps a single example of a third, and then another run of one of the favorite kinds. The longest uninterrupted run is of six items; perhaps we may see in this some effort to get away from at least one kind of thumping.

Is this asymmetry deliberate? The only reasonable excuse for it would seem to be a respect for chronology but, as we have noticed, chronology was not an overriding concern of our poet. I am inclined to think that this disposition too is a matter of intent; the effect is indeed casual as if to indicate that the collection grew up almost unobserved by the poet himself—and that is in fact in tune with the way Petrarch speaks of his *nugelle*. The variety of forms is new and seems, to one coming fresh from the *dolce stil nuovo*, original. But one must enter *caveat* here. The Provençal *canzonieri* with which our poet must have been quite familiar also present such higgledy-piggledy anthologies in which *cansos* were mingled with *planhs, tensos,* and other forms, although modern editors have rearranged them. If they are superficially regarded, one can easily say that the *Rhymes* are more reactionary than revolutionary from the point of view of their disposition, but this would be to disregard the record of history, for as we know, Petrarch's arrangement, whatever it may seem to us, and whatever be its intention, is not merely casual.

But if chronology is not always scrupulously respected it is nevertheless possible to see something of a story line in the *Canzoniere*. The anniversaries are faithfully marked, the poet gets older and so, alas, does Laura, who finally dies. There is even a progression of moods; in the very broad sense we can say that the early poems are centered on rather light and transitory motifs and become more and more sober and grave as the story progresses. Tonelli likes to see three stages of the poet's spiritual progress in the *Rhymes* (eager as he is to liken it to the *Comedy*),[11] but most readers will find this too sharp a distinction. If this be motion, as of a sort it is, then the *Canzoniere* tells a story, but in another sense it is static; the relationship between the poet and his Laura undergoes no change in her lifetime, and the heavenly Laura, more understanding and indulgent, also remains fixed in her posture. Frustration is the poet's constant condition, whether it be in the face of the unyielding Laura of life or of her who, with all her sweetness, must remain forever a dream to her mourning lover. The *Canzoniere* can be seen from one angle—although this is by no means the whole truth of it—as one long probing of the world of amorous despair. This too is in its essence a familiar situation, common from the complaints of the troubadours through Cino da Pistoia, Dante being the sole exception.

But we must now look more closely at the leading figure of the *Rhymes,* Laura herself. Let us begin by a consideration of the significance of her image in the intention of her worshiper. Envisioned as a concept or an ideal there are certainly two Lauras, at least in the first part of the *Rhymes.* One of them is the girl of the green laurel, the Daphne pursued by Apollo, the other is the virtuous guide to Heaven, with whom the poet fell in love on the very significant date of Good Friday. Calcaterra, whose terms I borrow here, offers a convincing analysis of these two elements.[12] The Daphne-Laura is the poet's shorthand for his poetic ambitions; as Apollo pursued Daphne so he pursues a cherished symbol of artistic accomplishment and, as a collateral, fame and recognition. His friend Giacomo Colonna affects to believe that the poet is not enamored of a living woman at all but has given to an imaginary woman a name suggestive of this ambition. Petrarch denies the charge (*Fam.* II, 9) insisting on the existence of a real Laura, but he does not deny the inference that the name may be associated with the pursuit of glory and poetic achievement. St. Augustine in the *Secretum* puts the argument the other way around, asserting that Laura's name had led the poet to seek for laurels.

These various Lauras are worthy of some detailed investigation. We shall not deny the existence of a Laura-Daphne although she is not always quite so easily and immediately detectable as one could wish. If this Laura lives in the aura of the laurel, signifying our poet's desire for excellence in the love lyric and for the glory that would follow upon his achievement, she does indeed seem to be visible in a fair number of earlier sonnets and other forms of the *Canzoniere.* This is undeniably the Laura of the second *sestina* (xxx), beginning "A young woman under a green laurel," and we may detect her presence elsewhere either by the attitude of admiration for her beauty, unmixed with any noticeable awareness of her ethical or spiritual influence, or by the wealth of classical associations that surround the particular item dedicated to her. As an example we may quote the aforementioned "introductory" sonnet (xxxiv):

> O Phoebus, if that fond desire remains,
> Which fired thy breast near the Thessalian wave;
> If those bright tresses, which such pleasure gave,
> Through lapse of years thy memory not disdains;
> From sluggish frosts, from rude inclement rains,
> Which last the while thy beams our region leave,
> That honored sacred tree from peril save,
> Whose name of dear accordance waked our pains!
> And, by that amorous hope which soothed thy care,
> What time expectant thou wert doomed to sigh,
> Dispel those vapors which disturb our sky!
> So shall we both behold our favorite fair
> With wonder, seated on the grassy mead,
> And forming with her arms herself a shade.[13]

There are a number of other poems wherein may be seen this same glittering and rather remote symbol: excellent examples are xix, xxiv, lxiv, clxxxv (where she is clothed in purple even as she is in the third eclogue), and cxciii.

The Laura who provides celestial direction, whom we may call here Laura-Beatrice, comes into her own really only in the second part; there are, however, indications of her presence in Part I and here we may cite the ode (xxxvii) in which, absent from Laura, the poet recalls her "angelic salutation" which could arouse him to virtue. I should say that I acknowledge the presence of this Laura only when I find in the text clear indications of her moral significance, and such items are rare in Part I though sonnets xciv and ccxxii recall the reverential tone of the *dolce stil nuovo*.

There is yet, it seems to me, a third Laura, who appears with tolerable frequency in Part I and reappears by a kind of negative inference in the very last sonnets of the second part of the *Canzoniere*. This is the Laura who may or may not be a symbol of artistic achievement but who is certainly beautiful and whose beauty is dangerous to the poet's soul. Perhaps we may call her Laura-Sophonisba. She is the Laura who is almost regularly repudiated on the anniversaries of the poet's enamorment, for example in the sonnet written in 1338 (lxii), "Father in Heaven, after my wasted days," wherein he speaks of his long servitude to an "unworthy passion." Some have seen in the *sestina* "To the sweet shadow of the lovely leaves" (cxlii) the moment of the poet's "conversion," for in the envoy he resolves henceforth so seek "other leaves" and even "another love." But other recognitions of the Sophonisba in Laura precede this statement, among them the sonnet we have just quoted—and Daphne will appear frequently again.

It should be said at once that these Lauras are not always distinguishable one from the other. One cannot always tell whether the poet's attitude is one of purely poetic admiration or quasi-religious reverence. We find occasionally a severely classical Laura, remote and scintillant, whose praises yet contain some reference to what seems to be the Christian frame of reference; for example, in such items as xc and cix we have the adjective "angelic" and the reference to Paradise; it is not easy to say whether in the first case we are to see a kind of syncretism which would make angels of nymphs and in the second case whether Paradise is a bold substitution for Olympus. In xli, "the tree that Phoebus loved in human form" of line 2 becomes in line 14 "the fair face awaited by the angels"; and in cxxxv we find ourselves confronted by the charming but somewhat discordant image of a *"fera angelica."* Of this blending of the two Lauras there are quite a few examples, particularly in the first part of the *Canzoniere*. It can be argued too that Laura-Sophonisba is merely the obverse side of Laura-Daphne; to put it in very simple terms the poet may well be saying that his poetic ambitions are an obstacle to his proper Christian concern for the salvation of his soul. I can only say that I find in most cases at least that the note of remorse and repentance seems to me a little too strong and personal to be attached merely to a misdirected ambition. I cannot but feel that Laura-Sophonisba is guilty of arousing the poet's carnal desires, which as a true penitent he must quite properly deplore.

This brings us to a consideration of a fourth Laura. When the acute and perceptive critics have finished with their analysis of the *Rhymes* in terms of the poet's classicism, Augustinianism, "*dolcestilnovism*," and the like, may we not after all possibly find room for Laura *qua* Laura? If we were to take out of the *Canzoniere* the items which are definitely packed with allusions to the laurel, Daphne, and Apollo and his *dolce famiglia* we should still have a good many left, and without the suggestion provided by the those that we have omitted, we might very well see in the *Canzoniere* not Daphne but simply Laura herself, a young woman with whom the poet fell in love on an April day of 1327. This I would say is particularly true of sonnets that refer to some incident; occasional sonnets, one might call them, lacking any universal signficance, too frail to bear the ponderous weight of Parnassus. My census shows me that there are quite a few of this character; let sonnet ccix serve as an example.

> The loved hills where I left myself behind,
> Whence ever 'twas so hard my steps to tear,
> Before me rise; at each remove I bear
> The dear load to my lot by Love consigned.
> Often I wonder inly in my mind,
> That still the fair yoke holds me, which despair
> Would vainly break, that yet I breathe this air;
> Though long the chain, its links but closer bind.
> And as a stag, sore struck by hunter's dart,
> Whose poisoned iron rankles in his breast,
> Flies and more grieves the more the chase is pressed,
> So I, with Love's keen arrow in my heart,
> Endure at once my death and my delight,
> Racked with long grief, and weary with vain flight.[14]

This is the Laura to be sure, on whom Daphne, Beatrice, and Sophonisba all depend, but it would be, it seems to me, a gross injustice, verging on callousness, to deny her a life of her own. This is the Laura of whom the poet can give us an occasional physical description. It is the Laura who can visit him and smile upon him or reject him, it is the Laura who can have trouble with her eyes or be sick, or travel, the Laura indeed who will eventually die. Since Daphne is unattainable and Beatrice would be inappropriate, I think it is also the Laura with whom the poet in the first *sestina* xxii would like to spend the night, even though the rest of that poem may have Apollonian implications. We have granted too that the Lauras often blend; there is a frequent fusion of Daphne and Laura, and it is of necessity the true Laura that gives Sophonisba her menacing reality. But I think it would be wrong to see only poetic allegory or religious symbolism in the girl of the golden hair and discreet reticence. I think the *Canzoniere* is not merely an exercise in lyric virtuosity or a revelation of the conflict within the poet's heart between love of beauty and Augustinian pessimism—although both of those themes are readily apparent—but also the record of a man in love with a woman. To be sure, Part II, written after Laura's death, is a little different. It would be tempting to say that this part marks the triumph of Laura-Beatrice, for indeed the beloved woman is now a saint who visits her mourning lover to cheer him with the prospect of his joining her in Paradise, but the mere mention of Beatrice suffices to remind us of the difference. Laura, when she visits her Francesco in his dreams, does not instruct him on matters of theology or even on the details of celestial topography; she is not a teacher, as Dante's Beatrice was, not really even a guide in any true sense of the word. She does not lecture or syllogize. She is a woman waiting. She is indeed, as De Sanctis remarked many years ago, much more human than she ever was on earth.[15] Any touch of lust would be, of course, out of the question, but her charm is the charm of a woman with whom the poet is in love and her beauty, although merely remembered, is still as important to the poet as her new status of sanctity. There is indeed almost a bourgeois realism in her approach to her bereaved worshiper; she behaves as we would expect any decent middle-class woman to behave who had left a widower behind her. That she is still a woman even though now innocuous is made quite apparent by the tone of the last three sonnets wherein this disembodied, and one would think essentially harmless, soul is in effect repudiated by the poet.

The *Canzoniere*, however, owes its charm and its vitality not to the identity or the definition of Laura, whether it be the Laura of fact or of poetic fiction, but rather to her effect upon her lover and his muse. Laura in turn is not so much the central personage as the pretext of the *Rhymes*. Many critics have pointed out, sometimes rather unsympathetically, what surely every reader can discover for himself; namely that the poet's principal concern is not with Laura's feelings or reactions, but his own. Indeed whether we think of Laura as Daphne or Beatrice or simply as a local matron we cannot fail to notice that her reactions to the poet are never analyzed. She is usually indifferent, sometimes cruel, occasionally indulgent, but the poet makes no effort to explain these reactions on the part of his beloved. It is true, of course, that in the poems written after her death she is allowed to explain her attitude; her secret and suppressed correspondence to the affections of her faithful swain and her firm resolution, for his sake as well as hers, to preserve her chastity. But there is no sign of this conflict while she is still alive, and the apology given after her death has about it an air not entirely convincing. One may fairly suspect that the poet is guilty of wistful rationalizing. Even this Laura, human as she is, one feels, is a creation of the poet. A real participation in Laura's emotional attitude might, we could argue, leave some room for the consideration she might have had for her husband, but it is not Laura's crisis which is the subject of the *Canzoniere;* it is Petrarch's. There is no reason that we should be distressed by this or indeed critical of it. It is the way of poets. We may be grateful for the result, for out of the poet's searching analysis, sometimes deeply moving and sometimes even faintly amusing though it may be, emerges some of the most sensitive poetry ever written. Laura, or the pondering on Laura, leads him far, and the currents of the *Canzoniere* set in motion by his devotion to her are deep and powerful.

For one thing the *Rhymes* are full of enchanting descriptions of nature. We shall not deny that they are formalized, but the basis of their formality is observation and, more than observation, the sincere and wholehearted appreciation of the beauties of this world we live in. In this connection we may note as others have before us that the amatory attitude of Petrarch is largely that of

the spectator. He does not seem—save for very rare references—
really so much to want to possess Laura as to contemplate her,
and he contemplates her against the background of nature. Laura
is always seen out of doors. This may be an aspect of the Laura-
Daphne, but I am inclined to think that is incidental; or perhaps
Daphne is the association with Laura because one can only think
of her out of doors. The happiest and most typical example we
can cite of what we have in mind here is the ode *"Chiare, fresche, e
dolci acque"* (cxxvi), in which one can see a kind of programmatic
foreshadowing of the Renaissance dream, later to be more consciously portrayed by Poliziano and Botticelli. In this dream the
young woman is the ultimate perfection of nature, but being such
she is not isolated but rather is a part of a truly earthly paradise.
Laura does not sit here for a studio portrait but is framed by the
fountain, the falling blossoms, and the aura of spring; and many
are the poems of the *Rhymes* in which Petrarch, Laura either
being visible or present only in his heart, finds comfort in the landscape, the streams, the fountain and the *deserti campi,* or the
riverbanks, fields, and hills that he can summon as his witnesses to
his love for solitary life. In truth in some of the most celebrated as
well as the most beautiful of the poems in the *Canzoniere,* Laura
is not needed at all save as a memory to sharpen his melancholy
perception. The landscape is always, like the poet himself, discreet, well bred, and a little melancholy; it is nevertheless a landscape more lovingly portrayed than any the world of poetry had
beheld before his time. Although the poet either despairing for
the hopelessness of his care or mourning his departed lady may be
sad as he looks upon this landscape, yet the trees, the brooks, the
hills, the valleys, the birds, and "the tiny fish" are not in themselves depressing—quite the contrary. They are consoling. The
sadness the poet feels on contemplating them does not come from
any lack of appreciation of this comforting element but rather
from the awareness that the fields, streams, and sympathetic hills
are, like Laura herself, expressions of the beauty of earthly life,
seductive but transient. Herein lies the true source of the Christian poet's uneasiness, unhappiness, dissatisfaction, and ultimate
rejection. If we reflect on this association of Laura—I shall not
call it an allegory—we shall see how wrong it is to vulgarize her,
to speculate on her age, civil status, possible pregnancies, even
identity. (For that matter I think it is equally unimportant

whether she is Daphne or Beatrice or Sophonisba.) The realistic
or naturalistic Laura fuses with the allegory and becomes one with
nature, one with this lovely world we can enjoy and must enjoy if
we are not to deny life itself but which is nevertheless destined to
decay and ultimately to pass away. This is the inescapable para-
dox. Platonists can tell us that the appreciation of earthly beauty
can be the first step on the divine ladder, that the rapture of the
love that we feel for the beautiful woman of our dreams, though it
may be sensual is pardonable, for it is translatable into the ultimate spiritual ecstasy, as Bembo will put it so eloquently in the
Cortegiano. But Plato is a pagan; St. Augustine knew better and
so did Petrarch. He can pretend not to, often enough; he can ask,
while Laura still lives, "in what divine ideal?" and after her death
he can see her as pointing the way upward to him and assuring
him that she awaits him above. He cannot, however, ultimately
convince himself. Doubts begin as early as the anniversary sonnet "Father in heaven, after my wasted days" (lxii); they reap-
pear at regular self-illuminating intervals; and they finally triumph with the complete abdication of the last sonnet, "I go a-
weeping for the time I've spent" (ccclxv). This poem is in fact the
end of Petrarch's statement, for his tension makes him what he is;
the hymn to the Virgin, technically admirable though it may be,
is, it seems to me, hardly a personal poem.

The woman and landscape are seen, as often as not, with the
eye of memory. The most haunting motif of the *Canzoniere* is that
of the passage of time; this is allied to, and indeed is another
aspect of the muse of memory, certainly Petrarch's most faithful
inspiration. We may note the frequency of verbs in the past tense
as contrasted with the use of the present by the older poets. Even
as Dante remembers, he puts his lady before us in the present
tense; Petrarch, so often, looking on Laura, is moved to recall her
as he saw her a year ago, a decade ago, and indeed, if it was only
last week, yet with an element of memory added to that of contemplation. Again we may cite *"Chiare, fresche, e dolci acque"* as
an example: the lovely vision is not so much seen as it is recalled,
for all its vividness. Another very beautiful sonnet (xc) is dedicated to the effect of time on his lady's beauty if not on his own
fidelity. Or we may call to mind the sonnet (ccxlvii) wherein he
bids all who wish to see earth's fairest thing to hurry, for such
beauty is at the mercy of the years. Even when Laura is present he

thinks of her not as she seems but as he well remembers her. And who does not remember, though the motif transcends the courting of Laura, the magnificent quatrain with which sonnet 231 (cclxxii) opens:

> Life, staying not an hour, flees before
> Onrushing Death whose forces follow fast:
> And present things and memories of the past
> Affright me and the future even more.

Probably the sense of time passing has been a part of man's psyche ever since he was foolish enough to chart the heavens and draw up a calendar. Surely the related motif of *carpe diem* is soundly classical, and the sense of the impermanence of mortal things is plain enough in many books of the Old Testament. As far as the lyric of the Western world is concerned, I believe it may be said that full awareness of this human condition and the self-conscious elaboration of it is essentially new with Petrarch. There are haunting lines in the old Provençal; again one may recall Bernart de Ventadorn and the beautiful stanza beginning "Time comes and goes and comes again/but always one is my desire."[16] But this and other such flickerings are not fed by the poet's further reflection; in the case of Petrarch the theme is recurrently and insistently explored, is indeed a part of himself, which he cannot but bring to light and which has, more than any other single element in his poetry, become a part of the Western lyric ever since. Unrequited love, chaste and cruel mistresses, these are constants, aye, even in the century we live in today, but the eternal impact of the *Canzoniere*, whether we think of it as a source of literary influence or in the sense of the reader's response, is the remorselessness of time and the sad and yet somehow consoling uses of memory. This wistful contemplator of earthly beauty, as sensitive to its appeal as he is, of course, aware of its fragility, is bound to find his consolation, and so his muse, in memory. It is true that if we do not care for the present we still have a choice and may as freely look to the future as to the past. Indeed Petrarch looked to the future too, for appreciation, for immortality, for an audience that might be worthy of him. But one cannot visualize the future, what the eye can summon to the heart are things seen, not things to come. The opening sonnet of the *Canzoniere* is much to the point here. We note that what it promises us is in fact the poet's memories. All poets remember, of course, but no poet before Petrarch can remember with such self-consciousness, such a bittersweet awareness of the then and the now. Other poets remember events and often, too, the emotions associated with them. But Petrarch cherishes and explores the operation of memory itself; he recalls the event not as a historian but with the full savor of the act of recalling. Memory, in fact, becomes obsessive; one has but to think of the anniversary sonnets or the frequent recollections of Laura in one pose or another. Relatively rare are the sonnets that speak of Laura in the present, as we have observed; when we come across them we are as like as not to say this must be the influence of the *dolce stil nuovo* for whose adherents beauty more often than not seems to lie in an eternal poetic presence. "So gentle and so modest *seems* my lady," [17] says Dante; but Petrarch, typically, writes, "her golden locks *were* spread upon the air";[18] this cult of memory, always deeply moving though occasionally approaching the morbid, is, in my opinion, Petrarch's great and lasting contribution to the lyric. What Leopardi made of this precious element we all know; without Petrarch we should either have had no Leopardi or would not have been prepared to understand him if we did. Pondering the true sources of his attitude it is helpful to remember, I think, that Petrarch is what we would call nowadays a displaced person. Not an exile, for an exile is forever *engagé;* not an expatriate, for an expatriate is such by choice. But a displaced person, with no true roots anywhere: everywhere at home and everywhere a stranger. This is the key, I believe, to both the restlessness and easy adaptability that his biography reveals. Of his homeland he can speak movingly as the land "that I first trod," but in fact he chooses to spend a lot of time in Vaucluse. To the city of his fathers he would not return although he might have. His affection for Italy indeed is fundamentally an affection for Rome, the love of a humanist, not an Italian. If we may say so, his language is also that of a displaced person, one who speaks his native tongue correctly and carefully but not quite colloquially. We have speculated elsewhere on how often and how regularly Petrarch actually spoke his mother tongue. We shall add no more to our discussion here but merely say that the "mother tongue" was, even in everyday life for Petrarch, not Tuscan at all but Latin. as Zabughin has asserted.[19] I would say that the language of the *Canzoniere* is an indication of a certain linguistic limitation. Petrarch has the art of making a virtue of this limitation, bringing out a kind of specialized vocabulary and a formalized style, a quotient of refinement and elegance—but not for him is the language of *"mamma e babbo"* or *"mo e issa."* This linguistic detachment not only parallels his experiential alienation but also accords with his temperament. Not for him either marriage or definite commitment to clerical orders; not for him either, to put the dichotomy of the *Canzoniere* in yet another way, the participant enjoyment of the sensual life of which Boccaccio was capable nor the abdication chosen by his own brother, whose example he admired but could not follow.

It seems clear to me that this alienation, this lack of inner security, to use the terms all too familiar to us nowadays, are at the root of the dominant motif of the *Canzoniere,* which, as above noted, is the sense of the impermanence of life, the uncertainty of human things, or rather the one great certainty of their mortality. Bosco is at some pains to indicate that with Petrarch this is not the simple and conventional Christian attitude, committed to a conviction that there is no permanence save in the eternal, nothing lasting but God Himself.[20] Bosco quotes Petrarch's letter to Philippe de Cabassoles (*Fam.* XXIV, 1) in which the poet tells how this awareness of mutability first reached him in his early readings of the Latin classics; while the others were reading to learn the grammar and the vocabulary, the lesson he derived was a deeper one. The Christian stance does not come into it. But the psyche of the boy does, and it is the psyche of a very young displaced person.

The introductory letter to the *Familiares* is eloquent and revealing; he writes to Socrates:

I was conceived in exile and born in exile. I cost my mother such labor and struggle that for a long time the midwives and physicians thought her dead. Thus I began to know danger even before I was born, and I crossed the threshold of life under the loom of death. . . . After the wanderings in Tuscany we went to Pisa. I was removed from there in my seventh year and transported by sea to France. We were shipwrecked by the winter storms not far from Marseilles, and I was nearly carried off again on the threshold of my young life. . . . Thenceforward certainly I have hardly had a chance to stand still and get my breath . . .[21]

There is no need to take the last sentence too seriously; Petrarch's middle years were hardly more breathless than those of many of his contemporaries, but the account of his early childhood cannot be overlooked if we are seeking the ultimate source of the *Canzoniere*.

We have noted how frequently and bitterly our poet laments the destiny that compelled him to live in what he considered—with some reason—a miserable age. Without refuting his opinion we may yet find it to be rather that of a wistful humanist than an objective historian. The statement is even a little ungrateful. Certainly within the possibilities offered by the society of his time he had a comfortable life—a life, in truth, of less trouble and torment than that of many poets. Handsome, courted by the great and well taken care of from the moment he met Giovanni Colonna until the day he died, he never knew need, rarely had any duties to perform that were not of his own choosing, never had any serious responsibilities, either political or professional. He was free to focus on his own interests and his own dilemmas, some self-made, but basically real enough because they were the truly human dilemmas. The *Canzoniere* is the story of this uneasy and restless intellectual; it is the distillation of a probing mind and a sensitive heart, given scope and freedom to examine man's ultimate destiny, and in its own formalized but beautiful language, to report on its discoveries and intuitions.

These voices of our poet's muse speak to us over the centuries and haunt us because they are not purely personal or rather because, being purely personal, they yet strike a chord that is universal and eternal. The worship of beauty, the appreciation of its fragility, the sad consoling uses of memory—these cannot fail to strike a responsive note within us and persuade us to realize, as we do with all great poetry, that the writer is speaking also for us. But it is not merely his themes that persuade and engage us; as much if not more so it is the art with which these sentiments are conveyed. It is one thing to have an emotional experience or a spiritual insight and another to transmit it to your audience, and Petrarch was a remarkable, one might almost say a unique, craftsman. We may dare go so far as to doubt the sincerity of his emotions or even to question the validity of his conclusions, although I think this would be difficult, but no one can turn a deaf ear to the music with which these convictions, these tender statements are

set forth. Our poet is not only a man of feeling but a master tech-
nician.

I believe the study of his technique in some detail will be worth
our while. Analysis and explication are impertinent exercises to be
sure, yet in the case of Petrarch they are certainly rewarding. If
we are to get at the ineffable pearl we must deal with the rugged
shell of the oyster. It would be unforgivable if in the process we
should crack the pearl, but your truly poetic pearl has a great
capacity for survival.

We could do worse than choose the first sonnet of the *Rhymes*
for our preliminary analysis. It has the advantage of being familiar to anyone who has ever taken up the *Canzoniere* in his hands;
it is a sonnet of the poet's full maturity, it is in many ways a very
fair specimen of his style, and it is, in my opinion, among the best,
both for what it says and the manner of saying it.

Let us spread it before us here:

> Voi ch' ascoltate in rime sparse il suono
>   Di quei sospiri ond' io nudriva 'l core
>   In sul mio primo giovenile errore,
>   Quand' era in parte altr' uom da quel ch' i' sono,
>
> Del vario stile in ch' io piango e ragiono
>   Fra la vane speranze e' l van dolore,
>   Ove sia chi per prova intenda amore,
>   Spero trovar pietà, non che perdono.
>
> Ma ben veggio or sì come al popol tutto
>   Favola fui gran tempo, onde sovente
>   Di me medesmo meco mi vergogno;
>
> E del mio vaneggiar vergogna è 'l frutto,
>   E 'l pentersi, e 'l conoscer chiaramente
>   Che quanto piace al mondo è breve sogno.

Perhaps we should observe first of all that, insofar as content is
concerned, the poem is not at all original. It is, in effect, a pali-
node, a metrical statement of recantation of a previous position, as
old as the language that is at the root of the English term. In the
literary tradition of which the *Canzoniere* is a part, recantation is
almost a recognized movement in the game. Does not even Andrew the Chaplain employ his last chapter to undo all that he said

in the earlier ones? The troubadours, if they lived long enough, regularly learned to see the unwisdom of their earlier earthly obsessions. Two specific statements come readily to mind, if we look for earlier models of this kind of statement. The oldest of all the troubadours, the very fountainhead of Western lyric poetry, William of Poitou, puts it with laconic brevity: "Pride and Pomp and Chivalry/and all that once was dear to me/I lay aside right willingly,/ as pleases my soul's Emperor." [22] Bertran de Born, of whom his biographer related that after a long life in the world he joined the Cistercian order, writes in a phraseology not very different from Petrarch's: "When I take thought of what I am and whence I came, I wonder in amazement that God should so long have been tolerant of my wickedness; but now may He who is strong and free and has been pleased to call me to Him consent to cancel my sins since my evil longings have died within me." [23]

In the *Divine Comedy* many souls exemplify this repudiation of the past; Guido da Montefeltro, Cunizza and Folquet, to cite a few. And perhaps Dante himself would have fallen into this category, as some passages of the *Convivio* seem to suggest, had he not translated Beatrice from the amatory to the theological sphere. We may also note that the form is not new. Petrarch in fact invented no new forms but rather gloried in employing some of the most dust-covered bottles, including even the *sestina,* for his new wine. The sonnet was nearly a century old by the time he used it; the ode or *canzone* was, of course, much older.

Is the wine in truth all that new? Chiorboli[24] notes classical references in line 2 of our sonnet, to both Ovid and Horace in line 9, and reminds us of the possible echo of Dante's *"Donne ch' avete intelletto d'amore"* in line 7, so that we may not say that it is the originality of the matter which wins us. It is rather the technique of expression.

Let us examine some of the tactics so cunningly employed. The device most apparent to the eye, at once the simplest and the most useful, is alliteration. There are in these fourteen lines a number of alliterative nuclei. Lines 1 and 2 contain three initial *s*'s and they are reinforced by the second syllable of *ascoltate,* unobtrusive to the eye but by no means so to the ear. In lines 8 *pietà and perdono* are effectively linked by the initial labial which looks back to *piango* and *prova* and ahead to *popol, pentersi* and *piace.*

Line 11 almost approaches caricature, and the ear of Tassoni in the seventeenth century was offended by it; yet most critics have found it effective, and the *vergogno* at the end of the line is picked up by the forceful combination *vaneggiar vergogna* in line 12. We may note, too, I think, that the *veggio* of line 9 and the *sovente* of line 10 lead the ear to enjoyment too of the climactic labial outburst.

In the area of vowel manipulation there is much subtlety; perhaps the happiest illustration is the association of *vario* and *vano* where the semantic ambiguity of *vario* comes into play too, since divers commentators have taken it as referring either to the style itself or to the conflicting currents of the poet's passionate obsession. And the long *a* echoes the keynote of the first line with the rhetorical *ascoltate* and the almost wistful *sparse*, again perhaps slightly ambiguous. Of the predominance of the sonorous vowel *o* in the sonnet it is unnecessary to speak; *o* has the first word and the last in this confession; more artful perhaps is the linking of *sospiri . . . nudriva* in line 2 with the *mio primo giovenile* of line 3 by means of the stressed vowel. The sonnet is, indeed, as much a musical composition as it is a statement. And yet the statement is clear enough; we may remark here once and for all that Petrarch, as far as syntax and diction are concerned, is an unusually straightforward poet. The best sonnets are all characterized by great syntactical simplicity. There are very few cases where the grammar is complicated or where the syntactical arrangements are at all puzzling. Petrarch's effectiveness and to a certain extent his later fortune have their source in the far-from-common combination of rhetorical and prosodic virtuosity with clarity of exposition. We may note, in connection with the syntax, that it is "modern" in the sense that the medieval pattern of coordinate clauses is gone. The fourteen lines contain but two sentences; the second, to be sure, has two independent clauses, but the word *e* appears only once as a clausal connective. This marks a major departure. The sonnets of the *Vita Nuova,* for example, and those of Cavalcanti show a striking incidence of "ands" by comparison. It is hardly necessary to say that the effect is to give the sonnet of Petrarch, as contrasted with those of his predecessors, a unity, one might better say an integrity, which strengthens the impact on the reader. His predecessors had composed line by line (one certainly has this impression reading the Provençal poets and the so-called Sicilians) or at best by quartets; the sonnet of Petrarch, like the Ariosto *ottava,* is fused into one very effective artifact.

The formula—and we do not use the term in a pejorative sense —the formula, then, as illustrated by the keynote sonnet of the *Rhymes,* is a straightforward statement of an emotional condition, adorned with rhetorical embellishment, musically set forth and conceived as a unity.

The musical impact of the sonnet is a matter of metrical beat as much as of vowel quality. In this area the poet's ear never fails him; and though from the point of view of content or manner one may find some compositions that do not charm, yet it is difficult to think of any that are not musically satisfying. Let us glance briefly at the metrical design of the opening sonnet. Some of the lines may be read in various ways, but as I read them I find lines 2, 3, 4, 11, and 14 all follow the same pattern, with regular iambic beat (to use the terms of English prosody; here, it seems to me, quite applicable). Lines 1, 8, and 10 differ only in that they contain an inversion in the first foot, another very common English scheme, as it happens. This gives us eight normal, one might say, reassuring lines. Another fairly normal variation is presented by lines 6, 7, 9, and 12; here the line begins with two anapests. The unusual lines are 5, where the movement becomes anapestic toward the end of the line and the very irregular line 13 which gives us three short syllables in succession and forces us to put a caesura after the fourth syllable, which is here unstressed. If one were to chart these lines with shorthand syllables, using *A, B,* and *C* for our major patterns we should come out with the scheme *BAAA XCCB CBA CXA,* in which we may note a cunning mixture of the normal and the irregular; there is just enough shock to avoid monotony, enough regularity to give the suggestion of incantation.

The simple statement, musically expressed and artfully phrased —this is the definition that could be applied to many of the best and most enduring items of the *Canzoniere.* This definition would certainly apply to such unique gems as "*Solo e pensoso i più deserti campi*" (xxxv), "*Or che 'l ciel e la terra e 'l vento tace*" (clxiv), "*La vita fugge e non s'arresta un' ora*" (cclxxi) among the sonnets, and the formula would also fit the magnificent *canzone* of honest and painful self-analysis: "*I' vo pensando e nel pensier m'assale*" (cclxiv), as sincere and musical a statement of a human dilemma as we can find in Italian literature before the coming of Leopardi. All of these incomparable lyrics, we may note, appear before us unadorned, without benefit of allegory. Not, to be sure, that allegory is missing from the *Canzoniere*. Many examples of its use will come readily to mind, nor is it always used playfully, though I think in fact more often than not. But playful or otherwise it is not an essential part of the poet's equipment.

Our first sonnet, with the characteristics we have assigned to it, is a pattern for many in the *Canzoniere*—the majority, I would venture to say. There is, however, one weapon in the poet's armory, and a very effective one, which does not appear in the magnificent prologue. Let us look at cccliii:

> Vago augelletto che cantando vai,
> o ver piangendo il tuo tempo passato,
> vedendoti la notte e 'l verno a lato
> e 'l dì dopo le spalle e i mesi gai;
> se, come i tuoi gravosi affanni sai,
> così sapessi il mio simile stato,
> verresti in grembo a questo sconsolato
> a partir seco i dolorosi guai.
> I' non so se le parti sarian pari;
> che quella cui tu piangi è forse in vita,
> di ch' a me Morte e 'l ciel son tanto avari;
> ma la stagion e l' ora men gradita
> col membrar de' dolci anni e di li amari
> a parlar teco con pietà m' invita.

Let us note, briefly, that the formula is much the same. This sonnet, too is a simple statement of a sentimental position, clearly stated in line 9, which is to say a comparison of the poet's state with that of the singing bird as in sonnet one. The fourteen lines contain only two sentences, there are no clausal connectives at all, and the euphonic elements are perhaps even more visible to the naked eye—or should one say audible to the natural ear? One stressed vowel, the grave and melancholy *a* carries the weight of all of the rhymes but one (this supplementary of rhyme with assonance is a frequent practice of our poet); alliteration and phonic correspondence play their usual role. We may admire the artful ambiguity of the initial "*vago*," and perhaps there is even a shadowy classical echo for those of us to whom Lesbia's sparrow may

come to mind. But it differs from sonnet i in that it is built around
an image. And our poet, though by no means every item in the
Canzoniere reveals it, is a master of imagery. And imagery, I
think, of such a personal kind and color that we may well be justified in calling it "new." Perhaps I can make an approach at defin-
ing it by calling it objective in depiction and subjective in intent.
Here a comparison with the practice of Dante might be helpful.
One does not like forever to be bringing these two into rivalry,
but history is stronger than our sense of decency and there is no
way out of it.

Dante's imagery (I have here in mind particularly the *Comedy*) is sharp, visual, and in a sense objective. Very often it is used
not to describe the poet himself but something seen by him; his
rightly celebrated lark that spreads its wings and satiates itself
with song (*Par.* xx, 73–75) is not introduced to describe the poet,
but the eagle of Jupiter. Likewise the famous log "that hisses for
the wind that issues forth" (*Inf.* xiii, 42), or the two ants meeting
and nosing each other on the road (*Purg.* xvi, 35), are there to
sharpen our perception of what the traveler sees on his journey
and not of his own condition. But even when Dante's figures are
applied to himself they are likely to be plastic or pictorial rather
than subjective. The peasant who, first depressed by what he
thinks is a late snowfall, and later cheered when the frost melts,
shares, to be sure, Dante's alternation of abasement and relief but
truly nothing of his guilt or subsequent satisfaction at being restored to the good graces of his mentor. But with Petrarch the
image is absorbed and devoured, and it is precisely this emotional
solidarity that the poet seeks. In the case of the sonnet in question
Petrarch hardly wants us to visualize him as seated on a bough of
a tree; he does want us to feel that the sorrow of the bird expressed for his missing mate is a sorrow akin to his own. To over-
simplify: Dante wants us to *see* with him and Petrarch wants us to
feel with him. The *"vecchierello canuto e bianco"* (xvi) does not
look like Petrarch or walk like him, but his emotional predica-
ment as he goes forth in a foreign land to look for a revered face is
exactly the same as the poet's. The succession of naturalistic vi-
gnettes in the canzone *"Ne la stagion che 'l ciel rapido inchina"*
(1), in which, tenderly depicted, the "old and weary pilgrim
woman," "the sober woodsman," "the shepherd," "the sailors on
their bark," and the unyoked oxen pass before us so naturally

etched that even Dante might have envied the sharpness of their outlines—they too are brought in to share the poet's all-embracing melancholy. These images are too sharply drawn to merge into the kind of emotional abstraction which will characterize much of the imagery of the Renaissance, but they are no longer simply aids to visualization. Is this new? Perhaps not entirely: one recalls Bernart's lark [25] (perhaps the begetter of Dante's) moving on wings of joy toward the sun (and it is the lover's joy), but no poet before Petrarch had so consistently brought life and nature to the service of his own responsive heart.

CHAPTER 13

The Enduring Petrarch

THE genesis of the work of any author lies in his experience, his reading, and ultimately, of course, in the mystery of his temperament which fashions these elements to his own purposes and his own style of expression. I believe it is safe to say that in the case of Petrarch reading played a much larger role than experience. He had, as we have observed in the sketch of his life, his meaningful encounters, his moments of crisis. Yet it was a serene life for the most part, not broken by exile as in the case of Dante, not embittered by frustrated love as was Boccaccio's. The crucial events were probably the happy association with the Colonna family, which launched his career, and the encounter with Laura. But one suspects that, given his personality, Petrarch was destined to attract some powerful patron sooner or later and, without being cynical, one may also suspect that some other lady might have served his artistic purposes as well as Laura had he not strayed into Santa Chiara on the fateful April day.

The sources of his inspiration are primarily in his reading. He has not concealed these sources; rather—save for one area—he seems to glory in them. Having reviewed his production in detail it will not be necessary here to labor our point: the Latin works show clear and freely confessed indebtedness to the classical authors, and this indebtedness is also apparent in the vernacular poems. He was the most widely read man of his time in the classics, and we have observed the influence, sometimes the outright imitation, of such writers as Virgil, Horace and Ovid, the uses of Livy and most persistently of all the recurrent invocation of Cicero. Indeed he confesses himself—and this in his old age when the "Christian" or "penitent" Petrarch was dominant—that he had fallen in love with Cicero in childhood when others were "yawning over Aesop," and goes on to tell of his lifelong efforts to get hold of the works and make suitable copies of those he could not buy (*Sen.* XIV, 1). We may refer the reader again to the statement in the invective *On His Own Ignorance and That of Many.*

All biographers of Petrarch have stressed his classical training: the actual books read, pondered, digested, and frequently annotated have been documented, most effectively of all, by Pierre de Nolhac.[1]

A second area of reading and study was the patristic. Gerosa in a recent publication summarizes our poet's knowledge of the writings of the Fathers, citing his knowledge of Jerome, Ambrose, St. John Chrysostom and the like and documenting the devotion to St. Augustine, which is indeed obvious enough not only in the Latin works but in the *Canzoniere* and the *Trionfi* as well.[2] It is only when we come to the third area that we find Petrarch a little reluctant to advertise his learning and reveal his sources. This is, of course, the area of vernacular literature. As we have seen, he knew the *Roman de la Rose;* in his invective in defense of Italy against France he shows some knowledge of medieval writers of French origin. He was familiar with at least some of the Provençal poets; one suspects he knew them better than he is prepared to confess, and also with the work of his predecessors in Tuscan, although here too the avowal is somewhat oblique. The *Canzoniere* is the work of a man who was thoroughly acquainted with the vernacular lyric tradition.

The influences on Petrarch are therefore so clear as to be immediately visible, and they are all, one might say, "bookish" (which is not to say that his own writings are stale or unoriginal). Sometimes imitation is too apparent, as in the *Africa,* or the burden of erudition is too heavy for free movement either for the author or the reader, as in many places in the *De viris* or the *Rerum memorandarum* or the *De vita solitaria* or the *Letters.* But at his best the "bookishness" is redeemed by the participation of the author, by his enthusiastic identification with his sources, and by the illuminating contribution of his own personality to a traditional and even hackneyed pattern. His originality lies in himself.

As for Petrarch's influence on others, if there is anything more difficult than to assess it, it is to exaggerate it. It was *in toto* ubiquitous, long-enduring, and profound. In order to estimate it one has to categorize the numerous areas in which this influence was felt. We may well begin with a quotation from Wilkins, who writes as follows:

From each of the three divisions of his work there proceeded, beginning in his lifetime, a specific wave of influence. While these waves were virtually simultaneous to their time of origin, they were by no means equal in their original strength or in their periods of greater strength. Generally speaking, the first wave, in point of original strength and with respect to the time when it reached its peak, was a wave that proceeded from the Latin works. Next came the wave from the *Triumphs;* and at last the wave from the *Canzoniere.*[3]

The wave proceeding from the Latin works is perhaps the one of greatest importance to historians of culture. As we have seen in our discussions of these individual works they give Petrarch a role of unique primacy in the origins of the Renaissance. His approach to the classics, a mixture of reverence and intimacy, with his eagerness to recognize their humanity as akin to his over the centuries and his reluctance to involve them in the ethos of traditional medieval values is, from the point of view of letters, the kernel of humanism. It is due almost solely to his inspiration that his contemporaries and those immediately following them read the classics with a new illumination, a better understanding, and a kind of spiritual emancipation which their forefathers had not been able to achieve. This is a fact of cultural history. But as Wilkins well suggests it is a moment in time—a crucial moment— and one which shifted the course of thought in the intellectual world—but a moment only. Petrarch's doctrine was readily and enthusiastically received. It may be said to have been well learned by the generation that followed him, and after that his insight and attitude simply became absorbed into the mainstream of cultural history. Indeed perhaps the lesson was learned too well for the enduring fame of the master. For, inspired by his perception and guided by his light, the generations that immediately followed learned, as might have been expected, to surpass their teacher. Humanism simply swallowed its father, and on the purely linguistic side there is even some rather sad irony to be noted; Latinists a hundred years later found Petrarch's Latin rather crude.

On the influence of the *Trionfi* we shall refer the reader to Chapter 11 and say little more here. It was indeed somewhat more enduring than that of the Latin works and, as a record of editions and commentaries will show, the *Triumphs* was read more widely and with more passionate participation than the

Rhymes during the *quattrocento* and the early *cinquecento*. For some time at least they rivaled the *Comedy*. I think we may say in all fairness that this popularity was due to a lingering medievalism; what appealed to the readers of the *Triumphs* was the allegory, the catalogues, the erudition, and of course the polish of the verses. But the *Triumphs* have not endured; did not endure, in fact, in popular favor after the Renaissance.

The enduring influence of Petrarch as a creative writer is in the third wave of which Wilkins speaks—that of the *Rhymes*. This is a broad subject indeed and may itself need some subdividing, but in its first or narrow historical sense it is not difficult to trace and makes a very interesting trail to follow. This influence too has quite an early beginning. I would be inclined to place it as not much later than the second wave of the *Triumphs*. The first of the so-called *Petrarchisti* was Serafino Aquilano, who wrote toward the end of the fifteenth century. Armed with a facile pen and a style which has been described as flamboyant he fell upon the *Rhymes* with a kind of famished delight, digested them, pounced on the ornamental and somewhat decorative elements of the poet's style, and reproduced a glittering Petrarch, playing up the conceits which the master himself had often borrowed from the classics. Serafino too had his little school, and collectively he and his followers were extremely important, not so much for their own contribution as for the influence they had in spreading the Petrarchan gospel (at least according to their reading) into foreign lands. Frenchmen such as Maurice Scève, Philippe Desportes, and Clement Marot were fascinated by Serafino and his school as were the famous pair Wyatt and Surrey in England. Apropos of England we may note one immediate and direct influence. Chaucer translated a sonnet which was essentially medieval in nature and perhaps more of a rhetorical exercise than an expression of the more authentic personality of the poet. So far as I know, no English poet imitated Chaucer imitating Petrarch, and the weight of Petrarch's influence comes into the British Isles through other sources. An Italian reaction against Serafino, best typified by Bembo writing in the first half of the sixteenth century, focuses not so much on the ornament and the rhetoric or on the Platonic content of many of the rhymes; here the brooding, meditative Petrarch in contrast to the stylist and rhetorician receives full attention; needless to say, the disciples are more often than not much more concerned with philosophical lucubrations than was the master himself. Such Platonists as Daniello and Varchi are associated with Bembo in this more respectable if somewhat less exciting branch of *petrarchismo*, and this group also had a strong influence abroad. Their outstanding conquest was that of the Pléiade in France and both Ronsard and Du Bellay may be counted *"bembisti"*; through them the influence of Petrarch passed indirectly to Watson and Sidney in England, and the legacy of both Ronsard and Desportes can be detected in the works of such English poets as Lodge, Barnes, and above all Drayton, whose successful adaptation of the lessons of Petrarch to his own needs had in turn an effect on Spenser and Shakespeare, and even on the later Jacobean poet Drummond of Hawthornden. Another trail less broad but precious to students of English literature comes through Giovanni della Casa. In the middle years of the sixteenth century his sonnets, blending the lessons of both the Serafino school and the *"bembisti"* and set forth with an original technique, had a direct influence on Milton.

In Spain, too, the influence of Petrarch is strong, beginning with the Marqués de Santillana (1398–1458), who had a true temperamental affinity with Petrarch and the Catalan Asías March (1379–1459). Petrarch is very much alive as well in the work of Garcilaso de la Vega and Boscán, central figures of the Spanish Renaissance. Over such broad highways the historians of literature may easily lead us following on the footsteps of our poet.[4]

But the heritage of Petrarch is not simply a matter of what may be dismissed as literary influence in the common sense of the term. Indeed I think, as in the case of all great writers, we must distinguish between "influence" and what can perhaps be called "presence"; and it is the presence of Petrarch, initially accompanying his influence but transcending it and lingering on long after all imitators have been successfully catalogued and pigeonholed, that we must contemplate. This presence is a part of our heritage and is so deeply absorbed that we are hardly conscious of it. To speak here only of the Petrarch of the *Rhymes*: he has fixed for us one of our permanent emotional attitudes. There is a sector of the psyche of Western man concerned with the sentimental rapport between men and women that Petrarch has not, to be sure, invented but so well revealed to us and so delicately explored that it may well be called his by right of discovery. In purely literary terms this is not easy to document. If we look at the *Rhymes* and analyze carefully all the emotional postures and nuances of feeling, we shall in all fairness have to admit that there is nothing very new in them. Commentators and footnoters can trace the essentials back to Petrarch's immediate Italian predecessors, before them to the Provençal troubadours, giving due credit to Ovidian suggestions as well. Petrarch is not an innovator; in fact, from one point of view he is a reactionary, as we have noted in our discussion of the *Rhymes*, but he is a reactionary who has not given up the essential gains of the sentimental revolution; he has rather consolidated them, withdrawing from the indefensible and dangerous frontiers. The troubadours could and did recognize the mystery of sex and could find in woman an object worthy of reverence; yet at the same time they did not lose track of her womanhood. If they lingered long in the season of courtship, they nonetheless preserved a realistic awareness that it was but a preliminary. If there was an underlying death wish in their dedication (whether it be the death of themselves or of the love affair) yet it was a risk that they were cheerfully, and sometimes in their expressions even crudely, willing to run, but by Petrarch's time the Provençal lady had been captured by the scholars of Bologna, which is to say the theologians, and something as abnormal as it was inspiring had been added to the tradition. One might say that it was no longer the lover who risked death; rather it was the lady who was certain of it, or how else could she be truly an angel? It is true, of course, that this fate also overtakes Laura, and we are to have no doubt of her position in the third heaven; but this befalls her only after twenty years during which she has been for the poet not only an incarnation of his dreams and ambitions but a living woman whose golden hair and winsome ways fed his male desire. We may say that he has taken us back to Languedoc, and this is true; but in his cultivation and rediscovery of this realm he has so brilliantly and tenderly restored it, embellishing, preserving, and refining, that he has made it an inevitable haven for lovers ever since. As long as man and woman in the Western tradition meet in the time of courtship, provided that they are man and woman and not simply animals, their meeting will take place in the kingdom that Petrarch has explored for them. The amatory attitudes of the *Rhymes* have in fact been built into our culture; it is possible, of course, that some day there may be a revolution in human emotions, whether it be a new morality or a new erotic, but until that day comes we shall live by the code that Petrarch elaborated with such instinctive perception and such compelling sophistication. This is not to say that the *Rhymes* should be read as a manual of love or a prescription for successful courtship (although they have been so read); it is rather to say that they are a record of a discovery on the part of a sensitive and discriminating man of a zone of eternal truth in the human heart. Nowadays as far as the lessons of the *Rhymes* are concerned, we do not need to read them at all. Indeed the reading of them only reveals to us what our own mores have inculcated in us, and in this inculcation Petrarch played a leading role.

In our culture at least and perhaps more universally than such a limitation would suggest, a man's attitude toward love is nothing more than an exemplification or perhaps a dramatization of his attitude toward life; and here the Petrarchan mood, if we may double back on our trail, has had its effect on our psyche. The Petrarchan mood—a mixture of melancholy, self-questioning, and lyric egocentricity—is found again in Tasso, the great poet of the Counter Reformation. Like Petrarch, Tasso is torn between the all-but-voluptuous enjoyment of the beauties of nature and the demands of a sincere and dedicated devotion to the truly Christian life with all its asceticisms, fervors, and abdications. The pattern of Tasso's life, whether we think of him as a man or as a poet, recalls that of Petrarch, with its restless wanderings, its shifts and reorientations and, in literary terms, its classicism and its authentic piety. The current flows on to include Leopardi, another restless pilgrim spirit. The orthodox piety of Petrarch is wanting in the poet of Recanati, but the strain of melancholy self-probing, the alternating fascination and disillusionment with nature, the searching analysis and the recurrent questions—who am I? where am I going?—these are all part of the Petrarch inheritance; it is not surprising that among the annotators of the *Rhymes* we find included also the greatest nineteenth-century poet of Italy and perhaps of Europe. Thousands who are neither Italian poets, nor indeed poets at all, on reading the *Rhymes* will discover themselves. Petrarch has given comfort to many among the breed of men that seek not for power nor even knowledge but for peace of mind and soul and self-understanding—and find no easy answer.

There is yet a third way in which Petrarch has left his mark on the world of letters and on Western culture. What I have in mind cannot be narrowly defined as influence, nor is it a matter of his presence. It might be better here to speak of his example. As in a very narrow sense we may say that the influence of the first wave to which Wilkins refers, that of the Latin works, might be also considered an example set, followed, and absorbed, so in a much wider, deeper, and enduring way we may look upon his whole career, taking into consideration both the style of his life and the general character of his works. His life indeed offers us the first clearcut case of the truly free and emancipated writer. He had, of course, his canonries and deaconries, and recurrently he depended upon the patronage of the great. But such offices, while necessary to his subsistence were not full-time occupations; they not only left him plenty of leisure but also allowed him a kind of spiritual independence of which he made full use. We may observe that although he accepted benefices he was always very careful to eschew those that would have given him a deep commitment to a priestly life; indeed he said that the cure of souls was beyond him, for he had enough to do with taking care of his own. This may strike us as egocentric and perhaps evasive, and it may indeed be so viewed, but it is also a declaration of independence. And as for his relationship to his patrons, we have seen how, whenever it was possible, he eluded a permanent commitment. Here again, if we are inclined to judge his conduct as a little ungrateful (as in the case of his break with Colonna) we must concede that this pattern too is indicative of the same not ignoble desire to dedicate himself to the proper study of mankind, which is man, focusing primarily but not exclusively on one Francesco. He will not be bound either by the demands of a career or by his obligations to a protector; as we watch him skillfully rejecting the one and evading the other, our admiration may at times, it is true, be mixed with a certain disapproval of his devices. But if his tactics are evasive and shifty, his strategy is bold, courageous—and original. Unaggressively, unpretentiously, but tenaciously and persistently he labored to create a design for living which suited his temperamental needs and for which there had been no true precedent in the world of letters before him. This accomplishment is the more admirable when we reflect on the good use he made of it. For in effect, if his life signified emancipation from many of the practical commitments others must face, he employed this freedom in the

service of intellectual culture, showing to what beneficial uses it
could be put, and by the force of this example created a new
image of the *letterato* which endures to this day. If he was free
from the tiresome trivialities of everyday life and routine occupations, his spirit likewise was free in its exploration of humanity,
and it was humanity which he did in fact explore. The sincerity of
his religious conviction is beyond dispute, but he never put his
mind to the exploration of the other world. To paraphrase the
excellent chapter of Whitfield,[5] Petrarch is not concerned with
such matters as metaphysics, eschatology, or even in a broad sense
philosophy itself. How to live the good life is what concerns him.
The first duty of a human being is to be human. Simply to be
good is the best and most human thing of all, but a simple good-
ness will not be marred but rather improved by a cultivation of
the intellect. It will depend, too, somewhat on man's relation to
his fellows. For this reason Petrarch never lost interest in politics.
He followed all the developments in his own country and abroad
with passionate interest, and he was always ready with advice.
Most of his advice was, as a matter of fact, quite sound and based
on experience, observation, and good sense. It is not unreasonable
to see in him a forerunner of Machiavelli, but there is another
rather fascinating aspect to this interest, somewhat paradoxical at
first glance. As we have frequently noted, Petrarch felt that his
own times were deplorable and in this sector of sentiment he is
frequently haunted by the thought of death and the old Christian
conviction that this life is after all but a vale of tears, a brief, unhappy, and irrelevant venture of the soul. In fact, however, he
never gives up hope. The very passion with which he offers advice
and counsel to Cola or to the Emperor is an indication of his tena-
cious belief that, given good will in the full sense of the term, and
of course the imitation of the classics, this can be made a better
world to live in. If he despairs of the conditions in which he finds
himself living, he never despairs of the potential of the human race
or indeed of his beloved country. Nor will he ever disparage the
uses of letters. He believes in literature even more strongly than
he believes in a fairer prospect for mankind—as strongly one may
say as he believes in God.

He loved nature too; if his descriptions in the *Rhymes* seem formalized and Arcadian, they are still beautiful and they are ever
recurrent. His Latin works, particularly the *Letters*, bear witness

to a more realistic appreciation. The ascent of Mt. Ventoux is perhaps more interesting in that the emotions that the poet recorded are not in fact unique but characteristic and enduring. In his crossing of the Alps he seems always to have found time for a glance at the plains below him and a moment at least of appreciation for the spectacle they afforded. One may think too of his description of the landscape around the Bay of Naples in the *Itinerarium syriacum*, and other examples would not be hard to find. Nor was this a mere literary pose: long before Voltaire, our poet cultivated his garden; there are detailed accounts of his labors in the rhymed letters. This activity he pursued not only in Vaucluse but also in Milan. He kept a record of the planting of his various trees and shrubs. This interest gave him a sympathy and understanding of the peasantry, of whom he writes with great admiration. He is the first man of letters who really cares about the life of that unsung but indispensable class of society, and in fact it was years before he had any rivals in this sphere of interest. He loved life as we live it in all of its manifestations. He could find it in him to admire the now lost murals of Giotto in Naples, the portentous Amazon that he found in the environs of that city, the monuments of Rome, the brave show of the Venetian galleys anchored not far from his house on the Canal. He did not care for violence; he deplored the blood sports that he was compelled to witness in Naples. And frequently in the course of his works either in Latin or in the vernacular he attacked the madness and the futility of war. He bids the princes of Italy to put aside that dreadful occupation and think rather of works "of wit or hand." If such a counsel may seem to some an intrusion of the classical Petrarch into the lyric world of the *Rhymes,* we must also grant that this is a counsel springing from a purely personal distaste for destruction and bloodshed.

Such, then, were our poet's motivations and convictions. They are all, for any century, decent and civilized. If his advice had little effect on the world he lived in, in the sense that the princes did not immediately take his advice, yet he won a hearing for his point of view and something more than a hearing. He won the respect and admiration of his world. His victory was due, certainly in part, to his own personality, and this personality continues to fascinate us over the centuries. Studying it one is aware of deficiencies, some of which are of such nature as to make his triumph somewhat puzzling, for if Petrarch was a man of broad interest and a man of reason and common sense, it is still fair to ask whether he was in truth what we might call a great man. He was not, for one thing, I believe, a very profound thinker. His dismissal of the medieval interest in philosophy and metaphysics enabled him to concentrate on what seemed to him the more immediate goal of human society, but at the same time it does reveal a certain lack of depth. If we may think of Dante's solutions to the ills of his world as basically too theoretical to be of use and *au fond* reactionary, it is still true that there is a quality of high seriousness in his approach which one misses in Petrarch. Dante probes much deeper into the mainsprings of human motivation and looks to goals of ultimately greater significance. Petrarch was a serious man but hardly, one would say, a profound one. At the other extreme he lacks also, it seems to me, a sense of humor. Occasionally in his letters there is a witty anecdote; now and again in his invectives a rather heavy-handed sarcasm, but humor in the sense that Boccaccio so well exemplifies is simply missing in Petrarch. It is perhaps significant of this fault that he could read the *Decameron*, which Boccaccio sent him, and find out of the hundred tales only "Griselda" worthy of his attention. He is the only poet in literary history who can quite seriously make Homer his press agent. The last lines of the *Africa* indicate a vanity so vast as to leave no room for humor. And yet his assets, for his purposes and our good fortune, far outweighed these serious limitations. His was a personality, this on the record, which was immediately attractive and fascinating to his fellows. When he tells us as much he is but recounting the simple truth. He had what we call today an outgoing temperament. If he enjoyed trees and mountains and spectacles, he enjoyed also the company of his fellow men. As we have seen, even in extolling the virtues of the solitary life he is careful to point out that he conceives of solitude as shared with a friend or friends. We cannot overlook his snobbery in his recognition of his own charm, in his overt statement that the kings of Sicily and France and the Emperor himself all sought his company, but we must recognize too that this weakness has its uses: ". . . . it meant much for humanism that its apostle should be able to play so brilliant a part in society." [6] At the same time, it is only fair to remember that he regarded his steward in Vaucluse as also a friend. He liked his fellow men; not unnaturally they reciprocated and, as he grew in years and erudition, and possibly also in wisdom, his friends drew increasing profit from his company. This not in spite of but rather because of a constant and conscious egocentricity, the motivation that endowed him with his "*docta pietas* . . . his desire to understand himself as a social animal and as an intellectual animal and as a literary animal." [7] He was (and I mean the phrase in no disparaging way) the best salesman of literature that the world has yet seen. It was he who gave the man of letters for the first time in the modern era a place in society not merely respected but honored; whether or not he had an "influence" on Montaigne and so on through Rousseau down to our contemporary commentators and essayists is irrelevant; without his example it is unlikely that they would have had a hearing. A historical determinist could argue that Petrarch was a product of his time, or, putting it the other way around, that the times were right for such a personality to emerge. To which we can only answer that if the times were right, the man was ready—and that man was Petrarch.

Notes and References

Chapter One

1. *Purgatorio* iii, 37.
2. *Ibid.*, xxx, 63.
3. J. H. Whitfield, *Petrarch and the Renascence* (Oxford, 1943), pp. 20–21.
4. Denys Hay, *The Italian Renaissance in its Historical Background* (Cambridge, England, 1961), p. 58.
5. By J. Huizinga, first edition in English, London, 1924.
6. By Wallace K. Ferguson (Boston, 1962).
7. Title given Part VIII of Norman F. Cantor's *Medieval History* (New York, 1963). It covers the early years of the century and is followed by Part IX, "An End and a Beginning."
8. *Europe in the Late Middle Ages*, edited by J. R. Hall, J. R. L. Highfield and B. Smalley (London, 1965), p. 13.
9. Robert S. Lopez, *La Naissance de l'Europe* (Paris, 1962), pp. 400–401.
10. From Boccaccio's Introduction to the *Decameron*. Translated from the text of Charles S. Singleton (Bari, 1953), pp. 12, 14.
11. Robert S. Hoyt, *Europe in the Middle Ages* (New York, 1957), p. 577.
12. Leonard Olschki, *The Genius of Italy* (New York, 1949), pp. 180–81.
13. *Croniche fiorentine*, xii, 10.
14. R. Caggese in *Enciclopedia italiana, sub voce Giovanna*.
15. Geoffrey Trease, *The Italian Story* (New York, 1963), p. 162.
16. J. A. Symonds, *The Renaissance in Italy*, Modern Library Edition, vol. I, p. 70.
17. *Fam.* XIX, 9.
18. Ferdinand Schevill, *History of Florence from the Founding of the City through the Renaissance* (New York, 1936), p. 263.
19. *Ibid.*, p. 261.
20. *The Shorter Cambridge Medieval History* (Cambridge, England, 1960), p. 863.

Chapter Two

1. "Letter to Posterity." In James Harvey Robinson and Henry Winchester Rolfe, *Petrarch, the First Modern Scholar and Man of Letters* (New York–London, 1898), pp. 60–61.

2. Edward H. R. Tatham, *Francesco Petrarca, the First Modern Man of Letters: His Life and Correspondence.* Vol. I (London, 1925), pp. 183–95.

3. *Sen.* VIII, 1; July 20, 1360.

4. G. Carducci, *Studi Letterari,* 2a ed. (Livorno, 1880), p. 234.

5. "Letter to Posterity," Robinson and Rolfe, *op. cit.,* p. 65.

6. *Sen.* X, 2. Translation of Morris Bishop, *Letters from Petrarch* (Bloomington, Indiana, 1966), p. 263.

7. E. H. Wilkins, *Life of Petrarch* (Chicago, 1961), p. 3.

8. Tatham, *op. cit.,* vol. I, p. 86.

9. *Sen.* XVI, 1.

10. *Secretum,* part III.

11. *Sen.* XVI, i.

12. *Sen.* X, 2; Bishop, *Letters* 267–8.

13. *Sen.* XVI, 1.

14. So most modern biographers, including Wilkins and Bosco. Some authorities would put it later. Tatham (I, 191–94) discusses the question.

15. *Ep. met.* I, 7 to Giacomo Colonna.

16. *Op. cit.,* I, 104–6.

17. *Life,* pp. 7–8.

18. *Fam.* X, 3. Bishop, *Letters,* p. 92–93.

19. *Europe in Transition,* p. 283.

20. Beryl Smalley, "Church and State 1300–77: Theory and Fact," in *Europe in the Late Middle Ages* (note 8 to Chapter I).

21. Marzieh Gail, *Avignon in Flower, 1309–1403* (Cambridge, Mass., 1965), p. 5.

22. C. B. Cayley's translation (London, 1879).

23. Richard Garnett's translation (London-Boston, 1896).

24. *Francesco Petrarca,* Bari, 1961, p. 275. The principal objection to the identification of the poet's Laura with Laurette de Sade is the statement (*Rhymes* iv) that the former was born in a small town ("*picciol borgo*"), which does not fit Avignon, the birthplace of Laurette. Chiorboli's introduction to his edition of the *Canzoniere* (Milano, 1924) discusses the various candidates.

25. *Secretum,* Book III.

26. In his note on her death. See page 75.

Chapter Three

1. *Fam.* X, 3. See Tatham I, p. 149.
2. See Robinson and Rolfe, p. 168.
3. *Fam.* I, 3; Robinson and Rolfe, p. 100.
4. *Fam.* I, 4; Robinson and Rolfe, pp. 300–305.
5. *Life,* p. 10.
6. *Fam.* I, 3; Robinson and Rolfe, p. 299.
7. *Sine titulo* 1. Probably written to Philippe de Cabassoles. Bishop, *Petrarch and His World,* p. 184, calls it "a really shocking letter."
8. *Fam.* IV, 1.
9. *Fam.* II, 14. Tatham's version, see *op. cit.,* vol. II, p. 338.
10. Translation of G. F. Cunningham, from *The Rhymes of Francesco Petrarca,* compiled by Thomas G. Bergin (Edinburgh-London, 1955), pp. 12–13.
11. *Op. cit.,* vol. I, p. 349.
12. *Petrarch and His World,* p. 101.
13. *Life,* p. 17.
14. *Ibid.,* p. 15.
15. Carlo Calcaterra believes that the magnum opus was the *Rhymes;* see his *Nella selva del Petrarca* (Bologna, 1942), pp. 55–57.
16. *Petrarch and His World,* p. 125.
17. From *Ep. met.* I, 6.
18. Aldo Bernardo, *Petrarch, Scipio and the "Africa"* (Baltimore, 1962), p. 11.
19. *Life,* p. 21.
20. *Petrarca's Leben und Werke* (Leipzig, 1878), p. 174.
21. Wilkins, *Life,* p. 25.
22. *Rime di F. Petrarca sopra argomenti storici etc.* (Livorno, 1876), p. 96.
23. *Petrarch and His World,* p. 175.
24. *Life,* p. 47.
25. Translation of G. F. Cunningham in Bergin, *op. cit.,* pp. 41–42.
26. Translation of Lady Dacre, *Translations from the Italian* (London, 1836).
27. *Fam.* V, 10. See Tatham, vol. II, pp. 344–45. (The couplet is Conington's translation of *Aeneid* IV, 123.)
28. *Ibid.,* p. 363.
29. Attributed to Thomas Wyatt by Harington in his *Nugae Antiquae* (London, 1769). See Chiorboli, pp. 351–52, on date of the poem.

Chapter Four

1. *Vita Nicolai Laurentii, sive di Cola di Rienzo,* in Muratori's *Antiquitates Italicae Medii Aevi,* Milano, 1740. I have translated from

the text in W. von Wartburg's *Raccolta di testi antichi italiani* (Bern, 1946), pp. 82ff.

2. *The History of the Decline and Fall of the Roman Empire.* I quote from the Heritage Press edition (New York, 1946), pp. 2397–2398.

3. *Vita Nicolai Laurentii, loc. cit.*

4. *Var.* 48.

5. *Var.* 38.

6. *Eclogue* v, 115–40.

7. *Fam.* XIII, 6. Translation from Robinson and Rolfe, pp. 343–44.

8. *Sine titulo,* IV. Robinson and Rolfe, pp. 348–49.

Chapter Five

1. Wilkins' translation, *Life,* p. 77.

2. *Fam.* XIII, 5.

3. "Petrarch and the Cardinalate," in *Studies in the Life and Works of Petrarch* (Cambridge, Mass., 1955), p. 80.

4. *Fam.* XVI, 1.

Chapter Six

1. Boccaccio's letter may be found in A. F. Messèra's edition of his *Opere latine minori* (Bari, 1928), pp. 136–40.

2. See Tatham, vol. II, p. 146.

3. *Petrarch's Eight Years in Milan, 1353–1361* (Cambridge, 1958), p. 149.

4. In the *Invectiva contra quendam* etc. See Wilkins, *Milan,* p. 101.

5. *Milan,* p. 15.

6. *Fam.* XIX, 3; translation of Morris Bishop, *Letters,* pp. 156ff.

7. Wilkins, *Milan,* p. 123.

8. *Fam.* XXII, 14; Wilkins, *op. cit.,* p. 222.

9. *Sen.* X, 2; *loc. cit..*

10. *Fam.* XIX, 16; Bishop's translation, *Letters,* pp. 161ff.

11. *Op. cit.,* pp. 174–75.

12. *Fam.* XXII, 7, *op. cit.,* p. 188.

13. *Fam.* XXII, 9; *op. cit.,* p. 189.

14. H. C. Hollway-Calthrop, *Petrarch, His Life and Times* (New York, 1907), pp. 212–13.

15. *Milan,* p. 212.

Chapter Seven

1. *Sen.,* XII, 1.

2. *Ibid.,* X, 7; Bishop, *Letters,* p. 274.

3. Bosco, *op. cit.,* p. 281.

4. *Life,* p. 237.

5. *Sen.* XVII, 2; translation from Robinson and Rolfe, pp. 426–28.

6. See *Petrarch's Testament,* edited and translated by Theodor Mommsen (Ithaca, New York, 1957).

Chapter Eight

1. See Wilkins, *Milan,* p. 182.

2. *Sen.* II, 1.

3. Nelly I. di Villadauro in *Dizionario letterario Bompiani delle opere e dei personaggi,* Vol. VIII (Milano, 1950).

4. *Sen.* II, 1.

5. Luigi Tonelli, *Petrarca,* (Milano, 1930), p. 106.

6. *Petrarch and His World,* p. 179.

7. *Purgatorio* vi, 118–19.

8. *Genius of Italy,* pp. 210–11.

9. *Petrarch, Scipio,* etc., p. 206.

10. *Francesco Petrarca: Prose* (Milano-Napoli, 1955).

11. *Life and Times,* p. 228.

12. *Francesco Petrarca,* p. 190.

13. *Prose,* p. xii.

14. Translated from the text of *Prose* (note 10, *supra*).

Chapter Nine

1. Tonelli, *Petrarca,* p. 124.

2. Pietro Paolo Gerosa, *Umanesimo cristiano del Petrarca* (Torino, 1966), p. 82.

3. Bishop, *Petrarch and His World,* p. 213.

4. *Petrarch and the Renascence,* p. 52.

5. Translated from *Francesco Petrarca: Rime, Trionfi e poesie latine* (Milano-Napoli, 1951), pp. 839–43.

6. *The Life of Solitude by Francesco Petrarca,* translated with introduction and notes by Jacob Zeitlin (Urbana, Ill., 1924), p. 240.

7. *Ibid.,* pp. 205–207. Here and occasionally elsewhere I have slightly revised Zeitlin's version.

8. *Ibid.,* p. 315.

9. *Ibid.,* p. 164.

10. *Ibid.,* p. 130.

11. *Ibid.,* p. 58.

12. *Ibid.,* p. 100.

13. *Ibid.,* p. 101.

14. *Ibid., loc. cit.*

15. *Ibid.,* pp. 112–14.

16. *Ibid.*, p. 242.

17. *Ibid.*, p. 250–52.

18. *Ibid.*, p. 152.

19. *Ibid.*, p. 262.

20. *Ibid.*, p. 156.

21. *Ibid.*, p. 139.

22. In *Dizionario letterario Bompiani*, Vol. VII, (1949), p. 842.

23. *Storia della letteratura italiana*, vol. I (Milano, 1947), p. 215.

24. *Petrarch and the Renascence*, p. 56.

25. *Umanesimo cristiano*, pp. 148–151.

26. *Leben und Werke*, pp. 560–561.

27. My English follows the Italian version of Casimiro Stolfi's edition, Bologna, 1867; vol. I, pp. 360–62.

28. Conrad H. Rawski's *Petrarch: Four Dialogues for Scholars* (Cleveland, 1967), which appeared during the preparation of this book, is a happy example of just such a selection.

29. *Milan*, pp. 161–64.

Chapter Ten

1. Carlo Cordié in the *Dizionario letterario Bompiani*, vol. III (1947), p. 156.

2. *Letters from Petrarch, cit. supra.*

3. *Ibid.*

4. See Ernest H. Wilkins and Giuseppe Billanovich, "The Miscellaneous Letters of Petrarch," *Speculum*, XXXVII, no. 2. (July, 1962).

5. *Essays on Petrarch* (London, 1813), p. 195.

6. Wilkins' translation; from *Petrarch at Vaucluse* (Chicago, 1958), pp. 64–67.

7. *Ibid.*, pp. 39–40.

8. Translated from text of Enrico Bianchi in *Francesco Petrarca: Rime, Trionfi, e Poesie Latine* (Milano-Napoli, 1951).

9. *Bucolicum carmen*, iii, 10–20.

10. Tatham, *op. cit.*, vol. II, p. 392. Tatham also refers to the letter of Boccaccio, p. 390.

11. Translated from the text of Pier Giorgio Ricci in *Francesco Petrarca: Prose, cit. supra.*

12. For the circumstances of the composition of the work see Hans Nachod's Introduction to his translation in *The Renaissance Philosophy of Man*, edited by Ernst Cassirer, Paul Oskar Kristeller, and John Herman Randall, Jr. (Chicago, 1948), pp. 23–33.

13. From the edition of Pier Giorgio Ricci in *Francesco Petrarca: Prose, cit. supra.*

Chapter Eleven

1. Calcaterra, *op. cit.*, vi, "La prima ispirazione dei *Trionfi*," pp. 145–99, discusses the question in some detail.
2. Calcaterra, *loc. cit.*, sees the *Roman de la Rose* as the direct inspiration of the *Trionfi*—although of a polemical nature. Petrarch, Calcaterra believes, felt that the *Roman de la Rose* was a good subject, mishandled by the author.
3. *Petrarch and the Renascence*, Chapter III, "Petrarch's Conflict: Ancient and Modern Against Medieval."
4. *Petrarch and His World*, p. 299.
5: *History of Italian Literature*, p. 100.

Chapter Twelve

1. *The Making of the Canzoniere and Other Petrarchan Studies* (Rome, 1951), p. 145.
2. *The Earlier and Later Forms of Petrarch's Canzoniere* (Chicago, 1925); see particularly Chapter V, pp. 173–88.
3. *Making of the Canzoniere*, p. 146.
4. *Life*, p. 34.
5. The poems excluded from the *Canzoniere* may be found in Angelo Solerti, *Rime disperse di Francesco Petrarca o a lui attribuite* (Firenze, 1909). There are approximately 150 presumably genuine items.
6. See G. G. Ferrero, *Petrarca e i trovatori* (Torino, 1959).
7. *Nella selva del Petrarca*, Chapter II, pp. 35–81.
8. According to E. Chiorboli, *Francesco Petrarca: Le "Rime sparse" commentate* (Milano, 1924), p. 2.
9. In his essay on Petrarch in *Poesia popolare e poesia d'arte* (Bari, 1933). Quoted—to be refuted—by Bosco, *op. cit.*, p. 80.
10. *Petrarch and His World*, p. 73.
11. *Petrarca*, pp. 209–24.
12. *Nella selva*, Chapters II and VII.
13. Translation of John Nott, *Petrarch translated . . .* (London, 1808).
14. Translation of R. G. MacGregor, *Indian Leisure* (London, 1854).
15. See his *History of Italian Literature*, translated by Joan Redfern (New York, 1931), vol. I, pp. 272ff.
16. *The Songs of Bernart de Ventadorn*, edited by Stephen G. Nichols and others (Chapel Hill, 1962), pp. 129ff.
17. *Vita Nuova*, xxvi.
18. *Rhymes*, xc.

19. V. Zabughin, *Vergilio nel Rinascimento italiano da Dante a Torquato Tasso* (Bologna, 1921), p. 36.

20. *Francesco Petrarca*, pp. 56ff.

21. *Fam.* I, 1; see Bishop, *Letters*, p. 19.

22. Original in Alfred Jeanroy, *Les chansons de Guillaume d'Aquitaine*, 2d ed. (Paris, 1964), p. 19.

23. Original in Carl Appel, *Die Lieder Bertrans von Born* (Halle, 1932), p. 97.

24. *"Rime Sparse,"* pp. 1–2.

25. Nichols, *op. cit.*, p. 166.

Chapter Thirteen

1. Pierre de Nolhac, *Petrarque et l'humanisme, d'après un essai de restitution de sa bibliothèque* (Paris, 1892); also the summarized English version, *Petrarch and the Ancient World* (Boston, 1907).

2. *Umanesimo cristiano del Petrarca*, Chapter X, "La cultura patristica del Petrarca," pp. 156–79.

3. *Studies in the Life and Works of Petrarch* (Cambridge, Mass., 1955), pp. 280–81.

4. Petrarchism is a vast subject. For the aspects briefly summarized here see further: G. Spagnoletti, *Il petrarchismo*, Milano, 1959; L. Russo, *Il petrarchismo italiano nel 500*, Pisa, 1958; M. Piéri, *Le pétrarquisme au xvième siècle*, Marseille, 1896 (reprinted New York, 1968); J. Vianey, *Le pétrarquisme en France au xvième siècle*, Montpellier, 1909; L. Einstein, "Petrarchism in England" in his *Italian Renaissance in England*, London, 1893; A. Lytton Sells, *The Italian Influence in English Poetry from Chaucer to Southwell*, Bloomington, Indiana, 1955; J. G. Fucilla, *Estudios sobre el petrarquismo en España*, Madrid, 1960.

5. *Loc. cit.*

6. "Petrarch the Man," in *Four Essays* by Murray Anthony Potter (Cambridge, Mass., 1917), p. 73.

7. "Politics and Culture in 14th Century Italy," in Denys Hay, *The Italian Renaissance in Its Historical Background* (Cambridge, 1961), p. 80.

Selected Bibliography

There is no modern edition of Petrarch's complete works. The *Opera quae extant omnia*, Basil, 1554 and the later edition, *ibid.*, 1581, are the most nearly complete collections that have been published. A National Edition is now in progress; it includes, so far: *L'Africa*, edited by N. Festa, Florence, 1926; the *Epistolae familiares*, in four volumes of which the first three are edited by V. Rossi and the last by U. Bosco, Florence, 1926–42; and the *Rerum memorandarum libri iv*, edited by G. Billanovich, *ibid.*, 1943. Two recent collections published by Riccardo Ricciardi (Milan and Naples) contain ample selections from Petrarch's works. The first, *Rime, Trionfii e poesie latine* (edited by F. Neri, G. Martellotti, E. Bianchi and N. Sapegno) includes the complete texts of the *Rhymes* and the *Trionfi* and selections from the *Rime disperse* and the Latin poems, including the *Africa;* the second, *Prose* (edited by G. Martellotti, P. G. Ricci, E. Carrara and E. Bianchi), 1955, contains the complete text of the *Letter to Posterity*, the *Secretum*, *De vita solitaria*, *De sui ipsius et multorum ignorantia* and the *Invectiva contra eum qui maledixit Italiae*, as well as selections from the *Letters*.

Principal editions of the individual works (excluding those mentioned above) may be usefully classified as follows:

I Latin works; verse
Bucolicum carmen. Padua, 1906; edited by A. Avena.
Epistolae metricae. Milan, 1831 and 1834; vols. ii and iii of the *Poesie minori del Petrarca*, edited by D. Rossetti.

II Latin works; prose
Epistolae sine nomine. In P. Piur, *Petrarcas Buch ohne Namen*, Halle, 1925.
De otio religioso. Vatican City, 1958; edited by G. Rotondi.
De viris illustribus. Bologna, 1874–79; edited by L. Razzolini.
Invectiva contra quendam magni status hominem sed nullius scientiae aut virtutis. Florence, 1949; edited by P. G. Ricci.

Invectivarum contra medicum quendam libri iv. Rome, 1950; edited by P. G. Ricci.
Itinerarium syriacum. See G. Lumbroso, *Memorie del buon tempo antico;* Torino, 1889.
Psalmi poenitentiales. Paris, 1929; edited by H. Cochin.

III Italian works
There are many editions of the *Rime* (or *Canzoniere*). The *Catalogue of the Petrarch Collection bequeathed by Willard Fiske* (Ithaca, 1916; compiled by Mary Fowler), a storehouse of bibliographical material, lists over 450 editions, beginning with the *editio princeps*, Venice, 1470, and there have been many more since the publication of the *Catalogue*. In addition to the Ricciardi edition, cited above, we shall mention here the two editions brought out by Ezio Chiorboli; the first, Milan, 1924, richly annotated; the second, Bari, 1930, of interest for the authoritative text.
The *Trionfi* are often published with the *Rime;* the Ricciardi edition, as noted, and Chiorboli's Bari edition contain both works.
The poems excluded from the *Canzoniere* may be found in Angelo Solerti, *Rime disperse di Francesco Petrarca, o a lui attribuite,* Firenze, 1909.

PETRARCH'S WORKS IN ENGLISH

I Latin works in translation
Letters. Selections may be found in *Petrarch, the First Modern Scholar and Man of Letters,* by James Harvey Robinson and Henry Winchester Rolfe, 2nd ed. revised and enlarged, New York, 1914; M. E. Cosenza's *Petrarch's Letters to Classical Authors,* Chicago, 1910; E. H. Wilkins' *Petrarch at Vaucluse,* Chicago, 1958 and, most copiously, in Morris Bishop's *Letters from Petrarch,* Bloomington, Indiana, 1966. Six letters are translated (some only partially) by Hans Nachod in *The Renaissance Philosophy of Man,* edited by Ernst Cassirer, Paul Oskar Kristeller and John Herman Randall, Chicago, 1948. All the biographers noted below have occasion to quote the letters, often in full.
Metrical Letters. E. H. Wilkins, *Petrarch at Vaucluse,* Chicago, 1958; a number of them also appear in Tatham's biography.
The *Secretum* has been translated by W. H. Draper, *Petrarch's Secret,* London, 1911. Bishop's *Petrarch and His World* contains an abridgment (Chapter XV, pp. 193–213.)
De remediis utriusque fortunae was translated by Thomas Twyne, London, 1597, under the title of *Phisicke against Fortune. Petrarch's View of Human Life,* Mrs. Dobson, *ibid.,* 1791, reproduces much of Twyne. Conrad H. Rawski has edited and trans-

lated *Petrarch: Four Dialogues for Scholars*, Cleveland, 1967, the only modern version of any of the dialogues, save as they appear in excerpts in various studies.

De vita solitaria was translated by Jacob Zeitlin, *The Life of Solitude by Francis Petrarch;* Urbana, Ill., 1924.

A translation of *On his own Ignorance and that of Others* may be found in *The Renaissance Philosophy of Man*, cited above.

E. H. Wilkins translated the Coronation Oration in *Studies in the Life and Works of Petrarch*, Cambridge, Mass., 1955.

Petrarch's Testament was edited and translated by Theodor E. Mommsen, Ithaca, 1957.

II Italian works in translation

The *Rhymes* have been a target for English (and American) translators ever since the Renaissance; indeed Chaucer leads the way with his version of cxxxii (*S'amor non è*) woven into a soliloquy of Troilus. Only two translators have published an English version of the entire *Canzoniere:* C. B. Cayley, *The Sonnets and Stanzas of Petrarch*, London, 1879; and Anna Maria Armi, *Petrarch: Sonnets and Songs*, New York, 1946. R. G. MacGregor's translation of the *Canzoniere* published in his *Indian Leisure*, London, 1854, lacks only one ode. A complete version in manuscript by John Nott (1751–1825) is in the possession of the Harvard University Library.

Joseph Auslander's *The Sonnets of Petrarch*, London–New York–Toronto, 1931, contains all the sonnets as does also the Limited Editions' *The Sonnets of Petrarch*, New York, 1965 (translated by various hands). Good selections may be found in Morris Bishop's *Love Rhymes of Petrarch*, Ithaca, 1932; Richard Garnett's *CXXIV Sonnets*, London, 1896; and (by various hands) in *Lyric Poetry of the Italian Renaissance*, collected by L. R. Lind, New Haven–London, 1954; and *Petrarch: Selected Sonnets, Odes and Letters*, edited by T. G. Bergin, New York, 1966.

The complete *Triumphs* were translated by Henry Parker, Lord Morley, London, 1554 (reprinted, *ibid.*, 1887) and recently by E. H. Wilkins, Chicago, 1962.

WORKS ABOUT PETRARCH

Biographical and critical studies on Petrarch are countless. Part II of the above-mentioned *Catalogue* of the Fiske Collection, which lists the critical works, runs to over two hundred double-columned pages and is of course more than half a century out of date. A short but substantial bibliography of significant works may be found in N. Sapegno's *Il Trecento*, Milano, 1955, pp. 266–74. Among relatively recent studies in Italian we shall mention here: Umberto Bosco's *Francesco Petrarca*, Bari, 1968; Carlo Calcaterra's *Nella selva del Petrarca*, Bologna, 1942; and P. P. Gerosa's *Umanesimo cristiano del Petrarca*, Torino, 1966. G. Koerting's *Petrarcas Leben und Werke*, Leipzig, 1878, is still useful; and Pierre de Nolhac's *Pétrarque et l'humanisme*, Paris, 1892, abounds in biographical and bibliographical information.

In English many excellent works are available. There are four biographical studies: Morris Bishop, *Petrarch and His World*, Bloomington, Indiana, 1963; H. C. H. Calthrop (sometimes styled Hollway-Calthrop), *Petrarch, His Life and Times*, New York, 1907; E. H. R. Tatham, *Francesco Petrarca, the First Modern Man of Letters: His Life and Correspondence*, London, 1925–26 (unfortunately incomplete), and E. H. Wilkins, *Life of Petrarch*, Chicago, 1961.

Recent special studies in English include:

BERNARDO, ALDO S. *Petrarch, Scipio and the "Africa,"* Baltimore, 1962.
WHITFIELD, J. H. *Petrarch and the Renascence*, Oxford, 1943.
WILKINS, E. H. *The Making of the "Canzoniere" and Other Petrarchan Studies*, Rome, 1951.
———. *Studies in the Life and Works of Petrarch*, Cambridge, Mass., 1955.
———. *Petrarch's Eight Years in Milan, ibid.,* 1958.
———. *Petrarch's Later Years, ibid.,* 1959.
———. *Petrarch's Correspondence*, Padua, 1960.

Index

Note: *Petrarch* is not indexed since the nature of the book makes it unnecessary to do so. Names of his immediate family are indexed under first names; e.g. Gherardo, Giovanni etc.